SIGN OF THE COVENANT

Society of Biblical Literature

Ancient Israel and Its Literature

Steven L. McKenzie, General Editor

Editorial Board

Suzanne Boorer
Victor H. Matthews
Thomas C. Römer
Benjamin D. Sommer
Nili Wazana

Number 3

SIGN OF THE COVENANT
Circumcision in the Priestly Tradition

Volume Editor
Benjamin D. Sommer

SIGN OF THE COVENANT

Circumcision in the Priestly Tradition

by

David A. Bernat

Society of Biblical Literature
Atlanta

SIGN OF THE COVENANT
Circumcision in the Priestly Tradition

Copyright © 2009 by the Society of Biblical Literature

All rights reserved. No part of this work may be reproduced or transmitted in any form or by any means, electronic or mechanical, including photocopying and recording, or by means of any information storage or retrieval system, except as may be expressly permitted by the 1976 Copyright Act or in writing from the publisher. Requests for permission should be addressed in writing to the Rights and Permissions Office, Society of Biblical Literature, 825 Houston Mill Road, Atlanta, GA 30329 USA.

Library of Congress Cataloging-in-Publication Data

Bernat, David A.
    Sign of the covenant : circumcision in the priestly tradition / by David A. Bernat.
        p. cm. — (Society of Biblical Literature ancient Israel and its literature ; 3)
    Includes bibliographical references and indexes.
    ISBN 978-1-58983-409-5 (pbk. : alk. paper) — ISBN 978-1-58983-410-1 (electronic library copy : alk. paper)
    1. Circumcision—Biblical teaching. 2. Berit milah. 3. P document (Biblical criticism). 4. Bible. O.T. Pentateuch—Criticism, interpretation, etc. I. Title.
    BS1199.C52B47 2009b
    296.4'422 22   2009004613

17 16 15 14 13 12 11 10 09   5 4 3 2 1
Printed in the United States of America on acid-free, recycled paper conforming to ANSI/NISO Z39.48-1992 (R1997) and ISO 9706:1994 standards for paper permanence.

In loving memory of my mother

Gladys Goldberg Bernat
זהבה בת רבקה ואברהם

אמי זכרונה לברכה
תעמד זכות הצדקת לנו ולכל ישראל
(H. N. Bialik, "My Mother of Blessed Memory")

Contents

Acknowledgments ix
Abbreviations xi

Introduction 1

Part 1: Actual Genital Circumcision

1. Introduction 13
2. Circumcision and ברית 27
3. Circumcision, Status, and Sexuality 43
4. Circumcision and the Cult 53

Part 2: Foreskin Metaphors

5. Introduction 79
6. Exodus 6: Moses' Foreskinned Lips 83
7. Leviticus 19: Foreskinned Fruit Trees 91
8. Leviticus 26: Israel's Foreskinned Heart 97

Epilogue: Circumcision and the Exile 115

Conclusion 123

Works Cited 133
Indices
    Primary Texts 149
    Modern Authors 160

Acknowledgments

This work is the revision of a Ph.D. dissertation completed at Brandeis University in Waltham, Massachusetts, in 2002. I affirm my gratitude to a number of people who have had a marked influence on the development of this work and upon my own professional growth.

Marc Brettler, my *Doktorvater*, is a model scholar and pedagogue whose exacting standards compelled me to play at the top of my game. His guidance has extended beyond the classroom and well past the moment I received my degree. My father, Rabbi Haskell Bernat, my first Torah teacher, remains an inspiration for me to this day. Friends and colleagues: Steve Geller—sent me, as an undergrad, on the path to academia; David Wright and Larry Wills—mentors during graduate school, discriminating and compassionate readers of my dissertation; and Barbara Geller—coached me toward a conclusion of this project. Stephanie White provided invaluable assistance in preparation of the indices and bibliography. Last, Ben Sommer, in the finest tradition of editors, compelled me to sharpen my focus and my prose.

My daughter Galia (not circumcised but welcomed into the community of Israel with due ceremony) and my son Micah (carries the sign of the covenant) bring constant waves of joy and wonder to our home. Finally, my wife Susan, whose support and patience has been of incalculable value.

Abbreviations

AB	Anchor Bible
ABD	*The Anchor Bible Dictionary*. Edited by David Noel Freedman. 6 vols. New York: Doubleday, 1992.
AnBib	Analecta biblica
BA	*Biblical Archaeologist*
BASOR	*Bulletin of the American Schools of Oriental Research*
Bib	*Biblica*
BibInt	*Biblical Interpretation*
BibInt	Biblical Interpretation Series
BJS	Brown Judaic Studies
BZ	*Biblische Zeitschrift*
BZAW	Beihefte zur Zeitschrift für die alttestamentliche Wissenschaft
CBC	Cambridge Bible Commentary
CBQ	*Catholic Biblical Quarterly*
CC	Continental Commentaries
ConBOT	Coniectanea biblica: Old Testament Series
CRAIBL	*Comptes rendus de l'Académie des inscriptions et belles lettres*
ErIsr	*Eretz-Israel*
ET	English translation
FAT	Forschungen zum Alten Testament
HAR	*Hebrew Annual Review*
HBM	Hebrew Bible Monographs
HDR	Harvard Dissertations in Religion
HSM	Harvard Semitic Monographs
HTR	*Harvard Theological Review*
HUCA	*Hebrew Union College Annual*
ICC	International Critical Commentary
IDB	*The Interpreter's Dictionary of the Bible*. Edited by G. A. Buttrick. 4 vols. Nashville: Abingdon, 1962.
IEJ	*Israel Exploration Journal*
Imm	*Immanuel*
Int	*Interpretation*

JANESCU	*Journal of the Ancient Near Eastern Society of Columbia University*
JAOS	*Journal of the American Oriental Society*
JBL	*Journal of Biblical Literature*
JNSL	*Journal of Northwest Semitic Languages*
JQR	*Jewish Quarterly Review*
JSNTSup	Journal for the Study of the New Testament Supplement Series
JSOT	*Journal for the Study of the Old Testament*
JSOTSup	Journal for the Study of the Old Testament Supplement Series
JSQ	*Jewish Studies Quarterly*
LBS	Library of Biblical Studies
LXX	Septuagint
NCB	New Century Bible
NICOT	New International Commentary on the Old Testament
NTS	*New Testament Studies*
OTL	Old Testament Library
OTS	Old Testament Studies
OtSt	*Oudtestamentische Studiën*
PAAJR	*Proceedings of the American Academy of Jewish Research*
RB	*Revue biblique*
RBL	*Review of Biblical Literature*
SAA	State Archives of Assyria
SB	*Studia biblica*
SBLDS	Society of Biblical Literature Dissertation Series
SBLSCS	Society of Biblical Literature Septuagint and Cognate Studies
SBLSP	Society of Biblical Literature Seminar Papers
SBT	Studies in Biblical Theology
SJLA	Studies in Judaism in Late Antiquity
SJOT	*Scandinavian Journal of the Old Testament*
SL	*Studia liturgica*
SubBi	Subsidia biblica
TDOT	*Theological Dictionary of the Old Testament.* Edited by G. J. Botterweck and H. Ringgren. Translated by J. T. Willis, G. W. Bromiley, and D. E. Green. 15 vols. Grand Rapids: Eerdmans, 1974–2006.
UF	*Ugarit-Forschungen*
VT	*Vetus Testamentum*
VTSup	Supplements to Vetus Testamentum
WBC	Word Biblical Commentary
ZAW	*Zeitschrift für die alttestamentliche Wissenschaft*

Introduction

The rabbis avowed "Great is circumcision, for it is of equal weight to all the commandments in the Torah" (b. Ned. 32a). More than a millennium later, Biblicists still employ the same lofty tones when considering circumcision's import. Von Rad's assertion (1972, 201) exemplifies this inclination: "Observance of the custom was a *status confessionus* ...a question of their [Israel's] witness of Yahweh and his guidance of history."[1] Scholars such as Skinner have also ascribed special consequence to circumcision within the Priestly pentateuchal tradition: "In P, it becomes a prescription of the highest magnitude, being placed above the Mosaic ritual, and second in dignity only to the Sabbath.... very few legislative acts have exercised so tremendous an influence on the genius of a religion" (1910, 297). Gunkel's succinct claim echoes that of the sages: "For P, it becomes one of the most important commandments of the law (1997, 265).[2] But are these statements mere hyperbole, or does circumcision merit pride of place in the Torah's ethos?

Despite the importance attributed to circumcision in the Hebrew Bible, the topic has not been accorded sufficient attention in the scholarship. To date, no book-length treatment of the rite has appeared.[3] Studies of circumcision have been more narrowly focused, on individual biblical passages[4]

---

1. For a sampling of analogous testimonials, see Davidson 1979, 58; Sarna 1966, 132; and Vawter 1977, 222.

2. On the centrality of circumcision in P, note also the comments of McEvenue (1971, 178), and Gevirtz (1990, 102).

3. The few works that exclusively treat circumcision in antiquity focus upon postbiblical contexts, such as Hoffman 1996; Kline 1968; and Cohen 2005.

4. The body of biblical circumcision passages can be easily delimited, based upon the occurrence of derivations of the roots מול (circumcise) and ערל (foreskin). Gen 17:9–14, 23–27; 21:4; 34; Exod 4:24–26; 6:12,30; 12:44–49; Lev 12:3; 19:23–25; 26:41; Deut 10:16; 30:6; Josh 5:2–9; Judg 14:3; 15:18; 1 Sam 14:6; 17:26, 36; 31:4 (= 1 Chr 10:4); 2 Sam 1:20; Isa 52:1; Jer 4:4; 6:10; 9:24–25; Ezek 28:10; 31:18; 32:19–31; 44:7,9. Hab 2:16 is excluded, reading הרעל "reel" for הערל "become uncircumcised," following LXX διασαλεύθητι καὶ σείσθητι "shake and stir." Note also 1QpHab 11:8–16,

or topics,[5] while attempts at synthesis tend toward summary, appearing as entries in encyclopedias,[6] excursuses in commentaries,[7] chapters of larger works,[8] and brief notices in survey literature and *Einleitungen*.[9] With the present monograph, I confront this lacuna by studying circumcision in the Priestly pentateuchal writings (P). The Priestly corpus has long been recognized as a discrete tradition with a distinct idiom and ideology. Its contents, more so than any other biblical authorial tradition, are ideal for a full-scale, in-depth, exploration of circumcision, as, uniquely, P's circumcision passages encompass both actual and metaphoric representations of the rite and are located in legal, narrative, and paranetic contexts.[10] Moreover, as will be determined, P's seemingly diverse collocation of circumcision texts bears witness to a relatively systematic and integrated conception of the practice.

The aim of the monograph is to provide new perspectives on circumcision in P and a deepened understanding of the narratives, laws, and general thought-world of the Priestly Torah. The contributions of the work have ripples, however, beyond the narrower focus of Priestly and pentateuchal studies. It is generally acknowledged that a Priestly hand gave the Torah its final edi-

---

where the lemma reads הרעל, while the pesher כיא לוא מל את עורלת לבו "because he [the Wicked Priest] did not circumcise the foreskin of his heart" assumes הערל.

5. Circumcision-related articles encompass a wide range of scriptural passages, including Gen 17 (Brueggemann 1991; Fox 1974); Gen 34 (Geller 1990; Bechtel 1994); Exod 4:24–26, by far the most extensively studied circumcision text (Kaplan 1981; Kosmala 1962; Morgenstern 1963; Blau 1956; de Groot 1943; Coppens 1941; Schmid 1966; Talmon 1954; Houtman 1983; and Propp 1993); Exod 6:12, 30 (Tigay 1978; Hurowitz 1989), Deut 30:6 (Brettler 1999; Le Déaut 1981); Jer 4:4 (Shields 1995; Althann 1981). Diverse topics include: circumcision and Gen 22 (Alexander 1983), the redemptive function of circumcision (Lods 1943; Flusser and Safrai 1980), circumcision and covenant (Isaac 1965), and circumcision in comparative perspective (Sasson 1966).

6. Lesêtre 1926; Hyatt 1962; Licht 1962; Mayer 1989; and Hall 1992.

7. Skinner 1910, 296–97; Westermann 1984, 265; Sarna 1989, 385–87; Wenham 1994, 23–24; Keil 1997, 467–70; and Propp 1998, 233–240, 452–54.

8. Hermisson 1965, 64–76; Morgenstern 1966, 48–66; Eilberg-Schwartz 1990, 141–76; Gevirtz 1990, 93–103; and Grünwaldt 1992, 6–70.

9. Wellhausen 1957, 340–41; de Vaux 1961, 46–48; Vriezen 1967, 151–52; Fohrer 1972, 312; Blenkinsopp 1992, 219; Albertz 1994, 407–8; and Lemche 1998, 122–23.

10. I recognize that the effective distinction between "narrative" and "legal" passages is not clear-cut in the Priestly corpus or the Hebrew canon generally. I follow Ruwe's opinion (2003, 57) that "the differentiation between 'narrative' and 'law'—... as a basic model of literary history has to be questioned."

torial shape,[11] that the crucial circumcision texts are pentateuchal, and that for Jews and Christians the Torah stands at the core of the Hebrew canon. Consequently, a grasp of P's circumcision traditions informs any potential study of circumcision in the Pentateuch or in the Hebrew Bible. Additionally, circumcision emerged, in the early stages of Jewish history, as a crucial point of distinction from formative Christianity and from Greco-Roman society more broadly. As such, the ritual became, and remains, a fundamental marker of Jewish identity.[12] Without understanding the pentateuchal roots of circumcision, it is impossible to accurately assess the later developments of circumcision ideology and practice in Judaism and anticircumcision theology in the New Testament and early Christian writings. Finally, as circumcision has been, and is, practiced by many peoples throughout the world, the biblical text provides one key anchoring point for any comprehensive cross-cultural examination of the rite and its significance.[13]

How does one assess the meaning and standing of a ritual such as circumcision, within a body of literature, when explicit statements of such meaning are few, far between, and, at best, laconic or opaque. This challenge is particularly acute for investigations of the Priestly corpus. Von Rad encapsulates the problem aptly: "in P, we are not dealing with a piece of writing in which the reader is freely addressed and given explanations: on the contrary, the separate traditions, and in particular, P's sacral ordinances … are presented without any interpretation whatsoever" (1962, 78). Geller similarly emphasizes the Priestly tradent's "reticence in verbalizing his underlying concepts. P certainly has ideas but he rarely presents them openly. His motto seems to be, 'Never Explain!'" (1996, 65). Even when P does explain, the reader is left short. For example, Gen 17:11 presents a rationale for the circumcision command: וְהָיָה לְאוֹת בְּרִית בֵּינִי וּבֵינֵיכֶם "It shall be a sign of the covenant between me and you." Fox avers that while "most seem to consider the phrase 'sign of the covenant' self explanatory … [its meaning is] far less transparent than scholars often appear to think." He inquires: "But how is it a sign of the

---

11. Knohl, Milgrom, and their adherents would argue that H was the redactor of Pentateuch. Still, most of the key circumcision texts engaged herein would be catalogued by them as Holiness material. Thus, the thrust of my thesis obtains whether one accepts the H hypothesis or not.

12. Monographs treating circumcision in Jewish writings over time include Barth 1990; Hoffman 1996; Marcus 1996; Kunin 1998; Mark 2003; Cohen 2005; Glick 2005; and Silverman 2006.

13. For a small sampling of works studying circumcision in diverse cultural and geographical settings, see Dessing 2001; Gruenbaum 2001; Biddick 2003; and Darby 2005.

covenant? For whom is it a sign—God, Israel or foreign peoples? What is the function of this sign? What does it signify, and what does it accomplish?" (1974, 558).

Geller observes that the biblical authors, unlike their Greek contemporaries, did not articulate doctrine through systematic, philosophical discourse. Rather, they gave voice to ideology and theology through narrative, law, and other modes of literary expression. Consequently, the extraction of meaning from the Hebrew Scriptures is an exegetical enterprise requiring close reading that "is sensitive to the lineaments of the text, and proceeds step by step within it" (1996, 30–31). That the study of biblical ritual must be, at its core, a text-based endeavor, cannot be overemphasized. For the most part, the exploration of biblical cult practice has been guided by ritual theorists and anthropologists. While the contributions in this oeuvre should not be discounted, there remains an inherent methodological tension that has not been adequately reconciled. Watts (2006, 5) points out

> The problem, in essence, is that we do not have access to ancient Israel's rituals, only to texts that happen to describe or refer to them. The authors of texts describe rituals to further their own interests in writing, not to reflect whatever purposes may have lain behind a ritual's performance.[14]

Ritual theorists will justifiably point out that rites have both official and unofficial meanings. The official meaning of a practice is that which is ascribed by authority figures, such as kings, priests, or shamans. Unofficial meanings are explanations of the ritual offered by members of the culture in question, which may differ from the testimony of the communal leaders.[15] In addition, the field anthropologist has the opportunity to observe a ritual as performed and to offer impressions independent of the gathered testimony. These impressions constitute yet another available layer of meaning. On the other hand, the present investigation is limited to one source of testimony, the Priestly Torah, and within it, in Watts's words, "the texts that happen to describe or refer to" circumcision[16] (ibid.).

---

14. Watts 2007 contains the author's fully fleshed out thesis of ritual rhetoric in P's sacrificial corpus.
15. For application of these analytical categories to the study of circumcision in rabbinic literature, see Hoffman 1993; 1996, 18–21.
16. On the problems attendant to analyzing the biblical text with an anthropologist's tools, see also Gilders 2004, 5–11. Admittedly, in some instances, an exploration of biblical ritual could integrate "testimony" external to the text. For example, a student of worship has access to many intact remains of temples, shrines, altars, stelae,

INTRODUCTION 5

The present monograph is largely influenced by a recent trend in the field, alluded to above, that draws a bold line of demarcation between the study of ritual texts and the study of rituals per se.[17] Watts (2007, 27–32) delineates the distinction quite simply by noting that "texts are not rituals and rituals are not texts." When examining written works that describe or refer to ritual activity, one must exercise due caution before treating these texts as if they are necessarily guides to, or full descriptions of, an actual practice. Rather, one can more profitably, and confidently, consider the message, ideological and theological, that is conveyed through the form and content of the ritual texts and the explicit and implicit attributions of meaning found therein. In this regard, ritual texts such as those in the Hebrew Bible can be approached with the same exegetical tools that are brought to bear on any literary genre, be it narrative, law, or parenesis.[18]

My endeavor is, therefore, at its heart, an exercise in close reading. Each of P's circumcision passages is carefully analyzed in its immediate and broader context. I do not look for a single, fixed, inherent, or essential meaning for circumcision. Rather, I examine circumcision within the full matrix of praxis and beliefs articulated in the Priestly Torah and underscore an array of implications for circumcision in relation to the core elements of P's thought-world and *Heilsgeschichte*.[19]

---

and a wide variety of implements. In the case of circumcision, however, no such data exist. Zevit 2001a is a recent exemplum of studies that integrate textual and material evidence to arrive at as complete a picture as may be possible of Israelite religious practice. It is worth noting that, because of the lack of archeological evidence related to circumcision, Zevit's compendious volume includes a bare four lines on the practice. His brief yet trenchant observation anticipates my conclusions regarding the question of circumcision as ritual: "Circumcision seems to have been a rather straightforward matter, more technical than cultic" (2001a, 665).

17. Scholars who exemplify this trend include Gilders 2004; Gane 2005; Klingbeil 2007; and Watts 2007. Gane's work, for example, illustrates the application of a literary approach to biblical ritual texts. In studying P's Day of Atonement prescriptions, he stresses that "Leviticus 16 portrays the character of YHWH, not by theological assertions, narrative, or even poetry, but by instructions for cultic deeds to be performed in his presence" (2005, xix).

18. This reading strategy is adopted explicitly by Watts in his application of analogous methods to the interpretation of ritual texts (2007) as he does to legal material in a previous monograph (1999).

19. This mode of attack borrows a leaf from Geertz's "cultural system" approach to the study of ritual (Geertz 1973; 1983; Hendel 1989). Geertz's anthropological perspective has led to a much-needed reconsideration of the essentialist approach to ritual that has long been regnant in the scholarship. For instance, Levine (1971)

At all times I prioritize the text's final form. This interpretive strategy is grounded in a conviction that, regardless of the potentially complex compositional and redactional processes that may have produced the P corpus, it is, in its present shape, a document that is internally coherent in style and content.[20]

---

questions Robertson Smith's overarching view of sacrifice as communion but replaces Smith's construct with another essentialist theory, arguing instead that sacrifice should be seen as a gift of greeting or appeasement to the deity. A similar essentialist debate has been carried out over the meaning or rationale behind the scriptural laws of purity. Is defilement a question of demonic possession (Levy-Bruhl 1937), the unnatural (Douglas 1966), or death (Milgrom 1990a, 641–1009, summarized in Milgrom 1990b, 344–46)? For a trenchant critique of Douglas, including an evaluation of the essentialist approach to purity, consult Klawans 2003. Barr's study of biblical philology (1974) similarly privileges contextual analysis over etymology and comparative linguistics in determining the meaning of words. Both Geertz and Barr owe a debt to Wittgenstein's "plain language" philosophical constructs. Wittgenstein argues in *Philosophical Investigations* §43: "For a *large* class of cases—though not for all—in which we employ the word 'meaning' it can be defined thus: the meaning of a word is in its use in the language" (2001, 18). On Wittgenstein's "meaning as use" doctrine, see Hallet 1967; 1977, 115–57; and Carver 1996.

20. Helpful reviews of the many issues and debates concerning the development of the Priestly writings can be found in Vink 1969; Nicholson 1998; and, most recently, Rendtorff and Kugler 2003. Implicit in my "final-form," synchronic approach to P is a position on one of the live questions in contemporary pentateuchal scholarship: Is there a Holiness School (H) whose authorial hand extends far beyond Lev 17–27 and is responsible for the redaction of the whole Torah? The H theory was first proposed by Knohl in an early article (1983/84) and comprehensively presented in monograph form (1995, the English translation of Knohl's published Hebrew University dissertation). Knohl's conclusions had, in some measure, been arrived at independently by Milgrom, as he notes (1991, 13–30). See also Knohl's responses to Milgrom's commentary (1995, 225–30). The pan-H scenario has gained purchase in several generations of scholars. A sample includes Wright 1999; Amit 1997; Olyan 2000; Kugler 1997; and Gilders 2004. Knohl's thesis, however, has been rejected by many exegetes, including Crüsemann 1996, 277–82; Propp 1998, 450; Warning 1999, 180; Levine 2003, 11–23; and Ruwe 2003, 55–78. Schwartz affirms the existence of Holiness material but treats it as a stratum of the larger Priestly corpus rather than as a distinct authorial tradition (1996a, 103–34; 1999, 17–24). Most recently, Olyan (2005), while not explicitly disavowing the H hypothesis in its broad strokes, questions Knohl's arguments regarding one specific pericope, opening up a broader challenge to Knohl's assumptions. I find there to be significant continuity in idiom and ideology across the entire Priestly corpus. This reading of P is borne out, at least as concerns the present study, by my demonstration of a fully integrated conception of circumcision across the boundaries of what some consider P and H (according to the chart in Knohl 1995, 104–15, Gen

Thus, a "synchronic" or "holistic" reading is fully sustainable.[21] Geller articulates the ethos incisively:

> Our approach holds that editing is as creative a literary task as composition, quite equivalent literarily with authorship, especially in ancient works in which the line between authors and editors is often very faint.... And the priestly editor of the Pentateuch was indeed an artist, producing not a patchwork aggregate signifying nothing, but a work meaningful in the whole, a tapestry more than the sum of its woven strands, a truly fit object of literary analysis. (1996, 62–63)

The goals of my inquiry, and the nature of the primary evidence under consideration, dictate certain limits in method and scope. By definition, in a context-driven study, heavy reliance upon comparative data is precluded. Thus, for example, the possibility that circumcision had been practiced as an initiatory or redemptive rite in Egypt, Canaan, and Israel is not unimportant. This knowledge, however, does not bring the reader any closer to understanding P's views about circumcision, except to acknowledge that P did not innovate the practice. Sarna's assertion is apposite: "The origin and meaning of a custom so old and so widely diffused cannot fail to be of absorbing interest to the anthropologist. Yet, his conclusions will be of little relevance to the biblical scholar, except in so far as they help to point up the remarkable transformation of the rite in Israel" (1966, 132).

Since the Priestly corpus is the object of my investigation, non-P biblical material will not be ignored but will also be regarded as comparative. Typically, Priestly texts can be fruitfully studied in their own right and against the background of other biblical authorial traditions, most notably, the Deuteronomic corpus. Thus, in a treatment of dietary regulations, one would naturally analyze Lev 11 in conjunction to Deut 14. With circumcision, however, such comparative opportunities are all but absent, as circumcision regulations appear only in the Priestly writings. Still, I do exploit innerbiblical comparisons when feasible, highlighting the distinctive facets of P's covenantal theology in contrast to Deuteronomic notions (see 27–32 below) and in my

---

17:7–8, 14; Exod 12:43–49; and Lev 26 are H, while the bulk of Gen 17 and Lev 12 are P. Knohl does acknowledge [1995, 102, 104] that the authorship of the key circumcision prescriptions of Gen 17 is "still unclear"). In sum, I stand squarely with those who are not persuaded by the "Holiness school" scenario.

21. The potentially dichotomous approaches to biblical interpretation, "synchronic, or holistic," as opposed to "diachronic, or, redactional," are well laid out in de Moor 1995, especially in contributions to the volume by Barr and Hoftijzer.

study of the foreskinned heart metaphor, which has a relatively wide canonical distribution (79–80, 104–5, 109–14, 126–29 below).

I take an assertively agnostic attitude toward historical questions, for two reasons. First, as I argue (115–21), there are no compelling grounds to link P's vision of circumcision to any particular circumstance or period in ancient Israel's history. More significantly, my "ahistorical" posture mirrors the Priestly agenda. The P narrative is set in the desert, in mythic time and space, thus "cleansing the cult's pristine and universal message from the contingencies of mere history, geography, and regnant political climate."[22] In like manner, the sacred cult site, the tabernacle, where the divine presence comes to rest, which is at the center of P's spatial and ideological maps, is imagined as fully portable. Thus, it is deliberately untethered to any particular geographical location or topographical element.[23] That the Priestly laws and ideals are meant to be "timeless," disconnected from the contingencies of the author/editor's own social and historical context, is reflected on the semantic level, in P's deployment of the word עולם, translatable as "eternal" or "perpetual." In the Priestly corpus, עולם appears as a component of several significant recurring phrases, the most common of which is חק/ת עולם, "perpetual statute" (33x). Other examples, in descending order of frequency, include ברית עולם, "perpetual covenant" (8x); אחזת עולם, "perpetual [property] holding" (3x); כהנת עולם, "perpetual priesthood" (1x); and גאלת עולם, "redemption in perpetuity" (1x). This pointed and insistent use of עולם has a rhetorical force. It underscores P's message that the laws, covenants, and landholdings presented in the text do not apply to any particular generation or generations. Rather, YHWH's mandates transcend any context, whether historical, political, or geographical, and are applicable to all Israel, for all time.

The articulated aim of the present study is to discern the meanings of circumcision as represented in the Priestly Torah. I should point out, however, that inherent in such an enterprise is a clarification of meanings that circumcision *does not* carry in the Priestly mindset. Accordingly, I demonstrate that, given the limited mention of circumcision in the Priestly corpus,[24] the ramifications of the ritual for P's covenantal ideology are quite extensive. On the other hand, I maintain that the Priestly tradent deliberately circumscribed the potential resonances of circumcision with respect to the cult. Thus, circumci-

---

22. The phraseology is borrowed from Appiah 2006. Appiah discusses issues unrelated to the Hebrew Bible, yet the language is apropos.

23. On the implication of P's tabernacle as a mobile shrine, see Sommer 2001.

24. A mere seventeen verses, within six chapters, attest derivations of מול and ערל (Gen 17:10, 11, 12, 13, 14, 23, 24, 25; 21:4; Exod 6:12, 30; Lev 12:3; 19:23; 26:41).

sion in P is not a sacrifice, a rite of dedication, redemption, or purification, nor does it have any implications for fertility or sexual function. Additionally, from the Priestly perspective, circumcision is neither a sign of ethnicity nor a national or communal boundary marker.

The questions engaged in a text-based study must, perforce, be engendered by the texts themselves. I include, therefore, a basic review of P's circumcision passages in canonical order, focusing upon narrative context and literary structure. In this process, instances of actual genital circumcision are treated separately from examples of circumcision metaphor (where circumcision terminology is utilized in connection to anything other than the penis). Admittedly, the text itself does not mark passages explicitly with labels such as "metaphoric" or "literal." Still, the P material does evince discrimination, semantically, and thus conceptually, between the two types of circumcision unit. Within all three of the genital circumcision sections (Gen 17–21; Exod 12; Lev 12), the verb מול, "circumcise," is found, along with forms of ערל, "foreskin." On the other hand, the three nongenital circumcision passages (Exod 6; Lev 19; 26) attest only derivations of ערל, and none employ the verb מול. While the "literal" and metaphorical units are treated separately for heuristic purposes, they are still regarded as parts of a conceptual whole. Thus the circumcision metaphors cannot be understood without reference to the instances of genital circumcision in the text. By the same token, the metaphors, particularly the foreskinned heart image in Lev 26, unquestionably flesh out our understanding of genital circumcision in P.

The treatment of genital circumcision thus commences with an introduction to the three germane units: Gen 17–21; Exod 12; and Lev 12. With this foundation, the implications of circumcision for P's understanding of covenant are explored. Next, I inquire as to how circumcision, or lack thereof, functions as an indicator of status, with respect to Israelites and various categories of outsiders in P's societal map. The rite is also situated against the background of P's larger constructs of gender and sexuality. Finally, the place of circumcision within the Priestly cultic system is contemplated. Vital questions in this chapter include: What sort of ritual is circumcision, and how does it function as ritual act? Why must circumcision be performed on the eighth day? What is the particular connection of circumcision and Passover observance? How does failure to circumcise relate to the full set of infractions that warrant the *karet* penalty?

The next stage entails an investigation of the relationship between "literal" genital circumcision and figurative ערלה. To develop a vocabulary for this inquiry, a theoretical consideration of metaphor and symbolic language is undertaken. Next, the relatively obscure and opaque images of Moses' foreskinned lips (Exod 6) and the foreskinned fruit trees (Lev 19) are scrutinized.

These bear, at best, a tenuous connection to the practice of circumcision. I attempt, nonetheless, to locate them, respectively, in the context of the Exodus narrative and P's system of food laws and offerings. Finally, the foreskinned heart metaphor in Lev 26 is unpacked and revealed as a lynchpin of P's covenantal historiography and notions of communal transgression and penitence. Additionally, in a historically focused epilogue, I confront the widely held view that circumcision gained currency in biblical Israel as a result of the Babylonian exile.

I conclude by synthesizing the findings of the study as a whole, emphasizing the wide-ranging implications of circumcision for P's ideological matrix, while also acknowledging the limits of the rite's significance within P's doctrinal arena. With that foundation, I explore, summarily, the ramifications of my inquiry into the Priestly corpus for investigations of circumcision in a canonical perspective and for studies of the ritual's evolution in subsequent Jewish textual traditions.

Part 1
Actual Genital Circumcision

1
Introduction

Genesis 17; 21:1–5;[1] Exod 12; and Lev 12 are the scriptural units that directly reference actual, genital circumcision in the Priestly literature. In the proceeding study, the contents of these chapters will be regarded as "of a piece" and approached synthetically, with treatments, by topic, of the circumcision-related questions raised within the texts. Since most of the discussion in the present work will draw upon these units, an introduction to them is warranted. The chapters will be treated individually, in canonical order, with the exposition focusing upon matters taken up throughout the study.

The three major circumcision passages under consideration, Gen 17:1–27; 21:1–5; Exod 12:43–49; and Lev 12:3 are, in the main, prescriptive. Despite this formal affinity, the units in question are found in diverse literary settings. The Genesis circumcision mandate is imparted during a dialogue between God and Abraham and is followed promptly by the narration of Abraham carrying out the directive. The Exod 12 circumcision regulations are part of a larger body of Passover law, located within the narrative context of Israel's departure from Egypt and the celebration of the first Passover.[2] The single germane Leviticus verse, 12:3, is situated in the midst of a block of purity legislation that is patently unrelated to circumcision.

---

1. In the final form of Genesis, chapters 17 and 21:1–5 do not form one contiguous unit. However, they do constitute continuous Priestly text and can be considered a full "circumcision tale" beginning with the command to Abraham and concluding with the fulfillment of that command in the circumcision of Abraham, Ishmael, Abraham's household slaves, and, finally, Isaac. The intervening chapters are recognized as emanating from a non-P hand.

2. Ruwe (2003, 57) rightly cautions against a strict differentiation between narrative and legislation, noting that "the so-called 'legislative material' itself is substantially determined by the fictional elements of the frame of the surrounding story."

Genesis 17, 21:1–5

Genesis 17 is the *locus classicus* for the circumcision injunction, which constitutes the only commandment incumbent upon the Israelite people that is delivered in the ancestral period, as opposed to after the exodus, when Israel has attained full-fledged nationhood. Moreover, the chapter provides the narrative foundation of God's ברית-promises[3] to Israel in the Priestly corpus. Genesis 17 exemplifies the elevated style of the Priestly legislator. The language and structure is complex and concentrated, typified by repetition of theme words and sophisticated devices such as inversion and paronomasia.[4] This style is often considered "semipoetic."[5] The stylistic and structural features of the chapter are of interest to exegetes beyond the matter of aesthetics. P's meaning and message are delivered quite effectively through the combination of content and form.

The chapter contains two distinct episodes: 17:1–22, which is almost entirely dialogue, recounts the intercourse between God and Abraham and consists of divinely delivered promises and circumcision instructions, along with Abraham's responses, verbal and nonverbal; 17:23–27 narrates the fulfillment of the commands: the circumcision of Abraham, Ishmael, and all the males of Abraham's household. Genesis 21:1–5, recording the conception, birth, and circumcision of Isaac, is P's continuation of the ancestral account.

The initial episode, which records God's interaction with Abraham, should be divided into five units: 1–3a, 3b–8, 9–14, 15–18, and 19–22.[6] These

---

3. ברית in P carries a particular range of meaning. This range is not well represented by the standard English term "covenant." Moreover, biblical "covenant," as it is typically understood, does not necessarily conform to P's technical understanding of ברית. Thus, throughout the present study, ברית will be left untranslated.

4. See McEvenue 1971 on this section and Warning 1999 on microstructure in P. On Priestly style in various key sections, see McEvenue (1971, 67–77) on the "rainbow-ברית" unit in Gen 9 and Schwartz 1991 on the Lev 17 prohibitions against eating blood.

5. See also Korpel 1987 and especially Paran 1989, 98–136 on the poetic nature of P's style.

6. To date, several differing scenarios have been proposed for the structure of the whole chapter. Westermann (1981, 306) sees three parts to God's speech to Abraham: Promise (3b–8), Command (9–14), and Promise (15–21). McEvenue (1971, 157–58) proposes five units with a chiastic (in his terminology "palistrophic") structure and six units in a "parallel panel." Williamson (2000, 147–48) rightly objects, observing that McEvenue forces certain elements to artificially conform to an order not really present. He further claims that, "while such complex literary arrangements (linear development, palistrophic pattern and parallel panels) may reflect the deliberated

units are demarcated by the initiation of divine speech, all employing forms of the verb אמר.⁷ They can be digested as follows.

1. 17:1–3A

This passage recounts God's appearance to Abraham and his disclosure of the divine name אל שדי. It contains the first promise—וְאֶתְּנָה בְרִיתִי בֵּינִי וּבֵינֶךָ וְאַרְבֶּה אוֹתְךָ בִּמְאֹד מְאֹד "I will grant my בְּרִית between me and between you and I will make you very very numerous"—and the first charge: הִתְהַלֵּךְ לְפָנַי וֶהְיֵה תָמִים "Walk before me and be blameless." Westermann (1984, 259) labels 1–3a a prologue, as it opens the scene and contains an apocopated form of the promise fully presented in the next unit. His view is plausible but a bit restrictive, as the verses do not contain only prefatory material. The charge הִתְהַלֵּךְ לְפָנַי ..., as a general moral imperative, stands on its own. Moreover, the promise וְאַרְבֶּה אוֹתְךָ is not merely introductory. It combines with וְהִפְרֵתִי אֹתְךָ in 17:6 to fully echo God's first words to humanity פְּרוּ וּרְבוּ (Gen 1:28). This diad is again found in the blessing received by Ishmael in 17:20: וְהִרְבֵּיתִי אֹתוֹ וְהִפְרֵיתִי אֹתוֹ.⁸

---

design of the author or compiler of this pericope, the presence of one seems to cast serious doubt over the existence of the others." Note Levine's generally applicable warning on the limited utility of chiasm as a structuring device: "Chiasm is a feature best restricted to small textual units. It enhances style and focuses the attention of the reader through the reinforcement that comes with repetition, and by shifting the order of the discrete components that comprise a complete statement. To characterize the sequential relationship of large textual units, of complete chapters or whole narratives, as chiasm is a questionable application of this feature" (1993, 80–81). The advantage of my division above is its sensitivity to the text's own cues and literary markers, rather than reliance on a solely conceptual analysis of content, per Westermann, or overly complex structures, per McEvenue.

7. Baker 1979 demonstrates the way in which introductory divine speech formulae such as וידבר serve as division markers in the Priestly legal corpus. Unit partition of this type has the advantage of relying upon linguistic markers within the text rather than more subjective content-based divisions such as that found in the work of McEvenue and others noted above.

8. On the resonance of פְּרוּ וּרְבוּ throughout the P material in Genesis, see Lohfink 1994, 166.

2. 17:3B–8

Here we have the name change and a more extensive promise configured of the following elements:[9]

- a. Progeny
  אַב הֲמוֹן גּוֹיִם "father of many nations" (17:4, 5)
  וְהִפְרֵתִי אֹתְךָ בִּמְאֹד מְאֹד "I will make you very very fruitful" (17:6)
  וּמְלָכִים מִמְּךָ יֵצֵאוּ "Kings will issue from you" (17:7)[10]

- b. Relationship[11]
  לִהְיוֹת לְךָ לֵאלֹהִים וּלְזַרְעֲךָ אַחֲרֶיךָ "To be God to you and to your seed after you" (17:7)
  וְהָיִיתִי לָהֶם לֵאלֹהִים "I will be God to them" (17:8)

- c. Land
  וְנָתַתִּי לְךָ וּלְזַרְעֲךָ אַחֲרֶיךָ אֵת אֶרֶץ מְגֻרֶיךָ אֵת כָּל־אֶרֶץ כְּנַעַן לַאֲחֻזַּת עוֹלָם "I will grant to you and your seed after you the land of your dwelling, all of the land of Canaan, as a perpetual holding" (17:8)

The unit is replete with typical grant and covenant-making formulas: נתן 17:5, 6, 8; and וַהֲקִמֹתִי אֶת־בְּרִיתִי בֵּינִי וּבֵינֶךָ וּבֵין זַרְעֲךָ אַחֲרֶיךָ לְדֹרֹתָם לִבְרִית עוֹלָם ("I will fulfill my ברית between me and between you and between your offspring after you, for their generations as a perpetual ברית").

3. 17:9–14

This passage is the crux of the Gen 17 pericope, the most fully developed circumcision regulation in the Torah, and the central circumcision text in the Hebrew canon.[12] It is reproduced and translated here in full:

---

9. On the promises in general, see Westermann 1976; Williamson 2000. Brettler (1978/79) and Weinfeld (1993, 1–21, 222–64) treat the land promise specifically.

10. This verse constitutes the sole mention of kingship in the Priestly corpus. This is in keeping with P's general apolitical, amonarchic tendency.

11. This is one half of what is typically called the "covenant formulary," on which see Rendtorff 1998.

12. The centrality of this passage vis-à-vis circumcision tradition obtains in post-biblical Judaism until this day.

(9) וַיֹּאמֶר אֱלֹהִים אֶל־אַבְרָהָם
וְאַתָּה אֶת־בְּרִיתִי תִשְׁמֹר אַתָּה וְזַרְעֲךָ אַחֲרֶיךָ לְדֹרֹתָם
(10) זֹאת בְּרִיתִי אֲשֶׁר תִּשְׁמְרוּ בֵּינִי וּבֵינֵיכֶם וּבֵין זַרְעֲךָ אַחֲרֶיךָ
הִמּוֹל לָכֶם כָּל־זָכָר
(11) וּנְמַלְתֶּם אֵת בְּשַׂר עָרְלַתְכֶם וְהָיָה לְאוֹת בְּרִית בֵּינִי וּבֵינֵיכֶם
(12) וּבֶן־שְׁמֹנַת יָמִים יִמּוֹל לָכֶם כָּל־זָכָר לְדֹרֹתֵיכֶם
יְלִיד בָּיִת וּמִקְנַת־כֶּסֶף מִכֹּל בֶּן־נֵכָר אֲשֶׁר לֹא מִזַּרְעֲךָ הוּא
(13) הִמּוֹל יִמּוֹל יְלִיד בֵּיתְךָ וּמִקְנַת כַּסְפֶּךָ
וְהָיְתָה בְרִיתִי בִּבְשַׂרְכֶם לִבְרִית עוֹלָם
(14) וְעָרֵל זָכָר אֲשֶׁר לֹא־יִמּוֹל אֶת־בְּשַׂר עָרְלָתוֹ
וְנִכְרְתָה הַנֶּפֶשׁ הַהִוא מֵעַמֶּיהָ אֶת־בְּרִיתִי הֵפַר

(9) God said to Abraham: "And you, my ברית must you keep, you and your seed after you for their generations. (10) This is my ברית that you must keep, between me and you and your seed after you: Every one of your males is to be circumcised. (11) And you must circumcise the flesh of your foreskins, and it shall be a sign of the ברית between me and between you. (12) Your eight-day-old shall be circumcised, every male of your generations, the home-born and the purchased slave from among the foreigners who are not of your seed. (13) Your-home born and your purchased slave must surely be circumcised so that[13] my ברית will be on your flesh as an eternal ברית. (14) And the uncircumcised male, the flesh of whose foreskin is not circumcised, that person will be cut off from his people; he has abrogated my ברית."

P's semi-poetic style is evident in the passage. It has a tight, interlocking structure where a key element from one line is repeated in the next, accompanied by the introduction of a new element. The text can be schematized as follows:

9   [Keep ברית]
10 [Keep ברית] [Circumcise Males]
11 [Circumcise] [Sign of the ברית].

---

13. The phrase הִמּוֹל יִמּוֹל is constructed of an infinitive absolute followed by an imperfect, whose combination has imperative force (*IBHS* 35.2.1b). This volitional form followed by the ו + suffix conjugation וְהָיְתָה can express a "consequent situation" (*IBHS* 32.2.2a), justifying the translation "must surely be circumcised *so that...*"

12	[Circumcise Males] [Eighth Day]	[Circumcise Slaves]	
13		[Circumcise Slaves]	[ברית]
14		[Circumcised]	[Abrogate ברית]
		[*karet* penalty]	

Verse 11, the pivotal verse in the prescriptive unit, is underscored in several respects. First, it is in the spatial center of the passage. Second, וּנְמַלְתֶּם interrupts a consistent pattern of מול conjugations: הִמּוֹל (17:10); יִמּוֹל (17:12); הִמּוֹל יִמּוֹל (17:13); יִמּוֹל (17:14). Moreover, the verb form is anomalous within the Priestly writings and the biblical canon as a whole.[14] Finally, אות ברית is

---

14. The idiosyncratic conjugation וּנְמַלְתֶּם in Gen 17:11 has engendered some confusion among commentators. Modern scholars have reasoned that, since the verb's root is מול, the נ must indicate a *niphal*. However the expected second masculine plural *niphal* would be נִמֹּלְתֶּם*. Commentators have typically relied upon Gesenius (GKC 67g,dd), who attributes the anomaly to "neglect of the strengthening in aramaizing forms" of the *niphal* in hollow and geminate verbs. (See Gunkel 1997, 265; Skinner 1910, 294; Wenham 1994, 15; and the BDB entry מול.) Nearly one thousand years ago, a more elegant solution was proposed by Rashi and Abraham Ibn Ezra. They read וּנְמַלְתֶּם as a *qal*, according to its vocalization, treating the נ as a first radical. (It is clear from their choice of ותגזרון that Targums Onqelos, Pseudo-Jonathan, and Neophiti all read ונמלתם as an active verb. LXX, on the other hand, uses the passive περιτμηθήσεσθε.)

The grammars (GKC 77; JM 84–85) note the close semantic relationship of particular weak verbs. Certain originally biliteral verbs display simultaneous development into two different triliteral root structures with the same meaning. In the case of ע"ו and פ"ן verbs, examples are נמג = מוג "melt," נפח = פוח "blow," and פוץ = נפץ "shatter." (Evidence of divergent root development from original bi-radicals is also evident between Semitic languages. A classic example is "give," which is נתן in Hebrew and יתן in Phoenician and Ugaritic.) Linear development from ע"ו to פ"ן is also possible. וּנְמַלְתֶּם is one such occurrence. Greenberg avers, concerning וְיִנָּזֵר in Ezek 14:7: "*nzr* is backformed from *nazoru* [Ezek 14:5, *niphal* of זור, 'fall away'], as though its *n* were radical (cf. *nmltm* Gen 17:11 backformed from *nmwl* 'be circumcised' from *mwl*)" (1983, 249). The same phenomenon is observable in conjugations of the root קוט "loathe." The verb is clearly attested three times in the *niphal* (Ezek 6:9; 20:43; 36:31). An additional occurrence, in Job 10:1 (נָקְטָה נַפְשִׁי בְּחַיָּי), is taken as a *niphal* in the lexica, grammars, and concordances but should be read according to its vocalization, as a third singular feminine *qal* first נ. The presence of a subject (נפש) and an object (חיים) lend credence to the assertion that נָקְטָה need not be parsed as a passive, and translators typically give the verb an active voice. I find that the above back-formations represent developments in the conjugations of the respective verbs. The first radical נ crept into the language because users were accustomed to hearing/reading the verb in the *niphal*, with its typical preformative נ.

4. 17:15–18

In this unit God tells Abraham of his wife's destiny. As with Abraham, she has her name changed by the addition of a ה element (17:15). Sarah is also the recipient of various promises (17:16). These promises, of nations and royalty descending from her, parallel those given to Abraham. However, while Abraham is the recipient of God's ברית, this term is never used with his wife. Rather, Sarah is blessed (ברך) by God. Abraham's surprised reaction וַיִּפֹּל אַבְרָהָם עַל־פָּנָיו וַיִּצְחָק "Abraham fell on his face and laughed" (17:17), anticipates their son's naming (17:19; 21:3).[16] Given the predicted birth of a son by his "chief wife," and the blessings conferred upon him, Abraham expresses concern about the fate of his existing son, Ishmael (17:18).

5. 17:19–22

God's response to Abraham is recorded. Isaac's birth is announced, and God promises, וַהֲקִמֹתִי אֶת־בְּרִיתִי אִתּוֹ לִבְרִית עוֹלָם לְזַרְעוֹ אַחֲרָיו "I will fulfill my ברית with him as an eternal ברית for his seed after him" (17:19), echoing the promise in 17:7. God continues with a blessing for Ishmael—

הִנֵּה בֵּרַכְתִּי אֹתוֹ וְהִפְרֵיתִי אֹתוֹ וְהִרְבֵּיתִי אֹתוֹ בִּמְאֹד מְאֹד
שְׁנֵים־עָשָׂר נְשִׂיאִם יוֹלִיד וּנְתַתִּיו לְגוֹי גָּדוֹל

> Behold, I will bless him so as to make him fruitful and very very numerous. He will give birth to twelve chieftains and I will make him a great nation (17:20)

—and then reiterates the Isaac promise: וְאֶת־בְּרִיתִי אָקִים אֶת־יִצְחָק אֲשֶׁר תֵּלֵד לְךָ שָׂרָה "But my ברית I will fulfill with Isaac, whom Sarah will bear for you" (17:21). Included in 17:21 is the detail that Abraham and Sarah's son will be born one year hence. The text here emphasizes the same ברית versus ברך

---

15. Schwartz 1991 makes a similar observation about form and content in the Priestly corpus, when he argues that Lev 17:11, which articulates the atoning power of blood, is the pivotal verse in the unit proscribing the consumption of blood.

16. On the use of anticipatory information as a literary technique, see Sarna 1981.

contrast with regard to Isaac and Ishmael that was delineated earlier with Abraham and Sarah. God's cessation of speech and departure in verse 22 neatly closes the pericope.¹⁷

The chapter concludes with verses 23–27. This section encapsulates Abraham's fulfillment of the circumcision command delivered by God in verses 9–14 by repeating key language from the circumcision regulation. The verb מול occurs five times, once in every verse, and the phrase בשר ערלה is attested three times (17:23, 24, 25). The narration also picks up on other terminology from 17:9–14, such as כל זכר, יליד בית, and מקנת כסף. The expression בְּעֶצֶם הַיּוֹם הַזֶּה דִּבֶּר אִתּוֹ אֱלֹהִים emphasizes Abraham's immediate and punctilious obedience to the divine injunction. The only aspect of the circumcision legislation missing in the passage is the eighth-day mandate. This element is actualized in the circumcision of Isaac, later in the account.

The Priestly portion of the ancestral narrative resumes with Gen 21:1–5. With this brief passage P concludes the circumcision pericope and inaugurates the Isaac episode of the patriarch cycle. Isaac is born, named, and circumcised on the eighth day. The text emphasizes both Abraham's obedience to God's command and YHWH's faithfulness to his own commitments. The notice in 21:5 that Abraham was one hundred years old signals that Isaac's birth was, as promised in 17:21, one year after Abraham's encounter with God.¹⁸

The Genesis passages are not only the first mention of circumcision in the Priestly Torah; they constitute the fullest expositions of the regulation of, and rationale for, the practice. The text enumerates the commands given to Abraham (17:9–14) and follows later with their execution (17:23–27; 21:1–5). The fact that the circumcision mandate is juxtaposed to God's ברית-promises and that circumcision is called a "sign of the ברית" between God and Abraham points to the ideological underpinnings of the practice in the Priestly worldview. These issues will be explored more fully in the chapters below devoted to the relationship between circumcision and ברית.

---

17. On literary closure devices, see Wyckoff 2006.

18. The repetition evidenced in Gen 17's two episodes follows a pattern that is well recognized in the Hebrew Bible and the literature of the ancient Near East. Parker (1989, 26–33) classifies this type of repetition as "transposition," of speech to narrative, specifically highlighting instructions and their execution, as with Abraham's adherence to YHWH's circumcision commandment, and prediction and fulfillment, as with God's promise to Abraham of a son through whom the ברית promises will be upheld.

Exodus 12

Exodus 12:1–13:16 narrates the beginning of Israel's departure from Egypt and recounts the celebration of the first Passover. It also presents regulations for the festival's observance, from the preparation and consumption of the paschal offering to abstention from leaven.[19]

The unit relevant to the present inquiry is 12:43–49, which, according to Noth, is "principally concerned with the question of admission to the Passover sacrifice" (1962, 100). The passage is reproduced and translated below.

(43) וַיֹּאמֶר ה' אֶל־מֹשֶׁה וְאַהֲרֹן
זֹאת חֻקַּת הַפָּסַח כָּל־בֶּן־נֵכָר לֹא־יֹאכַל בּוֹ
(44) וְכָל־עֶבֶד אִישׁ מִקְנַת־כָּסֶף וּמַלְתָּה אֹתוֹ אָז יֹאכַל בּוֹ
(45) תּוֹשָׁב וְשָׂכִיר לֹא־יֹאכַל־בּוֹ
(46) בְּבַיִת אֶחָד יֵאָכֵל לֹא־תוֹצִיא מִן־הַבַּיִת מִן־הַבָּשָׂר חוּצָה
וְעֶצֶם לֹא תִשְׁבְּרוּ־בוֹ
(47) כָּל־עֲדַת יִשְׂרָאֵל יַעֲשׂוּ אֹתוֹ
(48) וְכִי־יָגוּר אִתְּךָ גֵּר וְעָשָׂה פֶסַח לַה'
הִמּוֹל לוֹ כָל־זָכָר וְאָז יִקְרַב לַעֲשֹׂתוֹ וְהָיָה כְּאֶזְרַח הָאָרֶץ
וְכָל־עָרֵל לֹא־יֹאכַל בּוֹ
(49) תּוֹרָה אַחַת יִהְיֶה לָאֶזְרָח וְלַגֵּר הַגָּר בְּתוֹכְכֶם

(43) And YHWH said to Moses and Aaron: This is the law of the paschal offering: No foreigner may eat of it. (44) And any man's slave who is bought with money, you must circumcise him and then he may eat of it. (45) The household or wage laborer may not eat of it.[20] (46) In one house it shall be eaten. Do not remove any of the meat from the house to the outside and do not break any of its bones. (47) The whole community of Israel shall perform it. (48) And if a resident

---

19. The Deuteronomic counterpart is Deut 16:1–8. Other pentateuchal Passover-related prescriptions are contained in Exod 23:14–19; 34:18–26 (Covenant Code, JE); Lev 23:4–8 and Num 9–1–14; 28:16–25 (P). In the historical works Passover is mentioned in Josh 5:10–12, 2 Kgs 23:21–23; Ezek 45:21–25; Ezra 6:19–22; 2 Chr 30; 35:1–19.

20. The text specifies two types of hireling, the תושב and the שכיר. The former resided at his employer's premises, while the latter was a wage laborer who lived in his own home. The pair תושב/שכיר is attested in P in Lev 22:10; 25:6, 40. Lev 19:13 enjoins the Israelite to pay the שכיר every day without fail.

alien resides with you and performs a paschal offering to YHWH, all his males must be circumcised, and then he may approach to perform it. He shall be as a native of the land. No one uncircumcised may eat of it. (49) There shall be one law for the native and one for the resident alien who resides among you.

The language is straightforward as to paschal "eligibility." When the unit is read in conjunction with Gen 17, it is apparent that circumcision and eating of the Passover offering are both optional to the גר. The inclusive, gender-neutrality, of the phrase כָּל־עֲדַת יִשְׂרָאֵל יַעֲשׂוּ אֹתוֹ obligates males and females alike. It is reasonable to conclude that non-Israelite females were allowed to participate in the Passover according to the eligibility of their fathers, husbands, or masters.

The גר rule stipulates that the resident alien and his household may perform the paschal sacrifice as long as all his males are circumcised. Since all the males in an Israelite household include sons and slaves, we can assume this to be the case with the גר as well. Moreover, as with Israelites, the females in a גר's household are likely included by virtue of the males' admissibility. In sum, the unit underscores that circumcision is an inviolable criterion for participation in the Passover festival offering. As such, the Exod 12 pericope forges an important link between circumcision and Passover.

Leviticus 12

Leviticus 12–15 contains regulations pertaining to various types of ritual defilement and purification procedures.[21] Chapter 12 deals with the contamination incurred by a woman as a result of childbirth. The text distinguishes two levels of defilement: the more profound lasts seven days after the birth of a male child and fourteen in the case of a female. This defilement is articulated as equivalent to that of the menstruant. The language, כימי נדת דותה (12:2) and כנדתה (12:5),[22] implies that the restrictions enumerated in Lev 15:19–24 apply equally to the parturient. The second tier of defilement entails a further thirty-three day waiting period with a male newborn and double that with the birth of female. For this duration, the postpartum mother is

---

21. On the structure and content of these chapters, see especially Milgrom 1991, 742–1008).

22. See the commentaries of Milgrom (1991:744), Hoffman (1953:249), and Levine (1989:73) on the implication of these phrases and Magonet (1996) on the double duration of defilement in the case of the baby girl.

only denied entrance to the sanctuary and contact with sacred objects. After these waiting periods, the mother completes her purification by offering an עולה and a חטאת.

The chapter's legislation begins:

אִשָּׁה כִּי תַזְרִיעַ וְיָלְדָה זָכָר וְטָמְאָה שִׁבְעַת יָמִים
כִּימֵי נִדַּת דְּוֹתָהּ תִּטְמָא

A woman who conceives and bears a male shall be defiled for seven days. As the days of her menstrual illness shall she be defiled. (Lev 12:2)

The next verse interrupts this stream of thought by noting:

וּבַיּוֹם הַשְּׁמִינִי יִמּוֹל בְּשַׂר עָרְלָתוֹ

"And on the eighth day, the flesh of his foreskin shall be circumcised."

Leviticus 12:3 does not relate directly to the issue of birth defilement, yet the syntax of verses 2 and 3 is straightforward, with 12:3 following the preceding verse without a "bump":

אִשָּׁה כִּי תַזְרִיעַ וְיָלְדָה זָכָר וְטָמְאָה שִׁבְעַת יָמִים ... וּבַיּוֹם הַשְּׁמִינִי ...

"A woman who conceives and bears a male is defiled for seven days.... And on the eighth day...."

In fact, the pattern ... שבעת ימים ... ו/ב/מיום השמיני ... recurs in P.[23] The subject-object-verb relationships in the verse are straightforward. יִמּוֹל is a *niphal* (passive) whose object is the flesh of the foreskin. The referent of the pronominal suffix עָרְלָתוֹ is the male child, זכר, mentioned in the previous verse. The associative, seemingly tangential, reference to circumcision serves a specific function within the chapter wholly concerned with postpartum defilement. It reminds the reader/audience, "While we are on the subject of a baby boy's first week, don't forget the circumcision injunction." Such cross-references are part of P's legislative repertoire. They fulfill a uniform function.

---

23. See Lev 9:1; 14:1; 15:14, 29; 22:27; 23:36, 39 and Num 6:10.

They draw attention to a law found earlier in the canonical arrangement, which is also relevant to the new context.[24]

Synthesis

Genesis 17 is the key Priestly circumcision pericope. The specifics of the practice are detailed in 17:9–14. All males must be circumcised on the eighth day. The injunction applies not only to the Israelite and his family but to foreign slaves who are owned by the Israelite. Failure to circumcise brings a *karet* penalty. Though the mandate is delivered directly to Abraham, it will apply to all future generations emanating from the patriarch. Along with the presentation of the regulation, the chapter, and its continuation in 21:1–5, narrates Abraham's precise fulfillment of the divine command. He immediately circumcises himself and his whole household, including his then thirteen-year-old eldest son, Ishmael. One year later, the patriarch circumcises his newborn, Isaac, on the eighth day. The text provides a rationale, albeit laconic, for the practice. Genesis 17:11 avers that circumcision is the sign of the ברית between God and Abraham and his offspring, and 17:13 follows with an affirmation that circumcision ensures that the ברית sign is found on the flesh of each and every Israelite male.

---

24. Another example of the reminder appears among the festival prescriptions of Lev 23, where 23:9–21 details the customs of the עמר "first barley sheaf" and the בכורים "firstfruits" harvest offerings. An aside follows in verse 22:

וּבְקֻצְרְכֶם אֶת־קְצִיר אַרְצְכֶם
לֹא־תְכַלֶּה פְּאַת שָׂדְךָ בְּקֻצְרֶךָ וְלֶקֶט קְצִירְךָ לֹא תְלַקֵּט
לֶעָנִי וְלַגֵּר תַּעֲזֹב אֹתָם אֲנִי יְהוָה אֱלֹהֵיכֶם

When you harvest the harvest of your land, do not completely harvest the corners of your field, and the gleanings of your harvest do not glean. To the poor and the stranger you must leave them. I YHWH am your God.

The verse is an abbreviated, slightly altered, citation of Lev 19:9–10. Ibn Ezra and Nachmanides both assert that the verse serves to caution the Israelite that even when the proceeds of the harvest are devoted to God in the context of a festival, responsibility to the poor may not be neglected. Lev 19:10a, which deals with grapevines, is excluded from the extract. Wenham (1979, 305) notes "It [Lev 23:22] omits reference to the grape harvest, which would be inappropriate at this time of year, since grapes ripen much later. (On the parrallels between the verses Lev 19:10–11 and 23:22, see Schwartz 1999, 303).

The circumcision injunction is juxtaposed to a series of divine commitments granted to Abraham, Sarah, Ishmael, and Isaac. Abraham is guaranteed progeny, land, and a special relationship to God. This series of promises, which is characterized as God's ברית, is to be continued through Isaac. Sarah and Ishmael are, in their turn, assured great offspring. The promises to them are delivered through the act of divine blessing. ברית is never utilized in connection to Ishmael or Sarah.

Exodus 12:43–49 establishes an integral connection between circumcision and Passover observance by including a proviso to the core paschal legislation. Slaves who eat of their master's Passover offering must be circumcised. In fact, no uncircumcised male may eat the meat of a paschal sacrifice. Moreover, hired laborers may not eat from their employer's sacrifice under any circumstance. A section is also included, perhaps by a later P tradent, dealing with the גר. He has the option of eating the paschal offering with the Israelites among whom he resides. If he elects to do so, he and the males of his household must, like the Israelite native and his slaves, be circumcised.

Leviticus 12 deals with the defilement acquired by a mother upon giving birth. P includes in this chapter a seemingly tangential aside regarding circumcision. Engendered by the mention of the mother's seven-day period of severe defilement upon the birth of a male child, the text reminds the reader/audience that this male child must be circumcised on the eighth day. This type of associative reminder is part of P's standard legislative arsenal. Though nothing is added to the substance of the circumcision commands already detailed, the reminder does link the practice with other seven/eight patterns in Priestly law.

These scriptural passages underscore some crucial issues and raise some important questions regarding the Priestly conception of circumcision. The Genesis pericope foregrounds the connection between circumcision and ברית. However, this all-important relationship cannot be unpacked without a firm grasp of the meaning(s) attributable to the term ברית and to the pivotal phrase אות ברית. A canonical perspective on Gen 17 generates a pair of interrelated queries: Why infant circumcision? Why is the circumcision command imparted to Abraham, the "first Israelite," while every other law incumbent upon Israel is revealed after the exodus? The Gen 17 and Exod 12 regulations stress the circumcision of various classes of foreigner alongside all Israelite males. The Genesis passage also points up the circumcision of, and divine promises to, Ishmael. How is the circumcision of non-Israelites to be explained? Further, how does their circumcision bear on P's more general hierarchical concerns? Circumcision is performed on the penis. Does the practice, therefore, have any implications for male sexuality? Furthermore, how does circumcision, as an exclusively male prerogative, index the status of

Israelite females? Though not circumcised, are women still beholden to God's commands and beneficiaries of his promises?[25] While the circumcision mandate is introduced within the Genesis ancestral saga, it is reiterated in Exod 12 and Lev 12, in the context of purity and festival legislation. To what extent, then, does circumcision have a place within the framework of P's system of cultic practice? What are the ramifications for this system of the eighth-day stipulation, the special association of circumcision and Passover, and the imposition of the *karet* penalty for failure to circumcise?

---

25. Cohen (2005, 13) labels these issues, concisely, the "Sarah and Ishmael paradoxes."

2
Circumcision and ברית

Introduction

The word ברית appears thirteen times in Gen 17 (17:2, 4, 7 [2x], 9, 10, 11, 13 [2x], 14, 19 [2x], 21). The chapter's near saturation with the term and its associated verbs, הקים, הפר, שמר, and נתן, attests to the organic connection between circumcision and ברית in the Priestly worldview.[1] The natural first step in exploring this relationship is to cultivate an understanding of the word ברית in P's lexicon. Toward that end, a survey of ברית in the Priestly corpus outside of Gen 17 is undertaken. The resulting conclusions enable an analysis of ברית in Gen 17 and its link to circumcision.

ברית in P (outside of Genesis 17)

Throughout the canon ברית can represent a certain degree of mutuality that either indicates contingent obligations for both parties to the ברית or generally characterizes a relationship between the parties. Moreover, some type of ritual or ceremony often accompanies the establishment, ratification, or renewal of a ברית. Among many examples, Jacob and Laban erect a monument (Gen 31:44–54), Abraham cuts animals in half (Gen 15:9–10), as do the people of Jerusalem (Jer 34:8–21), and Moses throws blood on the people and the twelve pillars (Exod 24:3–8). We also find verbal affirmation of a ברית,

---

1. Rabbinic recognition of this terminological phenomenon is enshrined in the following statement attributed to R. Ishmael (m. Ned. 3:11): גדולה מילה שנכרתו עליה שלש עשרה בריתות, "Great is circumcision, for thirteen covenants were enacted because of it" (Note that the plural of ברית, unremarkable in rabbinic parlance, is nonexistent in the Hebrew scriptures.)

alone or in conjunction with ceremonial acts, such as in Exod 19:8; 24:3; Josh 24:16–18, 21; and 2 Kgs 23:3.[2]

The Priestly conception of ברית is more narrowly circumscribed. Two usage categories can be distinguished: (1) an obligation voluntarily undertaken[3] by God, or "promise"; and (2) an obligation or set of obligations imposed by God, or "command."[4] The first category is used with respect to God's promises to Noah and humanity (Gen 6:18; 9:9–7), Abraham, Isaac, and Jacob (Exod 2:24; 6:4; Lev 26:42), Phinehas (Num 25:12), the priests (Num 18:19), and corporate Israel (Lev 26:9, 44–45). The most common verb governing the ברית-promise is הקים (*hiphil* of קום, Gen 6:18; 9:9, 11, 17; Exod 6:4; Lev 26:9). Generally הקים ברית should be read as "uphold, fulfill," but in Gen 6:18 it carries the sense of "establish."[5] נתן is also used in this context

---

2. Patrick 1994 labeled such ritual and verbal affirmations "performative transactions." See also Watts's assertion that "God's authority therefore derives in part from a prior agreement establishing YHWH's role as law-giver" (1999, 95–96).

3. Kutsch's formulation, *Selbstverpflichtung* ("self-obligation"), captures the sense most simply (1973, 1–27).

4. These categories are based upon a model set by Kutsch 1973. He proposed that ברית did not denote any sort of covenantal bond (*Bund*). Rather, the term referred to obligations incumbent upon the parties in various types of relationships. His thesis does not fully account for the data. For example, the ברית enacted between David and Jonathan (1 Sam 18:3; 23:18) can indeed be termed a *Bund*. No specific obligations are enumerated. How their mutual אהבה "love, loyalty" will be manifested in practice is left open. Following a similar tack, Freedman 1964 discusses covenants of "divine commitment" and "human obligation." Haran, without developing the concept, also observes that for P, "the term *berit* actually approaches the meaning 'promise', 'obligation'.... it hardly means 'covenant' in the proper sense" (1985, 143). This view of ברית in P (or, for him, H) is also held by Knohl 1995, 137–48. Weinfeld 1975 accepts Kutsch's synthesis with some minor reservations, in line with the objections raised above. A comprehensive review of the scholarship regarding covenant, ברית, and Kutsch's challenge can be found in Nicholson 1986, 83–117.

5. The etymological meaning of הקים, "cause to stand," allows for both possibilities. Since Gen 6:18 contains the first mention of a ברית with Noah, הקים there should be taken as "establish." Sarna (1989:53), glossing this verse, observes accordingly: "in the present passage, it is uncertain whether the governing verb means to fashion a covenant anew or to fulfill one already made. Outside the flood narrative, biblical usages of the phrase favor the latter interpretation." Thus, in Exod 6:4, וְגַם הֲקִמֹתִי אֶת־בְּרִיתִי אִתָּם refers to God's "upholding" the ברית already established with the Patriarchs, who are mentioned in the previous verse. Brettler (1978/79:10) musters strong evidence that הקים ברית must denote "fulfillment" rather than "establishment" but does not deal with the problem of Gen 6:18.

(Gen 9:12; Num 18:19; 25:12). God is additionally portrayed as remembering זכר that which he granted or established (Gen 9:15–16; Exod 2:24, 6:5; Lev 26:42, 45). Finally, breaking the ברית-promise or command is represented by the idiom הפר (*hiphil* of פרר) + ברית (Lev 26:15, 44).

The "command" class of ברית is used in three instances of specific, single obligations imposed by God on Israel: Sabbath observance (Exod 31:16[6]), salting the מנחה "grain offering" (Lev 2:13), and baking and displaying the Sabbath loaves (Lev 24:8). One attestation of the ברית-command, Lev 26:15, stands out:

וְאִם־בְּחֻקֹּתַי תִּמְאָסוּ וְאִם אֶת־מִשְׁפָּטַי תִּגְעַל נַפְשְׁכֶם
לְבִלְתִּי עֲשׂוֹת אֶת־כָּל־מִצְוֹתַי לְהַפְרְכֶם אֶת־בְּרִיתִי

If you spurn my laws and reject my statutes, thereby not doing all of my commands, thereby abrogating my covenant ...

In this verse, the referent of ברית is the totality of the divinely commanded legislation, כָּל־מִצְוֹתַי, מִשְׁפָּטַי, חֻקֹּתַי.[7]

In the Priestly thought-world, ברית is unidirectional. The promises are made by God, and the obligations are imposed by God.[8] Moreover, there is no mention of voluntary acceptance or rejection of either the promise

---

6. ברית here is governed by a combination of the verbs שמר and עשה.

7. Schwartz (1996a, 126, 131) argues that covenant in P refers only to the divine promises, never to God's laws and statutes. He takes note of Lev 26:15 but dismisses it as a "rhetorical reflex" of the use of הפר ברית in 26:44. He goes on to posit that it may be "a case of innovative local rhetoric employed by H, rather than consistent terminology" and therefore should not "be taken as being reflective of any overriding viewpoint." Given the fairly few occasions where ברית-command terminology is actually found in the Priestly corpus, while the usage in Lev 26:15 is singular, it is not so anomalous as to be be utterly discounted. Milgrom (2000, 2305) critiques Schwartz's approach to the verse in question and affirms the connection here of ברית to the complete battery of YHWH's laws.

8. Failure to recognize the aforementioned distinction has led to confusion among scholars when dealing with Priestly material. Thus Joosten (1999, 120), when discussing the Sabbath loaves command in Lev 24:8, בְּיוֹם הַשַּׁבָּת בְּיוֹם הַשַּׁבָּת יַעַרְכֶנּוּ לִפְנֵי יְהוָה תָּמִיד מֵאֵת בְּנֵי־יִשְׂרָאֵל בְּרִית עוֹלָם, admits that, "The sense of the word *berit* in this verse is not entirely clear. Neither is it apparent—if the word means 'covenant'—to which covenant it refers." Despite this insight, Joosten misses the crux, that ברית in this context refers to the specific duty and not to any "covenantal" relationship. This is especially apparent in the way ברית עולם in verse 8 is parallel to חוקת עולם,

or the obligation and no ritual or ceremonial involvement.⁹ The unilateral, fully imposed character of the Priestly conception of ברית is manifest on the semantic level. Throughout the canon, with the exception of the Priestly literature, the idiom כרת ברית is employed to signify enactment of a covenant.¹⁰ The Priestly avoidance of כרת ברית can be attributed to two factors. The first involves the unilateral, fully imposed nature of ברית commands and promises. The use of כרת has its origins in the cutting of an animal.¹¹ This activity is indicative of a formal, ritualized agreement or treaty, which can be accepted or rejected, and is thus inimical to P's ideology. Second, P only allows ritual slaughter of animals at specific venues,¹² for clearly delineated functions, following authorized procedures. Although "between the pieces" killing is not strictly a sacrifice,¹³ it is still ritual slaughter for purposes other than eating. Moreover, in certain contexts a ברית is enacted or ratified by a sacrifice or sacrificial meal.¹⁴

Scholars have wondered why the Priestly tradition does not include a Sinai covenant event.¹⁵ In large measure, this "omission" turns on P's particular

---

"perpetual statute," in 24:3. On the ברית עולם and the bread ritual in Lev 24, see Gane 1992, 192–94.

9. It is no wonder that in fairly representative studies of covenant ceremony, no Priestly texts are adduced as examples. See, e.g., Baltzer 1971; Kalluveettil 1982; and Haran 1997.

10. Barr calls the pervasive use of כרת ברית the most "striking case of idiom in all biblical Hebrew" (1997, 27).

11. Though there is a substantial body of literature devoted to covenant and ברית, the definitive work on the phrase כרת ברית remains Bickerman 1976.

12. The altar at the entrance to the אהל מועד (Lev 17:1–9) and perhaps, with the paschal offering, the homestead (Exod 12). The issue of centralized and profane slaughter in P has been long debated. For the most recent contribution to the dispute, and comprehensive bibliography, see Schwartz 1996a.

13. For this assertion and discussion of opinions to the contrary, see Loewenstamm 1980.

14. A clear instance is Ps 50:5: אִסְפוּ־לִי חֲסִידָי כֹּרְתֵי בְרִיתִי עֲלֵי־זָבַח "Gather unto me my faithful, those who enact my covenant by means of sacrifice." Note also the meal hosted by David to solemnify the ברית between him and Abner (2 Sam 20:20).

15. The commonly accepted scenario, represented by Cross, is that the Priestly tradent simply relied upon the version found in the older "epic" tradition (1973, 318–20). See, more recently, Milgrom 1993, who affirms Cross's thesis. This default explanation falls short of explaining all of P's "missing" narrative elements. Priestly ideology must be taken into account when trying to understand doublets and omissions. For example, it is well recognized in the scholarship that the Priestly strand of the flood story does not include the seven pairs of clean animals taken on the ark (Gen

understanding of ברית. All the Sinai events (Exod 19; 24; and Deut 4–6), along with those connected to other mountains, such as Ebal (Deut 27), Gilgal (Josh 24), and Zion (2 Kgs 23), involve some marker of acceptance, in word, action, or both.[16] This would imply that Israel had the alternative of demur.

In Deuteronomy, free choice and reciprocity are explicit dimensions of the relationship between God and Israel. Deuteronomy 26:17–18 express a "tit-for-tat" type of relationship between YHWH and the nation, while the ideology of choice is most clearly expressed in Deut 30:19 The consequences of making the wrong selection may be calamitous. Nonetheless, Israel is absolutely offered an option. Moreover, the use of בחר in the verse is telling. D employs בחר to denote God's election of Israel (Deut 7:6; 14:2; 26:18).[17] Thus, as God chooses (בחר) Israel, so does Israel choose (בחר) God's path. Despite the fact that in D the relationship between God and Israel is not one of equals, the implication of mutuality is still manifest.

Mutuality and choice are not, however, part of P's theological vision, so the Priestly tradent does not compose a version of such a Sinai event. In the Priestly imagination, Sinai is not a covenant locus.[18] It is the site of the כבוד theophany, the place from which God issues the instructions on the building of the tabernacle. This structure becomes the venue of divine indwelling and the site from which God imparts the commandments to Israel.

In sum, the term ברית has a distinct character in the Priestly corpus. Its force is unilateral, connoting either promises made by God or divinely imposed commands. ברית-commands can entail observance of specific individual obligations, such as Sabbath observance or adherence to the totality of YHWH's injunctions. The distinction between the two classes of ברית, promise and command, can be made based upon the content and context of the verses or passages to be interpreted, as well as the presence of specific

---

7:2) or Noah's propitiating sacrifice (8:20–22). These lacunae cannot be explained by P's reliance upon the J account. Rather, as many commentators have noted, ommisions point to the fact that P does not acknowledge the existence of applicable dietary and purity regulations or a sacrificial cult until the Mosaic period. (For this observation pertaining to Gen 7:2, see Gunkel 1997, 62.)

16. The people's verbal assents to the covenants at Sinai are found in Exod 19:8; 24:3, 7; and Deut 5:24. At Ebal, the Israelites respond אמן to each individual curse recited by the Levites. The Gilgal declarations of obedience are recorded in Josh 24:21–24, and the communal affirmation of Josiah's covenant is cited in 2 Kgs 23:3.

17. On the election of Israel in Deuteronomy, see Weinfeld 1991, 60–62.

18. Schwartz 1996a, 128–29 makes the point nicely: "Obviously, for P no sacrificial ritual can be performed until the tabernacle has been constructed. And since for P, no covenant has been made at Sinai, no ceremony affirming it is made."

governing verbs. הקים and נתן always precede a ברית-promise, while שמר is typically linked with the command type of ברית. These distinctions are crucial to the understanding of ברית in Gen 17.

ברית in Genesis 17

Beyond the thirteen-fold occurrence of ברית in Gen 17, the connection of ברית and circumcision is further elucidated by the precise deployment of the term ברית within the chapter. P's strategic use of ברית constitutes a prime example of what Geller (1992) terms "literary theology." As noted earlier (3) central doctrines are often not articulated explicitly. Rather, they are driven home through literary structures such as juxtaposition and framing devices.

Both categories of ברית, the promise and the command, are attested in the pericope. However, the two categories appear, respectively, in distinct subunits of the text.[19] Sections 1, 2, 4, and 5 refer to divine promises, while section 3 contains the command ברית. The content of the relevant passages makes the division quite clear. Section 3, Gen 17:9–14, is comprised of a series of instructions governing the practice of circumcision. The other four units describe various commitments made by God to Abraham, Sarah, Isaac, Ishmael, and their descendants. That the individual units are distinguished by the category of ברית they describe is also evident by the verbs utilized within them. נתן and הקים, verbs whose subjects are all YHWH and are the indicators of the ברית-promise, are distributed in sections 1, 2, and 5 but absent in 3. Section 3, on the other hand, contains שמר, the lexical signifier of the ברית-command.

The above-described strict structural demarcation bears upon three important matters in P's conceptualization of circumcision: the status of non-Israelites and women; the conditional nature of "covenant"; and the interpretation of the key phrase אוֹת בְּרִית.

Sarah and Ishmael

Ishmael is circumcised and, like Abraham his father, is promised great and numerous descendants. However, P deliberately distinguishes the destiny of Ishmael from that of Abraham and Isaac. In connection to God's promises to Abraham, the term ברית is used four times (17:2, 4, 7 [2x]). The correlative passage regarding Isaac and Ishmael reads as follows:

---

19. See chapter 1 for the structure of the Gen 17 pericope, and the contents of its various sections.

CIRCUMCISION AND ברית

(19) וַיֹּאמֶר אֱלֹהִים אֲבָל שָׂרָה אִשְׁתְּךָ יֹלֶדֶת לְךָ בֵּן
וְקָרָאתָ אֶת־שְׁמוֹ יִצְחָק
וַהֲקִמֹתִי אֶת־בְּרִיתִי אִתּוֹ לִבְרִית עוֹלָם לְזַרְעוֹ אַחֲרָיו
(20) וּלְיִשְׁמָעֵאל שְׁמַעְתִּיךָ הִנֵּה בֵּרַכְתִּי אֹתוֹ
וְהִפְרֵיתִי אֹתוֹ וְהִרְבֵּיתִי אֹתוֹ בִּמְאֹד מְאֹד
שְׁנֵים־עָשָׂר נְשִׂיאִם יוֹלִיד וּנְתַתִּיו לְגוֹי גָּדוֹל
(21) וְאֶת־בְּרִיתִי אָקִים אֶת־יִצְחָק
אֲשֶׁר תֵּלֵד לְךָ שָׂרָה לַמּוֹעֵד הַזֶּה בַּשָּׁנָה הָאַחֶרֶת

(19) And God said "But Sarah your wife will bear you a son and you will name him Isaac and I will fulfill my ברית **with him,** as an eternal ברית for his offspring after him. (20) And as for Ishmael, I have heard you. See, I will bless him. I will make him fruitful, and I will multiply him exceedingly. He will give birth to twelve chieftains, and I will make him a great nation. (21) **But my** ברית **will I fulfill with Isaac**, whom Sarah will bear for you, at this time, next year.

It is clear from P's precise use of language, that while Ishmael receives a generous blessing,[20] he is not granted the ברית that is fulfilled through Isaac. The contrast is emphasized by the repetition of the formula הקים ברית את employed regarding Isaac and the fact that these declarations frame the Ishmael promise. The ואת that begins 17:21 has an adversative force:[21] I will bless Ishmael, *but* my ברית is only for Isaac. Equally weighty is the distribution of the promises. Ishmael will be the ancestor of a great nation. He does not, however, receive the land promise or the pledge of a unique relationship to YHWH that is the exclusive prerogative of the Israelite.[22]

The Priestly tradent was faced with a dilemma. Circumcision in Gen 17 is linked to a set of ברית-promises that served to distinguish Israel from other nations: the land and the special relationship to YHWH. Later in the canon, Israel is explicitly set apart from the nations (Lev 20:24–26). However, a number of Israel's neighbors practiced circumcision.[23] Moreover, P legislates

---

20. The commentaries note the correspondence of the twelve Ishmaelite chieftains to the twelve Israelite tribes. The genealogy of Ishmael is located in Gen 25:12–16 and 1 Chr 1:28–30.

21. See *IBHS* 8.3b.

22. The invidious contrast between Isaac and Ishmael is noted in the commentaries.

23. There is external evidence that Phoenicians, Egyptians, and Arabs practiced circumcision (see Sasson 1966). Jer 9:24–25 includes the Edomites, Ammonites, and

that slaves are to be circumcised along with their master's family.²⁴ How, then, can the connection of circumcision and the special position of Israel be preserved? The problem is solved with the Isaac/Ishmael, ברך/ברית dichotomy. Isaac is the elected son, recipient of the panoply of the ברית-promises. Ishmael, the paradigmatic foreigner, is circumcised but is never treated as a fully equal member of the community.

Genesis 17 also sets the tone for the subordinate status of women in the Priestly *Weltanschaung*.²⁵ The ברך/ברית dichotomy that contrasts Isaac's status to that of Ishmael also distinguishes Abraham and Sarah. The ברית is transmitted through Abraham, while Sarah receives a blessing, though not directly. The promise is also conveyed by God through Abraham (Gen 17:15–18). Since a female is not circumcised, she is included as a recipient of the ברית-promises through the person of her father or husband. This vicarious condition is consistent with Priestly legislation governing the consumption of תרומה (Lev 22:12–13) and the nullification of vows (Num 30:4–17). They establish, in the main, the cultic and legal status of females as the extension of a male's authority. The secondary character of a women's relationship to God is evident in Gen 17. The change in Sarah's name along with her blessing, the promise of a son from whom nations will arise, is delivered to Abraham. Sarah has no direct communication with God.

THE CONDITIONAL COVENANT

Four types of biblical covenant are delineated in the scholarship: the Noachide; the Abrahamic or patriarchal; the Davidic or royal; and the Sinaitic.²⁶ The first three are often categorized by the rubric "unconditional." God makes promises without any expectation of reciprocal obligations. In contrast, the Sinaitic is considered conditional because God's beneficence is contingent upon Israel's acceptance of the commandments. Some, utilizing compara-

---

Moabites in this category. Although there is no strong reason here to doubt the prophet's testimony, it is also unverifiable (see Holladay 1986, 319–20 on this passage).

24. P's view on the circumcision of non-Israelites is explored below, pp. 43–48.

25. The lesser hierarchical place of women is not, by any means, unique to the Priestly tradition. Among many examples in the non-P pentateuchal strata, see the covet commandment in Exod 20:17, which includes a wife as a part of the husband's estate, and the Hebrew slave law in the Covenant Collection, which does not allow a daughter the same rights of manumission as a male (Exod 21:7).

26. The scholarship on covenant is legion. Important contributions include Baltzer 1971; Bright 1977; Hillers 1964a; Kalluveettil 1982; McCarthy 1978; Mendenhall 1954; Nicholson 1986).

tive Near Eastern data, have framed the biblical covenants in political terms. Weinfeld (1970), for example, labels the conditional covenant a "treaty," an agreement entailing obligations for both parties. He likens the unconditional covenant to a gift of land, or movable property, granted by a king or high official to a subordinate in recognition of prior service or loyalty.[27]

The idea of an unconditional covenant between God and David is not supported in all the relevant texts. Nathan's oracle in 2 Sam 7:8–16 and Ps 89:20–37 affirm the promise of kingship to David and his descendants, even if they transgress God's law. On the other hand, Ps 132:11–18 makes a Davidide's holding the throne dependent upon the king's observance of divine commands. The same type of assertion can be made regarding the Abrahamic covenant. The unconditional covenant, or grant, is undeniably present in the non-P, Gen 15 account.[28] God makes repeated commitments to Abraham, of protection (15:1), offspring (15:4–5), and land (15:7, 18). No stipulations are attached to the promises. However, it is clear that the unconditional covenant of grant is not manifest in the Priestly patriarchal tradition. First of all, in Gen 17 there is no mention of Abraham's previous loyalty or service. God's initial words to Abraham, הִתְהַלֵּךְ לְפָנַי וֶהְיֵה תָמִים, containing a sequence of imperatives, are a charge to Abraham to behave ethically. Moreover, the ברית-promises that predominate in the pericope are clearly linked to the circumcision command. Israel's obligation, introduced by the words וְאַתָּה אֶת־בְּרִיתִי תִשְׁמֹר (Gen 17:9), is firmly embedded within a series of promise passages. It must be noted that Mesopotamian land grants of the type discussed by Weinfeld generally conclude with sanction clauses. These, however, pertain to future rulers or others who might violate the integrity of the gift. They never obligate the recipient to any duty or symbolic act.[29] In Gen 17, it is the beneficiary, Abraham (and, by

---

27. Num 25 contains a banner example of the "covenant of grant" in the Priestly corpus. While encamped at Shittim, a group of Israelite men join some Moabite and/or Midianite women in sexual intercourse and worship of Baal Peor. YHWH is incensed and calls for the execution of the offenders. Meanwhile, a Simeonite leader, Zimri, publicly displays his apostasy with Cozbi, the daughter of a Midianite chieftain. Phinehas, son of Eleazar, grandson of Aaron, takes his spear and kills the two in one stroke. The execution assuages God's wrath and averts the decimation of the people by a divinely sent plague. The grant language appears in 25:12–13, with key phrasing: "Behold, I give him my covenant of friendship" (הִנְנִי נֹתֵן לוֹ אֶת־בְּרִיתִי שָׁלוֹם), and "It shall be for him and his offspring after him a covenant of eternal priesthood" (בְּרִית כְּהֻנַּת עוֹלָם).

28. On this text, and its relationship to the royal covenant, see especially Clements 1967.

29. A representative sampling can be found in Kataja and Whiting 1995.

extension, Israel), who is bound by the obligation and threatened with sanction, the *karet* penalty, for failure to obey.³⁰

There is a possible tension inherent in the notion of a covenant whose promises are perpetual, and thus irrevocable, to which conditions are also attached. How are the obligations enforced, and can there be consequences to their abrogation when the promises are "forever"? This tension is resolved with recourse to the distinction between Israel as a collective entity (עם, עדה, קהל) and the actions and lives of individual Israelites. For individual community members, the ברית-promises can but do not neccessarily adhere forever. If one transgresses the commandments to a particular degree of gravity, the promises are withdrawn. In the Priestly view, such withdrawal is construed as *karet,* an irredeemable divine sanction.³¹ Corporate Israel, on the other hand, is never fully or irretrievable alienated from the ברית-promises of land and unique relationship with YHWH.

Sign of the ברית

In Gen 17: 11–14, circumcision is labeled a ברית or a sign of the ברית. Which class of ברית is referenced, the command or the promise? The use of שמר, along with apodictic language, and the inclusion of a penalty clause establish that the section manifests the command type of ברית. In 17:9–10, it is definitively the individual, specific command, equivalent to Sabbath observance and salting the grain offering. Genesis 17:11 provides a rationale for the practice: אֶת בְּשַׂר עָרְלַתְכֶם וְהָיָה בְּרִית בֵּינִי וּבֵינֵיכֶם וּנְמַלְתֶּם "And you must circumcise the flesh of your foreskins, and it shall be a sign of the ברית between me and you," The nature of the ברית reference in this verse is less clear cut. At first glance, there seems to be some dissonance: Could circumcision be a sign of itself? An analysis of the crux phrase אוֹת בְּרִית is necessary for the resolution of the problem. Much of the groundwork has been effectively laid by Fox 1974. He surveys אות in P and comes to the solid conclusion that the term indicates a cognition sign, or reminder. For example, the Sabbath is a sign to remind the Israelites that God has sanctified them:

כִּי אוֹת הִוא בֵּינִי וּבֵינֵיכֶם
לְדֹרֹתֵיכֶם לָדַעַת כִּי אֲנִי ה' מְקַדִּשְׁכֶם

---

30. Knohl (1995, 142) similarly argues against reading YHWH's ברית with Abraham here as a covenant of "grant" or "grace."

31. See my full discussion of the *karet* penalty and its implications for the study of circumcision, pp. 70–75.

For it is a sign between me and you for your generations to know that I am YHWH your sanctifier.

The postflood rainbow of Gen 9:12–17 is most germane, as it is also given the designation אוֹת בְּרִית. It functions as a reminder to God of his ברית-promise to never again destroy the world with a flood.

What, then, is the ברית that is referenced in Gen 17:11? Fox argues that "circumcision is a cognition sign … *whose function is to remind God to keep his promise of posterity*" (1974, 594–96). A similar claim, that circumcision is a reminder to YHWH of his promises, is made by a number of scholars.[32] This solution is problematic on several counts: As noted above, the most relevant attestation of אוֹת is Gen 9:13, 17, as it is the only occurrence, aside from Gen 17:11, of the full phrase אוֹת בְּרִית . In that case, the sign is placed by God and is explicitly a reminder to him. By analogy, circumcision should be understood as a sign for the one who affixes it, the Israelite male, not YHWH. Second, the distribution of the key phrase זכר ברית does not support the thesis that circumcision is a reminder for God. In the flood pericope, the notion that the rainbow-אוֹת is a cognition sign, or mnemonic, for God, is made explicit by the use of the verb זכר. God will see the rainbow and *remember* his ברית (Gen 9:15–16). זכר ברית is utilized four more times in the Priestly corpus (Exod 2:26; 6:5; Lev 26:42, 45), always with God as the subject. However, it is never circumcision that jogs the divine memory. Rather, in every instance, it is Israel, in the straits of slavery or exile, crying out or acknowledging guilt that moves God to remember his promises. Additionally, I established, on semantic and structural grounds, that the two classes of ברית were deployed in distinct sections of Gen 17 and that my unit 3 (17:9–14) was the locus of the ברית-commands. Thus, אוֹת בְּרִית in Gen 17:11 must entail a command type of ברית.[33] Furthermore, it is unlikely that the Priestly tradent

---

32. See, e.g., Skinner 1910, 294; Sarna 1966, 132; McEvenue 1971, 178; Schwartz 1999, 340; and Cohen 2005, 11.

33. So Westermann 1985, 266; Wenham 1994, 24. Kline (1968, 47–48, 87) fittingly links circumcision with human obligation rather than divine promises. However, he identifies circumcision as a curse ritual, invoked to deter against violation of God's covenant. This theory does not fit the biblical text. In Gen 17:14, the penalty is invoked for failure to circumcise. By extension, Kline's conceptualization would entail imposing a penalty upon those who neglect the curse ritual in a treaty. In ancient Near Eastern treaties, however, symbolic curses are invoked for failure to follow the terms of the agreement. No treaties are in evidence with built-in measures to guard against ignoring a part of the treaty ritual. On biblical analogs to Near Eastern treaty curses, see Hillers 1964a.

would attribute to circumcision, or any ritual, a primary significance related to fertility or sexuality. (This issue is addressed below, 50–52.)

Understanding ברית in 17:11 as the command type still does not address the tautological tension of אות ברית as a "sign of itself," that is, circumcision as a reminder of the command to circumcise (per 17:9–10). The logical discord, however, is resolved when ברית in Gen 17:11 is read in light of the term's clear connotation in Lev 26:15: the obligation to follow the aggregation of God's commands. אות ברית, then, should properly be interpreted as a sign of Israel's commitment to observe the totality of YHWH's dictates. By the same token, in 17:13 וְהָיְתָה בְרִיתִי בִּבְשַׂרְכֶם לִבְרִית עוֹלָם can be read as implicitly seconding אות ברית, referring to a perpetual sign of YHWH's ברית-commands evident in the flesh of every Israelite male and his male dependents. By extension, the phrase בְּרִיתִי הֵפַר, whose usage is also consistent with Lev 26:15, establishes the presence of a foreskin on an Israelite male beyond the age of eight days, or his male slaves, as a sign of the rejection of the divinely imposed commands.[34]

Finally, I will anticipate a later discussion (part 2, ch. 8) by illustrating how the foreskin metaphor in Lev 26:41 helps to confirm the meaning of אות ברית in Gen 17:11–14. Leviticus 26:15 equates rejection of God's commands with abrogating the covenant (הפר ברית). According to Lev 26:41, the condition that symbolizes Israel's abrogation of the covenant is the foreskinned (ערל) heart. If the foreskinned heart is a metaphor for Israel's abrogation of the ברית through rejection of YHWH's commands, then by clear analogy the foreskinned penis as sign of an individual's abrogation of the ברית must also signify rejection of that individual's commitment to heed those commands. By considering all of P's circumcision passages as a coherent whole, it

---

34. The study of ברית in Gen 17 does present an unavoidable linguistic quandary. Ideally, a single word will maintain a consistent meaning within the span of two or three continuous scriptural verses. In this case, however, such consistency is untenable and is not claimed by any commentators. Here, close, context-based reading must trump any single, essential meaning for ברית. This methodological problem is all too common in biblical interpretation. For example, Schwartz (1991) argues that כפר has two distinct meanings, "cleanse/purge" or "ransom/make restitution," each deriving from different etymologies. Usage determines which sense is applicable in a particular verse or passage. Recently Sklar (2005) challenged this notion, proposing that כפר as "atone" carries both meanings simultaneously. The latter approach, in general, allows for philological stability and maximal interpretive potential. However, it also suffers from what Barr (1961, 218) terms "illegitimate totality transfer," the faulty concept that one lexeme, in every incidence, carries its full range of meanings. Barr's admonition is apropos for the present discussion.

becomes more apparent that אות ברית in Gen 17:11 cannot be read as a sign of YHWH's ברית-promises, as has been suggested in the scholarship.

Understanding ברית in Gen 17:11–14 as denoting the totality of God's precepts (consistent with Lev 26:15) resolves some important interpretive obstacles in the pericope but leads to a new difficulty: How could Abraham have been bound by a set of commandments that are imparted much later in the text's chronology? The rabbis asserted, אין מוקדם ומאוחר בתורה, "There is no early or late in scripture."[35] Structuralists have more recently labeled the same literary trend "anachrony." Anachrony refers to a disruption in a text's narrative timeframe. This phenomenon has been isolated by narratologists throughout the biblical canon.[36] Anachrony can take various shapes. One manifestation is the nonsequential narration of events in a larger episode.[37] Another type of anachrony would entail an obscuring of the chronological perspective between the narrative context and the context of the author and the author's implied or intended reader. With respect to the Pentateuch, the narrative is set in a quasi-mythic ancestral or desert epoch, while the author could be situated in monarchic Israel or postexilic Yehud.[38] Often, the perspective distance is self-consciously bridged with generalized narrator's statements such as עד היום/(ה)כ/יום הזה "to this day"[39] and more pointed explanatory glosses such as "In those days there was no king is Israel" (Judg 17:6; 18:1; 19:1; 21:25) and "he arrived proximate to Jebus, which is Jerusalem (Judg 19:10).[40] Finally, there are instances where the blurring may not be intentional. This type of anachrony is present in the use of ברית in the circumcision mandate. Genesis 17:9–14 has a patently atemporal quality. While the superficial context of the chapter is God's dialogue with Abraham, the circumcision injunction is intended for Israelites in future generations. Thus, commentators have noted that the passage reads as if it were taken directly from one of P's legal collections. Here the author of Gen 17 retrojected into the ancestral saga the obligation to a set of laws yet to be presented. This

---

35. See y. Meg. 1:4, b. Sanh. 6b; 49b, Num. Rab. 9; Cant. Rab. 1; Ruth Rab. 4; Qoh. Rab. 1; and the discussion in Melamed 1975, 18–21.

36. For discussion and bibliography relating to manipulation of time in biblical narrative, see Ska 1990, 7–15.

37. On this phenomenon, which is typically labeled "chronological displacement," see Glatt 1993.

38. This last judgment depends, of course, upon one's view as to the date of pentateuchal and Priestly authorship, issues that are far from settled in the scholarship.

39. Stock phrases in Deuteronomy include 2:22, 30; 3:14; 4:20, 38; 6:24; 8:18; 10:8, 15; 11:4; 29:3, 27; 34:6.

40. For a discussion of this type of statement, see Greenspahn 1991, 1–2.

retrojection establishes, at the beginning of the patriarchal account, a link between circumcision, God's ברית- promises, and YHWH's commandments that are given to Israel after they become a nation.[41]

Summary

ברית is the *Leitwort* in Gen 17, occurring thirteen times. P employs the term strategically in service of an aggressive ideological agenda. First, by framing the distinction between ברית and blessing, P contrasts the status of Abraham and Sarah, and Isaac and Ishmael. More broadly, these dichotomies set the tone for the Priestly views about women and foreigners, which are laid out more comprehensively in the law and lore.

Additionally, the juxtaposition of promissory passages with the circumcision mandate establishes P's view that the "unconditional covenant" is nonexistent. Most important, by labeling circumcision אות ברית, the Priestly tradent articulates a command-centered concept of ברית. P composes an overture to Israel's *Heilsgeschichte* by imparting a set of promises to Abraham, the first patriarch, and wedding these promises to the practice of circumcision. The promises will not be realized until Israel, as a nation, is liberated from Egyptian servitude. Similarly, circumcision signals each Israelite's obligation to comply with all of God's commands. These commands will also be imparted when Israel achieves nationhood. Just as the promises to Abraham are inextricably linked to the practice of circumcision, so will Israel's ability to receive divine grace be bound to her observance of YHWH's commands. Setting the precedent for P's unilateralist theology, the ברית-promises and commands are dispensed by God to Abraham with no occasion for ritual ratification (per Gen 15) or verbal affirmation.

Fundamental Priestly doctrine is also played out in two important but curious facets of the Abrahamic narrative: the institution of *infant* circumcision; and circumcision as the only regulation intended for Israel, introduced in the ancestral period. A sign of commitment to a set of obligations is

---

41. A nearly identical, and even less subtle, retrojection can be found in a non-Priestly patriarchal pericope. In Gen 26:3–4, God reaffirms to Isaac the promises he made to Abraham. Gen 26:5 provides the reason for God's commitment to Abraham and his progeny: עֵקֶב אֲשֶׁר־שָׁמַע אַבְרָהָם בְּקֹלִי וַיִּשְׁמֹר מִשְׁמַרְתִּי מִצְוֺתַי חֻקּוֹתַי וְתוֹרֹתָי: "because Abraham heeded me, keeping my charge, my commands, my statutes, and my directives." Nowhere, however, within the ancestral saga is there any mention of laws and commands communicated to Abraham. Collocations such as מִשְׁמַרְתִּי מִצְוֺתַי חֻקּוֹתַי וְתוֹרֹתָי are apposite in a postexodus and Sinai milieu (Lev 26:46; Deut 11:1) but are misplaced in Genesis.

imposed upon a newborn male who is unable to dissent or consent, just as the commands, and attendant promises, are imposed by God upon the Israelite collective, who are given no option of acceptance or rejection. Because of the anachrony embedded in the narrative, Abraham carries the sign of God's ברית-commands and is informed of the ברית-promises, neither of which will be put into effect until his seed grows to peoplehood. Abraham, as a literary type, embodies Israel *in potentia*. A circumcised infant carries the sign of God's ברית-commands, which he will be unable to operationalize until he grows up. He is, in effect, an Israelite *in potentia*.

3
Circumcision, Status, and Sexuality

The Priestly tradent envisioned a stratified society in which the rank and role of its members was clearly delineated.¹ In P's worldview, circumcision and status are, in certain respects, closely intertwined. Circumcision does not function as an index of hierarchy for Israelite males, as there is no distinction made between the circumcisions of priests, Levites, and Israelites or between elders and their tribal consitutents. Still, it is an indicator of the subordinate place of non-Israelites and women in the Priestly system more broadly, a phenomenon that is encapsulated and anticipated in the relationship of Sarah and Ishmael to God and his ברית-promises in Gen 17 (see above, 19–20, 24–26, 32–34). In this chapter, the social standing of women and non-Israelites is explored in the context of the circumcision mandate.

Circumcision and the Non-Israelite

Priestly circumcision legislation includes regulations pertaining to various types of non-Israelites. Genesis 17:11–12 mandates that all slaves are to be circumcised. These fall into two categories: מקנת כסף, the purchased slave; and יליד בית, those who are born of existing slaves.² Exodus 12:44 seconds this law, commanding that all slaves must be circumcised before eating the paschal offering. The verse in Exodus uses the collective phrase כל עבד "every slave," modified by the more specific designation מקנת כסף. The status of the עבד is specified in Lev 25:44–46. The עבד can be male or female, must be non-Israelite, and can be purchased, retained, disposed of, and/or inherited,

---

1. For an excellent full-length study of societal status in the Priestly system, see Olyan 2000.
2. Other biblical traditions, such as Deut 20:10–14, along with ancient Near Eastern data indicate that prisoners of war are used as slaves. It can be assumed that these prisoners of war would be subject to the same circumcision regulations as the categories of slaves specified in the text.

as with any movable property. Based upon the inclusive phrase כל זכר "every male," the law of eighth-day circumcision should apply equally to the Israelite's offspring and the יליד בית.

There are no detailed prescriptions regarding the circumcision of the purchased slave. It is plausible to assume that the Israelite must circumcise the slave upon, or soon after, his acquisition. Minimally, the מקנת כסף would have to be circumcised in time for the next Passover. In P, the slave is contrasted with the hired laborer, of which the text articulates two categories: the שכיר and the תושב. The latter is a worker who lives on his employer's property; the former is a wage laborer who returns to his own home.[3] According to Exod 12:45, the שכיר and the תושב, whether circumcised or not, may never eat of the paschal sacrifice.

Exodus 12:48 mentions the גר as having the option of participation in the paschal festival. If the גר chooses to take part, he must be circumcised. Under other circumstances, there is no requirement for the circumcision of the גר. The גר in P is a foreigner who lives among the Israelite people.[4] The גר enjoys certain protections equivalent to those of the Israelite and is, at the same time, bound by some of the same laws.[5]

---

3. On the two categories, which are mentioned throughout the economic legislation of Lev 25 (25:6, 23, 35, 40), see Levine 1989, 170–71. He notes that the תושב, also labeled גר תושב (25:35) may be a foreign laborer or an indentured servant. Lev 25:39–43 specifies that an impoverished, indebted Israelite may not be treated as a slave (עבד) by his creditor or redeemer. Rather, his status is the same as that of the שכיר and the תושב. Lev 19:13b protects the salary of the hired worker: לֹא־תָלִין פְּעֻלַּת שָׂכִיר אִתְּךָ עַד־בֹּקֶר "Do not retain the wages of the שכיר until morning."

4. The distinction between the גר and the Israelite is highlighted by such phrases as אִישׁ אִישׁ מִבֵּית/מִבְּנֵי יִשְׂרָאֵל וּמִן־הַגֵּר אֲשֶׁר־יָגוּר בְּתוֹכָם "Any person from among the house/people of Israel or from among the גר who lives in your midst" (Lev 17:8, 10, 13; 20:2; 22:18.) The Israelite is also labeled אזרח (native born), from whom the גר is also differentiated (Exod 12:48; Lev 17:15). On the אזרח, see Levine 1993, 298.

5. In P, the גר is mentioned in Exod 12:19, 48, 49; Lev 16:29; 17:8, 10, 12, 13, 15; 18:26; 19:10, 33, 34; 20:2; 22:18; 23:22; 24:16, 22; 25:35, 47 (3x); Num 9:14 (2x); 15:14, 15 (2x), 16, 26, 29, 30; 19:10; 35:15. The general status of the גר vis-à-vis the Israelite throughout the canon is similar to that which is detailed in the Priestly corpus. The differences lie in the details. Milgrom (1990, 398–402) provides a helpful summary of the גר tradtions in P and other scriptural texts. Ramirez Kidd's study of the גר in the Bible is quite comprehensive and offers many important insights. I dissent only with his historical conclusions. He considers the Priestly גר regulations an "accommodation to the *status quo* acquired by non-Jews, who joined Jewish communities during the Persian period" (1999, 68). However, there is no extrabiblical data that speaks to the relative permeability of Israelite or Jewish community boundaries during any par-

Three related questions emerge: (1) How do we account for the specifics of P's circumcision regulations pertaining to non-Israelites? (2) Given Israel's status as YHWH's people, does the slave or גר merit the same rank by virtue of his circumcision? (3) Similarly, since God's ברית-promises are conditioned upon Israel's circumcision, does the circumcised slave or גר become a beneficiary of these privileges? Societal stratification and hierarchy can be conceived of politically, with regard to spheres in which power is exercised; economically, in terms of material assets; or sociologically, with reference to contexts in which group or personal identity is self-determined or lost. All Israelites, as God's people, are completely subordinate to him. They reside on YHWH's land, are under his control, and constitute his possession; their identity is not independent of YHWH. Circumcision marks Israel's commitment to follow YHWH's commands. The purchased or captured foreign slave is the property of his Israelite master and, as a result, is fully subordinate to him. As such, he also falls into YHWH's sphere of influence and must be circumcised.[6] However, the slave's involuntary submission carries with it no privilege or distinction, nor does he have any claim to the land promise. Gunkel states the case succinctly: "The slave is not a person, not even in religion. Obviously, he will practice his master's religion" (1997, 265). Olyan, approaching the problem from a sociological perspective, also penetrates to the heart of the matter. He observes:

> At first glance, these texts [Gen 17:10–14; Exod 12:43–49] appear to privilege the foreign slave: unlike nonresident foreigners and uncircumcised

---

ticular segment of the biblical epoch, let alone the Persian period Yehud. It is equally plausible to situate the גר regulations in the monarchic period, when foreign soldiers or laborers retained by more prosperous kings were housed in the urban centers. For example, the Arabs and mercenaries (*urbiu u ṣabīšu damqītu*) in Hezekiah's employ, mentioned in Sennacherib's annals (III:39), or the Kittim of Arad ostraca 1 and 2 could have been subject to rules and protections such as those dilineated for the גר. That said, it must be acknowledged that P's גר traditions may be rhetorical and ideological constructs, with no basis in the demographic, political, economic, or cultic realities of the biblical world.

6. An analogous situation is evident in Neo-Assyrian royal inscriptions. A vanquished people is typically portrayed as bearing the yoke of their conquering king. The standard formulation is *kabtu nīr bēlūtiya ēmissunūti* "The heavy yoke of my rule I imposed upon them." Surrendering to the rule of a king also entails submission to the power of the victor's patron diety. Thus in the same text genre, we read formulaic declarations such as *nīr Aššur ... ēmissunūti* "The yoke of Ashur ... I imposed upon them." For such declarations, see, e.g., the annals of Tiglath-pileser I.2:54–55 (Budge and King 1902) and Sennacherib 2:36 (Luckenbill 1924).

resident outsiders, he eats the Passover; like free Israelite males, and in contrast to all women, bond or free, he bears the sign of the covenant in his flesh. Upon closer scrutiny, however, it is evident that privileging of the slave is not what these texts really suggest.... [The slave] is subject to the same ritual requirements as his master and has access to ritual privileges, *but only as an extension of his master's person,* not in his own right. Paradoxically, the slave's apparent privilege at first blush really stems from the extent of his debasement. He is his master's possession, with no independent place in the social order apart from his master. Thus he is circumcised as the free Israelite male is circumcised and eats the Passover as native Israelites eat it. His diminished status is realized and underscored by the very ritual means that appeared at first glance to produce and signal privilege: eating the Passover with his master's household. (2000, 96)

That the slave is, as Olyan phrases it, "an extension of his master's person," is starkly highlighted in the syntax of Gen 17:13:

הִמּוֹל יִמּוֹל יְלִיד בֵּיתְךָ וּמִקְנַת כַּסְפֶּךָ וְהָיְתָה בְרִיתִי בִּבְשַׂרְכֶם לִבְרִית עוֹלָם

"*Your* home born and *your* purchased slave must be circumcised so that my ברית will be in *your* flesh as an eternal ברית."

The command here regards the slave as a direct extension of his master's body.

As opposed to the slave, who is part of the master's domain, the שׂכיר and the תושׁב are fully independent, and their relationship to the employer consists simply of an exchange of labor for payment. Thus, they are ineligible to eat from their employer's paschal offering, whether circumcised or not. An Israelite שׂכיר or תושׁב would offer his own sacrifice, while the foreign worker could not participate in a Passover celebration. As delineated in Lev 22:10–11, similar conditions attach to the laws of the תרומה, the sacred, donated food that is the prerogative of the priest and his household. The slave, who is fully subsumed into the priest's household, may eat the תרומה along with the members of the priest's family. The תושׁב and the שׂכיר, as with the Passover, are always ineligible to eat the תרומה.

The גר occupies the middle ground. He lives as guest in Israelite territory.[7] He does not have the total independence of the wage laborer, nor does he enjoy the full range of protections and privileges afforded the Israelite

---

7. Standard גר formulary attests to this fact: וְכִי־יָגוּר אִתְּךָ/כֶם גֵּר (Exod 12:48; Lev 19:33; Num 9:14; 15:14); וּמִן הַגֵּר /וְלַגֵּר הַגָּר בְּתוֹכָם/בְּיִשְׂרָאֵל (Lev 17:10, 13; 20:2; Num 15:26, 29; 19:10).

אזרח. Most significantly, he and his family may be enslaved in perpetuity by an Israelite (Lev 25:45). On the other hand, a גר who prospers and acquires an Israelite debt slave must allow for redemption of the Israelite. If redemption is not forthcoming, the גר is compelled to release his debtor at the Jubilee (Lev 25:47–54).

While the גר does not have parity with the Israelite, he is also not completely subordinated to the Israelite and YHWH. For example, while the אזרח is bound to observe Sukkot, the גר is not so compelled. However, the גר, like the Israelite, must abstain from leavened products for the duration of Passover/Massot (Exod 12:19–20). This statute is in force because the laws of מצות/חמץ apply בְּכֹל מוֹשְׁבֹתֵיכֶם "in all your habitations." By implication, the presence of any חמץ, whoever its owner, affects the community. Consumption of the paschal sacrifice is compulsory for every Israelite (Exod 12:47; Num 9:13) but optional for the גר. If the גר wishes to participate, he must observe its regulations scrupulously (Exod 12:48; Num 9:14). The גר who elects to partake of the Passover, in effect, more fully enters into the fold of the host community of Israelites in order to celebrate the quintessential ברית-centered festival. To gain the privilege, he must forfeit some of his independent status and subordinate himself to the Israelite and YHWH. He must signal this commitment by being circumcised.

The status of the foreigner relative to the Israelite and YHWH can be broadly represented by the following analogy: the foreigner is to the Israelite as the Israelite is to God. The foreigner who resides in Israelite territory is classified as a גר. The גר has no rights or claims to the land and dwells on it at the Israelites' sufferance. However, the same land is also regarded as YHWH's property, upon which the Israelite resides at the deity's pleasure. A family may not dispose, at will, of its stake. In this context, the text specifies that, relative to YHWH, the Israelite is a גר:

וְהָאָרֶץ לֹא תִמָּכֵר לִצְמִתֻת כִּי־לִי הָאָרֶץ כִּי־גֵרִים וְתוֹשָׁבִים אַתֶּם עִמָּדִי

"But the land may not be sold irretrievably[8] because the land is mine, for you are aliens resident with me" (Lev 25:23).

The same equation applies to slavery: any foreigner may be enslaved by an Israelite; the Israelite is, however, YHWH's slave (Lev 25:42, 55).

The circumcision of Ishmael in the narrative (Gen 17:23–27) and the legal matter pertaining to the circumcision of foreigners (Gen 17:9–14; Exod

---

8. On the technical term לצמתת, see Levine 1989, 174.

12:43–49) suggests that the practice is a status indicator within the Israelite community and an eligibility factor for one particular ritual, the Passover offering. However, circumcision in P is not a symbol of Israelite ethnicity, nor does it ritually demarcate communal borderlines. For P, at least as far as males are concerned, the communal boundaries, delineated terminologically as between אזרח, on the one hand, and גר or בן נכר, on the other, are impermeable. As such, circumcision does not effectuate a crossing or blurring of these boundaries. Moreover, the narrative of Ishmael's circumcision conveys, on one level, P's implicit acknowledgment that other nations may practice circumcision. Thus the lack of a foreskin in and of itself would not in any way distinguish Israelites from other nations.

Circumcision, Gender, and Genitalia

Like a slave, a female in P is in most cases subordinate to her father or husband and classified according to the sphere of influence of these males.[9] An Israelite wife or daughter is still, however, higher on the social ladder than any non-Israelite, slave or גר. Three groups of laws illustrate the subordinate status of women in the Priestly societal order. The first involves the eating of the תרומה (Lev 22:1–16). A priest eats the sacred food along with his household. His household includes all those in his sphere of influence. Thus, his slaves partake, as do his wife and unmarried daughter. As with the Passover, no hired laborer may eat the תרומה, and a priest's daughter, if she marries, no longer eats her father's תרומה. If she marries another priest, she shares his donated food, but if she weds outside the clan, she is considered a part of her husband's family and, in this context, a זרה, an outsider.[10] This status attaches because she moves from being subordinate to her father to her husband's sphere of influence. If she is widowed or divorced and has borne no children, she may return to her father's house and share again in his תרומה.

The second regulation that indicates the subordination of women pertains to the annulment of vows (Num 30). A husband or father, within certain limits, may annul the vow of his wife or daughter. The widow and the divorcee are not fully relegated to the jurisdiction of their father. The laws of vows

---

9. The lower status of women is not, by any means, unique to the Priestly tradition. Among many examples in the non-P pentateuchal strata, see the covet commandment in Exod 20:17, which includes the wife as part of the husband's estate, and the Hebrew Slave law in the Covenant Collection, which does not allow a daughter the same rights of manumission as a male (Exod 21:7).

10. In the context of the regulations governing the priesthood, זר/ה, "outsider," refers to anyone not of priestly lineage.

in Num 30 accord them independent status. With regard to the divorcee and the widow, the law states:

וְנֵדֶר אַלְמָנָה וּגְרוּשָׁה כֹּל אֲשֶׁר־אָסְרָה עַל־נַפְשָׁהּ יָקוּם עָלֶיהָ

"But the vow of the widow and the divorcee, whatever she has imposed upon herself, shall be fulfilled" (Num 30:10).

Thus, while the widow and divorcee may avail themselves of certain privileges attached to their father, they retain independent status under the law.[11]

The third case, of the daughters of Zelophehad, involves inherited property (Num 27:1–11). Zelophehad, a Manassehite, died without male heirs, and his five daughters appealed to Moses to give them the inheritance, lest the property fall out of the clan's hands. Moses brought the case to God, who found in their favor. A principle was then codified whereby a daughter can inherit if there are no sons in the family. A later continuation of the matter leads to a qualification of the law (Num 36:1–12). The members of Zelophehad's clan feared that, if the daughters married into another tribe, the land that they had inherited would pass to that tribe. The resultant ruling allowed a daughter to retain her father's property if she married within the tribe. If she married outside the tribe, the land reverted to a male relative within the original tribe. The disposition of this case assumes that a woman is part of her husband's domain. Her property, movable or not, becomes his property. Leviticus 25:8–17, 23–34 shows the importance in P's ideology of keeping landholdings within the family or clan. This ethic was upheld in the case of the daughters of Zelophehad.

The Priestly tradent's designation of circumcision as a sign of God's ברית-commands dovetails with P's general view of the place of women in the societal hierarchy (see Jay 1988, 70). Females stand below males,[12] and their status is tied to the man in whose domain they reside. It is only a male who can carry the sign. A woman is thus part of the community by proxy, an extension of her father or husband.

The specifics of the male-female power dynamic are fleshed out in P's legal material. However, the proxy character of a woman's membership in

---

11. For a domain-based taxonomy of women in the Bible, see Wegner 1988, 14.

12. The privileging of males in P's hierarchy is manifest most notably in the fact that women cannot serve as priests. The role of women in the biblical cult is treated by Bird 1987; Gruber 1987. It is also evident in the laws of ritual defilement from genital discharge. On this issue, see Wegner 1998; *contra* Milgrom 1991, 944.

the community is grounded in Gen 17. As explained above (25–26, 32–34), in that context God communicates directly only with Abraham. Notice of Sarah's name change and her blessing is delivered to Abraham. Additionally, the term ברית is used exclusively in reference to Abraham and his primary male descendant, Isaac.

From the Priestly traditions pertaining to the Israelite women, we can extrapolate some conclusions about slaves and the גר. If a male slave is circumcised, his wife/wives and daugther/s can eat of the Passover. Similarly, the גר's wife/wives and daughter/s are eligible to partake of a paschal sacrifice based upon the presence or absence of their husband's or father's foreskin. P minimizes, ignores, or eliminates any connection of circumcision to the penis or its function and did not "choose" the penis as the locus for an important body mark. Rather, the Priestly tradent inherited a practice and ascribed new meaning to it. As such, it would be an exaggeration to assert that P configured circumcision as sign of the ברית in order to subordinate women. Nonetheless, the secondary, proxy status of women attendant to circumcision is absolutely congruent with the Priestly author's gender ethos.

Circumcision Has No Fertility Implications

The fact that circumcision is performed on the penis does enable the Priestly author to perpetuate a patriarchal ethos. Beyond this, circumcision in P has nothing to do with the penis and its function. Throughout the Hebrew canon, and in the extant ancient Semitic witnesses to circumcision (per Sasson 1966), there are no references to the effect of a foreskin, or its absence, on the utility of the penis. Von Rad is on point when he explains that "circumcision is understood quite formally, i.e., without significant reference to the procedure itself, as a sign of the covenant" (1972, 201). Eilberg-Schwartz, with his claim that circumcision was a fertility rite (1990, 141–48), completely misapprehends the character of the Priestly literature. Geller (1990, 5–8) notes that Priestly and Deuteronomic religion attempted to expunge the cult of any influence of "Canaanism," that is, elements of fertility and sexually related practice. He maintains that

> beyond all doubt it is the sexual sin which looms largest in the roster of Canaanite iniquity, especially in the Priestly formulation of covenant theology. After a long inventory of tabu sexual relations, Leviticus proclaims that it was precisely for such acts that the former inhabitants of the land were destroyed, a punishment which is ascribed, not to Israel, but, in a remarkable turn of phrase, to the physical reaction of the land itself: it "vomited out" the Canaanites (Lev. 18 and 20).

CIRCUMCISION, STATUS, AND SEXUALITY   51

Given the extent to which this ethos colors the Priestly writings as well as other biblical traditions, Fox's reading of אות ברית, in Gen 17:11 as a sign of YHWH's promise of fertility appears less than credible (see above, 37–38). Eilberg-Schwartz (1990, 145–46) cites a panoply of fertility-related symbolism and activity in Ndembu circumcision ritual to support an argument about circumcision in the Torah. He fails to recognize, however, that circumcision in P is all but devoid of such symbols or ritualization. He further buttresses his thesis with a "measure for measure" scenario, based upon the fully valid idea that the *karet* penalty may carry the sense of extirpation of one's offspring. Eilberg-Schwartz reasons that, since an uncircumcised Israelite will incur the *karet* punishment and be rendered infertile, the opposite, increased fertility, must attach to those who do comply with the circumcision commandment. Implicit in the logic of his argument is the invalid assumption that circumcision is the only precept whose abrogation brings *karet* upon the violator. In fact, the *karet* penalty is imposed for many transgressions besides failure to circumcise, such as working on the Sabbath (Exod 31:14), eating blood (Lev 17:10–14), and inappropriately using sacred substances such as anointing oil (Exod 30:33) and sanctuary incense (Exod 30:38). Eilberg-Schwartz would be hard-pressed to connect most of these to fertility. For his formulation to stand, however, the same "measure for measure" test must be applicable to each and every transgression that bears the *karet* penalty.

It is well-established that circumcision has fertility connotations in many cultures. Moreover, even if there is no available data to suggest it, circumcision may have been a fertility ritual in ancient Canaan or Israel. However, it definitively has no such significance in the Priestly literature. The twofold argument, albeit valid and supported by the text, that (1) the Priestly corpus has no rituals with any ascribed sexual valence and (2) in P's mindset, circumcision has little or nothing to do with the penis or its functionality, leaves one vulnerable to the following challenge: Why, then, would the Priestly tradent choose the penis, a sexual organ, as the locus of the ברית sign? Any answer to such a question, will, by nature, be speculative. I suggest, in line with a traditional viewpoint, that P did not choose the penis. Circumcision must have had an ancient provenance and been deeply embedded into the fabric of the society out of which the Priestly community emerged. Thus, the rite had to be integrated into a new ideological framework and marked with a new set of meanings. In Gevirtz's words, for P, "making the removal of the foreskin an indispensable component of a covenant between deity and man … imbued it with a religious significance it seems never to have had before" (1990, 102). The detachment of circumcision from any implications of fertility or genital function is fully congruent with P's broader engagement with matters of sexuality. Passages in the P corpus dealing with sexuality suggest an effort to define ethical boundaries, with Canaanite behavior as a foil (Lev 18; 20), or to manage the defilement that is a natural byproduct of the sex act or any kind of genital flow.

4
Circumcision and the Cult

Circumcision as Ritual

In order to ascertain the place of circumcision within the larger matrix of Priestly ritual and cult practice, it is profitable to determine how circumcision is presented in the text as a ritual act. This line of inquiry must, by nature, begin with a cogent understanding of ritual and its dynamics. While scholars have, in many quarters, attempted to define "ritual" as against nonritual activity, such a definition, if not elusive, is ultimately of little use in the present inquiry.[1] I follow Wright (per the note below) in asserting that I know a ritual when I see one. Therefore I start from the premise, as have all students of circumcision to date, that it is indeed a ritual. The crux of the examination, then, is to determine what kind of ritual it is. Thus, in this regard, the work of thinkers who describe and characterize ritual becomes more germane. Bell eschews the identification of any essential feature to distinguish ritual from ordinary activity. She argues that certain practices are "ritualized," thereby setting them apart from the mundane. Ritualization, in her view, creates and privileges "qualitative distinctions." These distinctions between the ritual and

---

1. Those striving for a definition of "ritual" include Turner 1967; Goody 1977; and Alexander 1991. Zeusse asserts that, "although it would seem to be a simple matter to define *ritual*, few terms in the study of religion have been explained and applied in more confusing ways" (1987, 405). Staal stresses, similarly, that efforts to "define the meanings, goals and aims of ritual" have proved inadequate (1979, 8). Moreover, in his view, there have been "so many different answers and theories, not only often contradictory between themselves, but of such disparate character that it is difficult to even compare them." Goody observes that definitions of ritual have become so inclusive that they "are likely to block research" (1977, 27). In the same vein, Wright points out that "researchers have often noted that one knows ritual when one sees it, but that it is otherwise difficult to define" (2001b, 8).

the ordinary resist an essentialist approach because they are specific to individual cultures and communities (1992, 74).[2]

Wuthnow, like Bell, shies away from either/or dichotomies. He avers that

> the distinction between expressive and instrumental activity is not a hard and fast rule that can be used to divide the world into two categories. The distinction is, rather, an *analytic* distinction that allows activities to be arranged along a continuum, from those at one end that are primarily expressive to those at the other end that are primarily instrumental. Most behavior falls somewhere in the middle, having aspects that are expressive and aspects that are instrumental. For example, meals are heavily imbued with both.... The fact that expressivity and instrumentality represent an analytic continuum has important implications for the study of ritual. Ritual is not a *type* of social activity that can be set off from the rest of the world for special investigation. It is a *dimension* of all social activity. (1987, 101)

Although Bell does not use a term such as "continuum," she also avoids characterizing an activity as "ritual" or "not ritual." Rather, she evaluates the activity based upon the degree to which it displays evidence of ritualization.[3] Gruenwald's approach is akin to that of Bell and Wuthnow. In a manner analogous to Bell's focus upon aspects of ritualization, Gruenwald is attentive to the "operational structure," or "processual logic," of ritual acts "as they are done in their programmed sequence," often at a specific place and time (2003, 2, 5). Similarly, Staal asserts that ritual is instrumental, "pure activity," where "what is essential ... is the precise and faultless execution, in accordance with rules, of numerous rites and recitations" (1979, 9), in order to achieve a desired end. Exploiting this theoretical perspective, Klingbeil sets up a typology of biblical ritual, delineating a lexicon of ritual elements such as structure, order, sequence, space, time, objects, action, participants, and language, then classifying rituals based upon the presence and nature of these elements. He

---

2. For example, observant Jews ritualize eating by reciting prayers at the start and conclusion of any meal. Among the elements of ritualization in a traditional Japanese meal is the seating hierarchy, based upon proximity to the entryway and the *tokonoma* (ceremonial alcove; see Kondo 1996, 171–75). Bell uses meals as one of her main examples (1992, 90–91), and Wright (2001b, 12–13) focuses on banquets as important ritual settings in the Ugaritic Aqhat narrative. A 2001 issue of *Semeia* (86) is fully devoted to "Food and Drink in the Biblical Worlds" and includes many references to, and discussions of, ritual and ritualization.

3. Bell's discussion of meals (1992, 90–91) is in accord with Wuthnow's statement. For her classifications of ritual and ritualization, see Bell 1992, 69–170; 1997, 138–70.

also dissects rituals, or what some call "ritual complexes"[4] into components that he labels "sub-rituals."

Circumcision, as represented in the Priestly Torah, is absent any Turnerian "symbols." Similarly, it is not a "structured" or "processual" practice comprised of deliberate, sequential components, nor is it portrayed an aggregation of rites, subrites, or recitations. The sole indication of ritualization is the time-bound nature of the commandment. Even then, no particular time on the eighth day is stipulated. The P texts do not specify any personnel, venues, tools,[5] or procedures for making the cut, nor do they enumerate any regulations for purification, before or after, or any accompanying offerings, declarations, or liturgical accompaniment.[6] If we apply Klingbeil's system of classification, it is apparent that the Priestly presentation of circumcision is completely silent with respect to structure, order, sequence, space, objects, action, participants, and ritual language. According to the Genesis narrative, Abraham circumcises his sons and slaves (Gen 17:23; 21:4). One might argue that P utilizes the narrative to convey a sense of expected normative practice. In that scenario, the father's participation in, or supervision of, the cutting could be construed as an element of ritualization. However, the regulations in Gen 17 and Lev 12 consistently use passive forms of מול, suggesting that there is no requirement as to who carries out the circumcision. P's silence regarding the performative elements of the circumcision mandate is particularly resonant. The Priestly corpus is replete with explicit detail pertaining to ritual performance. Any divergence from the prescriptions has dire consequences.[7] It would seem that, beyond the eighth-day regulation, P was not invested in describing the particulars of circumcision. Rather, it is the removal of the foreskin that is of signal, and nearly sole, importance.[8]

---

4. This rubric is used, for example, in Gilders 2004.

5. Contrast Exod 4:25 and Josh 5:1–2, which both specify stone knives for circumcision (צר in Exodus, חרבות צורים in Joshua.). The significance of these implements is highlighted in LXX Josh 24:30, which recounts the burial of the knives with Joshua. On the symbolism of the stone knives, see Heger 1999, 115.

6. The Mishnah is replete with very detailed circumcision regulations (e.g., m. Šab. 19:1–6; m. ʿArak. 2:2, m. Neg. 7:5; m. Ned. 3:11; m. Pesaḥ. 6:2), but there is no way to date the origin of many of these customs and rules. Moreover, there is no reason to assume that ancient Israelites did, or did not, circumcise their sons according to any conventions or laws. We only know that P chose not to include such stipulatons.

7. The fatal result of nonconformance and/or disobedience in ritual matters is illustrated by the Nadab and Abihu episode in Lev 10.

8. In rabbinic law, when a son is born without a foreskin (נולד מהול), a ceremonial bloodletting (הטפת דם ברית) must still be performed. This prescription is in

As an illustration or test of the aforementioned characterization of circumcision in P, circumcision will be compared with two body-marking practices attested in the Hebrew Bible and its Near Eastern cognates that involve some sort of cutting: the ear piercing of the perpetual Hebrew slave (Exod 21:2–6, Deut 15:12–18); and the marking of slaves generally, as articulated in a variety of sources.

SLAVE MARKING IN THE ANCIENT NEAR EAST

Ancient Near Eastern slaves were marked by various methods, such as a tonsure (*abbuttu gullubu*) or a hanging tag.[9] The most common form of marking was the tattoo, where the name of the owner was inscribed on a body part, usually the arm, of the slave. This type of slave mark is attested throughout the Near East of the biblical epoch, from Mesopotamia to the Jewish garrison on Elephantine. The Akkadian terms for the tattoo, *šimtu*, *šindu*, and *šintu*,[10] are cognate to the equivalent Aramaic term שנת. For example, Cowley 28 deals with a division of slaves and other property. Line 6 reads

שנית על ידה בימן שניתת מקרא ארמית כזנה למבטחיה

"The mark on her right arm is marked in the Aramaic language 'Mibtahiah's.'"

The slave tattoo is also mentioned in biblical texts such as Isa 44:5, where God's name is inscribed on an Israelite's arm.[11]

זֶה יֹאמַר לַה' אָנִי וְזֶה יִקְרָא בְשֵׁם־יַעֲקֹב

---

line with the highly ritualized rabbinic model of circumcision in which the drawing of blood is quite significant. By contrast, in P blood plays no role in the practice. Given the instrumental nature of the activity in the Priestly mindset, it can be inferred that a child born with no foreskin would not need to be circumcised.

9. On slave marks, see Hurowitz 1992; Mendelsohn 1949, 42–49.
10. See CAD *šimtu*.
11. See also Ezek 9:4, where the Judeans are branded on their foreheads. Isa 49:16 may present a fascinating case of role reversal: God declares הֵן עַל־כַּפַּיִם חַקֹּתִיךְ "See, I have incized you on [my] hands," possibly equating his commitment to Israel as that of slave to master. Such divine-human role reversals are characteristic of Deutero-Isaiah. On this tendency, see Sommer 1998, 91, 250 n. 50. Note a rabbinic tradition, in the same spirit, that has God wearing phylacteries inscribed with scriptural verses trumpeting Israel's uniqueness (b. Ber. 6a).

וְזֶה יִכְתֹּב יָדוֹ לַה' וּבְשֵׁם יִשְׂרָאֵל יְכַנֶּה:

This one will say "I am YHWH's," and this one will be called by Jacob's name, and this one will inscribe his arm "YHWH's" and adopt the name Israel.

While the available data delineate the types of slave marks in use, there are no extant descriptions or regulations as to marking practices, in terms of specific steps in the procedure, or their order, tools, the timing of the marking with respect to the acquisition or birth of new slaves, and who must apply the mark. Thus, the branding of slaves seems to be absent any aspects of ritualization. Addionally, the marking of a slave is not a transformative act. A person is made a slave by capture or purchase and is a slave whether marked or not. The aim, and outcome, is purely instrumental: the identification of a slave's ownership. As with any piece of property that is lost (or, in the case of slaves, escapes), the mark facilitates restoration to the rightful owner.[12]

THE PIERCED EAR IN EXODUS 21 AND DEUTERONOMY 15

According to the regulation in the Covenant Code, the עבד עברי "Hebrew slave" works for six years and must be emancipated in the seventh. When set free, he may depart only with property and family that he brought with him at the beginning of the period of his servitude. If he marries a woman provided by the master and has children, the woman and children remain the possession of the master. However, the עבד עברי can opt to forgo his freedom. The process begins with a statement on the part of the slave (Exod 21:5): אָהַבְתִּי אֶת־אֲדֹנִי אֶת־אִשְׁתִּי וְאֶת־בָּנָי לֹא אֵצֵא חָפְשִׁי "I love my master and my wife and my children; I will not depart as a free person." A procedure follows the slave's declaration (21:6):

וְהִגִּישׁוֹ אֲדֹנָיו אֶל־הָאֱלֹהִים
וְהִגִּישׁוֹ אֶל־הַדֶּלֶת אוֹ אֶל־הַמְּזוּזָה
וְרָצַע אֲדֹנָיו אֶת־אָזְנוֹ בַּמַּרְצֵעַ וַעֲבָדוֹ לְעֹלָם

---

12. Cuneiform law is quite stringent about the requirement to return fugitive or lost slaves. Rewards are mandated for those who discharge the obligation and grave punishment legislated for those who do not (Ur Nammu 17; Lipit Ishtar 12–13; Eshnunna 50; and Hammurapi 15–20). Hammurapi 226–227 also prohibits shaving a slave's *abuttu* without the owner's consent, on pain of corporal or capital punishment, depending upon the circumstance. In contrast, Deut 23:16–17 forbids the return or ill-treatment of escaped slaves.

His master shall bring him to the God, and bring him to the door or to the doorpost, and his master shall pierce his ear with an awl, and then he [the slave] shall serve him [the master] in perpetuity.

The law in Deut 15:16–17 outlines a similar process for a Hebrew man or woman who elects perpetual servitude.[13] A declaration: לֹא אֵצֵא מֵעִמָּךְ "I will not go out from you" is followed by a piercing procedure. The piercing described in both versions is not necessarily permanent, since a newly pierced ear left unfilled would close fairly quickly. Consequently, the piercing in and of itself would have no value as a slave mark. Biblical sources (Gen 24:30; 35:4; Exod 32:2; 35:22; Hos 2:15; Prov 25:12; Job 42:11) suggest that Israelite men and women wore נזמים (rings) in their ears. Thus, an earring in the new hole would not be an effective indicator of perpetual servitude. Influenced by his knowledge of Mesopotamian custom, Mendelsohn attempts to resolve the problem by suggesting "that the hole was made in order to push through it a ring, or cord, on which was fastened a tag made of clay or metal" (1949, 49). Unfortunately, Mendelsohn has speculated beyond the scope of the evidence. With all the detail provided in the texts, if the ultimate purpose was the insertion of a tag or cord, why was this crucial element omitted in the regulation?

It is preferable, then, to view the purpose of the piercing as something other than marking the slave. This purpose is revealed by the various ritualized aspects of the piercing. The laws delineate the actors, tools, and place of performance. Moreover, the practice is initiated by a formal declaration of intent. Viberg characterizes the piercing as a "legal symbolic act" (1992, 77–88). He defines a legal symbolic act as a "[n]on-verbal act which fulfils a legal function when it is performed under the proper circumstances and when the legal function is different from the physical result of the act" (9). The piercing can be grouped with symbolic acts such as shoe removal (145–65), which confirms property transfers (Ruth 4:8) or marks the rejection of Levirite responsibility (Deut 25:9). Viberg asserts, justifiably, that "the legal function of the act of piercing the ear of the slave is that the owner officially ... accomplishes the transference of the legal status of the Hebrew slave from that of being a debt-slave for a limited duration of time, to that of being a slave of the owner forever" (88). He explains that "the ear, as a symbol for the obedience of the slave, was pierced, which symbolizes the submission of the slave to his owner" (88). If the ear does not, as Viberg maintains, symbolize obedience per se, it may, as

---

13. The range of differences between the Hebrew slave laws in the Covenant Collection and D have been fully treated in the scholarship. See the still-classic commentary of Driver (1895, 181–85).

one of the extremities, have a synecdochal purpose, representing the whole body of the perpetual slave. Additionally, the door or doorpost may also carry a communicative function. Affixing the person's ear to the door represents the binding of the slave to the master's household and domain of influence. In sum, the ear-piercing in Exod 21 and Deut 15 is a ritual whose procedures, singly and in consort, have communicative value and a transformative effect. The desired end is not a mark on the ear of the indentured person. Rather, it is the solemnification of their new status as an עבד עולם, "slave in perpetuity."

A comparison of the ear piercing of the עבד עברי (per Exod 21 and Deut 15) to the extant evidence pertaining to slave marks yields a simple conclusion. The ear piercing of the perpetual slave is about process; the "how" is of utmost importance. In contradistinction, slave marking is wholly concerned with product. The mark is essential, but we have no access to information regarding the "how." Circumcision, as epitomized in the P corpus, is akin to the marking of slaves. The process, the "how" of circumcision, is almost completely ignored by the Priestly tradent. With both circumcision, and the branding of slaves, it is the mark, the sign, that counts, not how the mark is made or how the foreskin is removed.[14]

From the standpoint of quantity and significance of ritualized elements, when set against the background of any given ritual from among the vast array of cultic activities laid out in the Priestly legislation, the ear-piercing procedure must be judged quite "minimalist." All the more so does circumcision seem out of place in P's highly detailed, densely ritualized, punctiliously processual cultic system. Nonetheless, three aspects of the circumcision regulation call for examination in the context of P's cultic system. The first is the mandate that circumcision of infants be performed on the eighth day, the sole specified aspect of the practice. Moreover, this time element links circumcision with other aspects of the cult that evince a seven/eight-day pattern. Second, Exod 12:43–49 contains a seemingly redundant command: no uncircumcised male may eat of the Passover sacrifice. This rule compels an

---

14. Traditional Jewish commentators Joseph Bechor Shor (eleventh-century France) and Malbim (Meir Lev ben Yechiel Michael, nineteenth-century Russia) opined that circumcision in the Torah was a slave mark, indicating Israel's servitude to God. Unfortunately, the comments were offered without any accompanying explanations. The hypothesis is attractive and borne out by the explict characterization of Israel as YHWH's slaves (Lev 25:42, 55) and the affinities I have suggested, from the perspective of ritual theory. However, a comprehensive comparison of the two practices and their wider implications suggests that the analogy is limited. For example, circumcision is a recognition sign between God and Israel, while a slave mark identifies the slave to others beside the owner.

Circumcision and the Eighth Day

examination of circumcision in the context of P's Passover and festival legislation. Finally, since failure to circumcise warrants the *karet* penalty, the practice must be understood within the framework of the other *karet*-bearing transgressions.

The typological use of numbers and number patterns is attested throughout the literature of the ancient Near East. Zakovitch (1977, iii) has shown that the three/four pattern, with its derivatives, pervades the Hebrew Bible. He attributes this pervasiveness to the fact that in ancient cultures three constituted "the limit of mathematical consciousness and ... an expression of superlative." In the Priestly literature, the number seven predominates and would seem to represent a round number or discrete set. In P, seven and its derivatives mark quantities of time, weight, population, or age. Seven appears as a discrete integer,[15] in multiples such as fourteen,[16] forty-nine,[17] and seventy,[18] and is the climactic component of the six/seven pattern.[19]

Circumcision is one of eight instances of the seven/eight pattern in P, all of which entail a count of days and display the same formulaic language: ...שבעת ימים ... ו/ב/מיום השמיני... "... seven days ... and/on/from the eighth day...." The מצרע[20] (Lev 13–14), the male and the female with abnormal genital discharge (Lev 15), and the Nazirite affected by corpse contamination (Num 6:6–12) must undergo a waiting period of seven days of

---

15. Examples include the duration of Passover observance (Exod 12:15, 19), the lamps of the מנרה (Exod 25:37; 37:23), the sequence of חטאת blood applications (Lev 4:6, 17; 16:4; Num 19:4), a standard purificatory period (Lev 15:19, 28; Num 19:11, 14), and the quantity of lambs offered for the new moons and festivals (Num 28:11, 19, 29; 29:2, 4, 7, 10).

16. Fourteen lambs are offered daily on Sukkot (Num 29:12, 17, etc.).

17. Forty-nine are the years preceding the Jubilee (Lev 25:8).

18. The largest attested multiple of seven in P accounts for the life span of various antediluvian characters (Gen 5:12; 11:26), the quantity of Israelites who went down to Egypt (Gen 46:27), and the weight in shekels of the מזרק holding the grain offering donated by each tribe (Num 7:13, 19, etc.).

19. The six/seven pattern connects the creation of the world (Gen 1–2:4a), Sabbath observance (Exod 31:12–17; Lev 23:3), and the agricultural sabbatical law (Lev 25:2–7).

20. While "leper" is the standard English translation of מצרע, Milgrom uses the apellation "scale disease." He demonstrates that, although biblical צרעת cannot be precisely identified, it is clearly not leprosy (1991, 816–26).

purification, during which they are isolated from their community or dwelling place. On the eighth day, they are to bring an expiatory sacrifice, after which their purification is complete.[21] According to Lev 8:33–9:24, the high priest's ordination ceremony requires the ordinands to remain at the entrance of the tent of meeting for seven days. On the eighth day, an elaborate complex of sacrificial rituals is performed, after which the priest is ready to carry out his duties.[22] P's Sukkot legislation directs the Israelite to dwell in booths and bring festal offerings for seven days, after which an additional festival day, termed an עצרת, is mandated (Lev 23:33–43; Num 29:12–38). Leviticus 22:27, which has the most affinity to the circumcision law, restricts the use of sacrificial animals until they are eight days old.

שׁוֹר אוֹ־כֶשֶׂב אוֹ־עֵז כִּי יִוָּלֵד
וְהָיָה שִׁבְעַת יָמִים תַּחַת אִמּוֹ
וּמִיּוֹם הַשְּׁמִינִי וָהָלְאָה יֵרָצֶה לְקָרְבַּן אִשֶּׁה לַה׳

When an ox or a sheep or a goat is born, it shall be under its mother for **seven days. From the eighth day** onward, it shall be acceptable as a gift offering to YHWH.[23]

In Gen 17:12 and Lev 12:3, only the eighth day of circumcision is mentioned. That the child remains seven days with his mother is implied. Additionally, though the standard formula ... שבעת ימים ... וביום השמיני... is present in Lev 12:2–3, it involves a change of subject, from the mother to the male infant (see above, 22–24). Despite these formal distinctions, circumcision is of a piece, conceptually, with the other instances of the seven/eight pattern.

In all but one of the seven/eight-day sequences, the eighth day is not a particularly auspicious or climactic day.[24] Rather, it is the first day following the

---

21. On the specifics of purificatory waiting periods and offerings and their relationship to the various conditions of defilement, see Wright 1991.

22. On the ordination ceremony, see Gorman 1990, 103–48.

23. This law is a revision of a similar regulation in Exod 22:29. The Covenant Code prescribes the waiting period only for firstborn animals. P extends it to all sacrificial animals.

24. Contra Westermann (1981, 266), who asserts, without providing examples, that "the number eight is a lucky number."

crucial seven days.²⁵ Thus with the מצרע, the corpse-contaminated Nazirite, and people with abnormal genital discharges, the eighth day is picked for the sacrifice because it follows immediately after the period of purificatory separation that is standard in all cases of severe defilement.

Common to the seven/eight pattern in the cases of the ordained high priest, the sacrificial animal, and the circumcised infant is the concept of ritual or sacral viability. All must wait seven days before they are eligible to be involved in their designated community/cultic functions.²⁶ The priest's status is hereditary. At birth, he enjoys certain privileges and is bound by specific restrictions.²⁷ Still, he may only officiate following ordination and attains his eligibility after he has undergone the seven days of separation. The complex of rituals confirms his viability and is the final act of sanctification. The case of the sacrificial animal and the male infant can be further distinguished from the other examples of the seven/eight-day pattern. Neither are separated and then reintegrated. Rather, for both newborns, the eighth day marks the first occasion of entry into the mainstream.²⁸ The ritual-viability equation plays

---

25. This is in contrast to the six/seven sequences where the seventh day/year is the momentous one. The exception is the Sukkot עצרת, which is a distinctive celebration in its own right. The significance of the עצרת has not been fully understood. See von Rad 1965, 174–75; Levine 1989, 162; and Haran 1978, 296–97.

26. The altar law in Ezek 43:18–27 is a further example of ritual viability and the seven/eight pattern. For seven days (שבעת ימים) the altar is purified and ordained. (The same technical language, מלא יד [*piel*], is utilized here and with the high priest in Exod 28:41.) From the eighth day forward (והיה ביום השמיני והלאה), sacrifices may be offered upon it. הלאה is common to Ezekiel's altar law and the newborn animal regulation (Lev 22:27).

27. Any member of a priest's household may eat the תרומה (Lev 22:16). Additionally, the limitations on marriage, shaving, laceration, and corpse contact are not age-specified (Lev 21:1–8).

28. The rabbis note this parity (Lev. Rab. 27:1), as does Eilberg-Schwartz (1990, 122–23), who highlights a number of similar animal-human homologies. In this vein, Cohen (2005, 20) argues that because an animal may not be sacrificed until the eighth day and a boy may not be circumcised until the eighth day, "circumcision is analogous to, and a surrogate for, sacrifice," observing also that the equivalence is "explicit in later Jewish tradition." This type of conclusion is no doubt influenced by rabbinic hermeneutic principles such as *heqesh* ("analogy") or *gezerah shavah* ("equivalent ordinance"). These intertextual interpretive modes, usually applied in halakic contexts, suggest that two scriptural passages evincing terminological or other content-based affinity can be treated as more generally comparable. This reading strategy is less appropriate to a "plain sense" approach to the text. First, as in the case of the sacrifice-circumcision analogy, a single common element is insufficient to support a more

out differently in the cases of the sacrificial animal and the male infant. The animal may be sacrificed any time from the eighth day forward, while the baby boy *must* be circumcised on the eighth day. Thus, the eighth day is significant as regards circumcision, not because the eighth day has any special ritual power, but because it is the first possible day in the infant's life when the rite can be carried out. In this respect, we can point up P's intent to have an Israelite infant circumcised immediately. Beyond that, the specific time-bound nature of the practice is indicative of P's attention to seven-day cycles and the typological import of the number seven in the Priestly mindset.

Circumcision Is Not Purificatory

Due to the juxtaposition of the eighth-day circumcision notice and the purificatory procedures for the parturient in Lev 12, a number of scholars have erroneously posited a connection between circumcision and purification in the Priestly writings. Levine opines that "there is undoubtedly a correlation between the eight-day period between birth and circumcision and the duration of the initial period of the mother's impurity after giving birth to a male" (1989, 73). Levine cites Hoffman to buttress his claim. Hoffman actually takes an opposite position (consistent with my own). He observes that

> Many modern critics have connected this law [eighth-day circumcision] to the law of purification.... However, we have not located, anywhere in scripture, even a hint that a boy is defiled as a result of his birth.... The assignment of circumcision to the eighth day ... is connected to the laws of defilement and purification, only in regard to their basic timing.... The newborn may only be consecrated to serving the Creator, by means of circumcision, on the eighth day.[29]

---

thoroughgoing kinship. Additionally, *heqesh*, *gezerah shavah*, and their modern iterations often rely upon "out of context" exegesis. In order to assert a common guiding principle, circumcision and sacrifice should not be interpreted as a pair of practices in isolation. Rather, they must be considered in light of all cases of seven/eight patterns and eighth-day rites. From that perspective, the ritual-viability thesis is more solidly grounded and posseses the greater explanatory power. No medical or ethical motive should be imputed in the case of the animal regulation. There is no suggestion that removing a suckling infant from its mother on the eighth day, as opposed to the seventh or ninth, has any positive or negative emotional or nutritional implications that could have generated the law. Thus, the eighth-day viability discussed here is not a biological or medical matter.

29. Hoffman, 1953, 259–60. Milgrom (1991, 746–47) also objects to any link between circumcision and purification in Lev 12. Cohen (2005, 19) takes a more cau-

Hoffman continues by pointing out the relationship of circumcision to the regulations regarding an animal's sacrificial viability.

Eilberg-Schwartz (1990, 180) goes even further than Levine, maintaining that the circumcision of the boy purifies the mother from her initial postpartum defilement. His claim, however, has no validity. As noted earlier, the seven-day period of purification is not unique to the parturient. It is observed for corpse contamination (Num 6:10; 19:11; 31:19), genital discharge (Lev 15:13; 19; 28), and skin disease (Lev 13–14). Moreover, no ritual is necessary to bring the mother from the initial level of defilement to the less severe. Had one been required in the case of the male newborn, a comparable rite would be necessary on the fifteenth day after the birth of the female. A sacrifice is brought by the postpartum mother, but only following the passage of thirty-three or sixty-six days. Additionally, Lev 12:2 equates birth defilement to that of the menstrual blood, and a purification ritual is not needed for the menstruant. She simply observes a seven-day waiting period.[30]

There may be a practical element in the relationship of the mother's seven-day period of defilement to eighth-day circumcision. While the postpartum mother is a primary carrier of defilement, it would seem that the infant is not.[31] However, if we assume that the parturient's defilement is equivalent to that of the menstruant, then the baby would acquire secondary defilement from the mother. It is unlikely that an infant could be considered a human bearer of defilement, since it could not undertake the appropriate purificatory

---

tious middle ground. He suggests that the alignment of the purification cycle of the postpartum mother with the circumcision of the infant is not a coincidence. However, he qualifies the comment by admitting that "the association of circumcision with purification is, at best, implicit."

30. Eilberg-Schwartz (1990, 180) attempts to draw an invidious contrast between male circumcision blood and female menstrual blood in P's ideology. While the latter defiles, the former purifies and "creates covenant." Beyond the above-mentioned problems with his scenario, Eilberg-Schwartz ignores the fact that circumcision blood is never mentioned in the Priestly literature. In the Hebrew Bible, circumcision blood is only mentioned in Exod 4:24–26. It is unclear, however, what ritual role, if any, the blood plays in that episode. For discussion of this enigmatic tale, see Propp 1998, 233–43 and the scholarship catalogued above at 2 n. 5. Circumcision blood is highlighted in early exegesis of the "bloody bridegroom" pericope (see Vermes 1957/58) and attains significance in the rabbinic period. Note for example, y. Ned. 3:9, where the sacrificial דם הברית "blood of the covenant" thrown upon the Israelites by Moses in Exod 24:8 is reread as circumcision blood. A summary treatment of the emerging significance of circumcision blood in postbiblical Jewish traditions can be found in Cohen 2003 and Bernat 2009.

31. See Hoffman, above, and Milgrom 1991, 746.

sacrifices or lustrations. However, the baby, a physical entity, might acquire defilement in a manner analogous to inanimate objects, such as clothing or vessels that the mother touches during her period of immediate postpartum defilement. This defilement could be communicated to anyone who comes into contact with the mother and child. For this practical reason, the child is best kept isolated from the community until the eighth day. This implication is mostly likely coincidental and, as such, is not the reason behind eighth-day circumcision nor the motive for including the circumcision notice in Lev 12. Most significantly, it is clear that the circumcision of the newborn boy has no bearing upon his mother's purity.[32]

Wold divides the infractions that warrant the *karet* penalty into five subcategories (1978, 257– 61). He labels one of the groupings "Neglect of Purification Rituals" and includes circumcision in this rubric.[33] Wold supports his categorization with evidence of the link between circumcision and purity in African and Arab cultures, classical texts, and Philo.[34] While his data are unimpeachable, Wold never explains how these nonbiblical sources have any specific bearing on the meaning of circumcision in the Priestly Torah, nor does he adduce any direct biblical evidence.

Propp adduces a broad range of biblical and extrabiblical sources in a discourse on the purificatory and apotrapaic virtues of circumcision (1998, 453). The evidence he brings from Priestly tradition involves the circumcision-Passover nexus (see my discussion below, 66–70). Propp avers: "The connections between *Pesaḥ* and circumcision transcend the fact that each is a rite of passage.… There is evidence that circumcision, too, purifies.… Blood impurity (Num 9:6–14) and noncircumcision alike bar participation in the *Pesaḥ*." While it is accurate that corpse defilement or possession of a foreskin renders a man (and, by extension, his dependents) ineligible to offer a paschal sacrifice, Propp implies a connection between the two conditions that simply does not exist. First of all, corpse defilement is not an obstacle particular to the paschal offering. A person must be in a pure state to eat any sacrificial

---

32. One might pose the following challenge: If there is no essential link between circumcision and purification, why include the circumcision notice in Lev 12? I address this concern (ch. 1) by highlighting the "reminder" or "cross-reference" as a feature of Priestly legislation.

33. Milgrom (1990, 406) upholds Wold's characterization. However, he seems to contradict himself, as elsewhere Milgrom denies the connection of circumcision and ritual purification in P.

34. On the circumcision-purity nexus in these sources, along with the Septuagint, Symmachus, the New Testament, and rabbinic tradition, see Propp 1998, 220, 236, 453; Cohen 2005, 15–21; and Bernat 2009.

meat (Lev 7:19–21). Moreover, anyone who acquires corpse contamination must be removed from the camp altogether (Num 5:1–4). The reason the issue of defilement is raised pointedly with respect to the Passover is that the Passover is the only festal offering where failure to implement it by any Israelite brings the *karet* penalty (Num 9:13).

Leaving aside the specific claims addressed above for a circumcision-purity nexus in P, the matter can be put to rest more simply. Early in his career Milgrom wrote: "In the Priestly legislation we meet with a precision of terminology and formulation unmatched by other biblical codes" (1967, 115). This relative precision is certainly applicable to P's purity system, which in its concrete and technical aspects is detailed and comprehensive. The legislation is fully explicit as to substances and conditions that defile and appropriate modes of ritual purification. P never raises the notion of the foreskin as defiling and circumcision as purifying.[35]

Circumcision and Passover

The regulations in Exod 12:43–49 limit participation in the paschal offering to those who have been circumcised. Such a stricture is not specified for any other practice. To a certain extent, these laws are redundant: Gen 17:9–14 already mandates, without qualification, that all Israelite males and their male slaves must be circumcised. Thus, the only legal innovation of these verses pertains to the גר.

The redundancy serves to emphasize, generally, the special status of the Passover celebration and, specifically, the integral connection of Passover and circumcision. The Priestly literature is replete with indicators of the unique standing of Passover. The offering itself has many features that distinguish it from the standard sacrifice. While the שלמים, the type of sacrifice whose meat is eaten by the offerer, is typically boiled (Lev 6:21; Num 6:19), the פסח is roasted (Exod 12:8–9).[36] Additionally, it is the only sacrifice that must be

---

35. It is worth noting that for Ezekiel, who shares much with P in idiom and ideology, circumcision is better subsumed within the categorical dyad קדש/חול (sacred/profane), rather than טהר/טמא (pure/defiled). The distinction is aptly illustrated as follows: the prophet in 5:11 chastises the people for defiling God's sanctuary with their idols and abominations; on the other hand, according to Ezek 44:7 the presence of an ערל, a man with a foreskin, profanes the sacred precincts, just as one who transgresses the Sabbath profanes, rather than defiles, the holy day.

36. In the Deuteronomic tradition, the Passover is boiled (Deut 16:7). Note also the harmonization in 2 Chr 35:13: וַיְבַשְּׁלוּ הַפֶּסַח בָּאֵשׁ כַּמִּשְׁפָּט. On the culinary aspects of the offering, see Hendel 1989, 384–87; Propp 1999, 439–40.

performed in the evening time (Exod 12:8). Moreover, while, according to Lev 17:3-9, all animals must be slaughtered at the tabernacle, the paschal offering may be the exception. The ceremonial placement of the sacrificial blood on the doorpost further distinguishes the Passover observance (Exod 12:7).[37] The singular status of Passover is also signaled by two unique and interconnected legal provisions. First, Passover is the only festival where failure to celebrate incurs a *karet* penalty. Second, with no other observance is there a stipulation such as that of the second Passover of Num 9:6–13. If an Israelite misses the offering by reason of journey or defilement, there is an opportunity to carry out the observance one month later.[38]

Passover is also the most historicized of all the festivals in P.[39] The first Passover is set within the exodus narrative. Moreover, specific elements of the observance are anchored to specific aspects of the exodus/desert experience.[40] The only other festival tethered to a "historical" event is Sukkot, and its etiological notice is quite brief (Lev 23:43).[41]

The thorough raveling of Passover and the exodus in the Priestly mindset accounts for the linkage of circumcision to the festival. The exodus is the event through which God begins to actualize the ברית-promises first imparted to Abraham in Gen 17. Israel is redeemed from Egyptian bondage to become YHWH's slaves, attaining the unique relationship with him that is fully articulated in the standard *Bundesformular*. Moreover, they are on the path to the promised land and to reception of the commands to which they had

---

37. One could maintain, following the rabbinic differentiation between פסח מצרים "The Passover of Egypt" and פסח דורות "The Passover of Generations" (m. Pesaḥ. 9:5, Mek. Bo' 3, 4, 11, 14), that many of the customs of the first Passover are unique to that occasion and are not to be maintained in perpetuity (see Propp 1999, 445–52). This distinction would easily resolve the tension between a domestic sacrifice and the altar regulations of Lev 17 but would not negate the unique standing of Passover in P's ethos.

38. See the references above and note Haran's discussion of the unique aspects of the Passover obesvance in JE and P (318–22). In general, celebration of the paschal sacrifice in D is more in line with the other pilgrimage festival observances.

39. Passover is also the most historicized festival outside the Priestly corpus. The Covenant Code (Exod 23:15–17 = 34:18, 22–23) and D (Deut 16:1–17) link Passover to the exodus, while the other two pilgrimages are given no such etiologies.

40. Examples include hurried consumption of the Passover (Exod 12:11), the blood rite (12:13), and the second Passover (Num 9:6–14).

41. סכות in the motive clause is generally understood as referring to booths. However, the text may be establishing a festival practice based on a pun. Sukkot in P is the first stop in the desert itinerary (Exod 12:37; Num 33:5–6; and note the place-name etiology for Sukkot in Gen 33:17).

already committed by means of circumcision. The first Passover functioned as a community rite of passage marking the transformative moment.[42] Subsequent Passovers would reenact and commemorate this passage. Passover is thus the quintessential celebration of God's ברית-promises made real. Given P's command-centered theology, it is quite logical that any Passover celebrant must be circumcised, bearing the sign of his commitment to the ברית-commands. The slave, an extension of his master, would be also be compelled to bear the mark. The גר in choosing to partake of the paschal offering, in effect, voluntarily draws closer to the Israelite by sharing in an important communal event. Consequently, he must also be circumcised, thereby subordinating himself to a greater extent. Whether Israelite or not, bound or free, circumcision, the sign affirming commitment to the ברית-commands, is a perquisite for anyone celebrating the communal rite of passage solemnifiying Israel's attainment of the ברית-promises.[43]

Origins of the Circumcision-Passover Nexus

The link between Passover and circumcision is not unique to P. Joshua 5:2–9 records the mass circumcision of the Israelites following their miraculous Jordan crossing. The next three verses mention a communal Passover celebration. There is a general consensus that these texts represent a pre-Deuteronomistic tradition. Nelson (1997, 6–9, 71–79) and Boling (1982, 182–193) attribute the Gilgal narratives to an ancient stratum in Joshua. Soggin (1972, 73–76) considers Josh 3–5 part of the Deuteronomic redaction. He asserts, however, that the Passover account is an older tradition that was integrated by the Deuteronomist. Thus, it is unlikely that the juxtaposition of circumcision and Passover in Joshua was due to Priestly influence. By the same token, there are no literary markers to indicate that P drew upon Joshua directly. I would posit that the circumcision-Passover nexus was an extant cultic or cultural phenomenon that contributed to the formation of the narrative in Joshua and the Priestly regulations.

---

42. In the historical works of the Bible, Passover also serves as a communal rite of passage. In 2 Kgs 23:21–23 (= 2 Chr 35:1–19) and 2 Chr 30:1–27, the Passover celebration marked covenant renewals enacted by Josiah and Hezekiah. Additionally, the returnees from Babylonian exile, under the leadership of Ezra, observe a Passover (Ezra 6:19–22). On the Passover as a community rite of passage in the Bible, see Prosic 1999.

43. On the circumcision of non-Israelites, see above, chapter 3.

Scholars have attributed the unique connection between circumcision and the spring festival to four possible factors.[44] (1) Weber (1952, 90–93, 336) offers an idiosyncratic interpretation of the evidence. He sees the origin of circumcision in the initiation rites of warriors. Thus, the Josh 5 narrative, which is a prelude to the conquest of Canaan and constitutes the earliest link between Passover and circumcision, is part of ancient Israel's holy-war tradition. His formulation fails the test of credibility, as it is unsupported by any comparative ancient Near Eastern evidence and rests solely on the Joshua passage.

(2) Since antiquity, exegetes have linked the apotropaic efficacy of the blood of the paschal lamb with the similar power of circumcision blood. This connection is exemplified in early interpretations of the episode of the divine attack on Moses (Exod 4:24–26).[45] Although the natural association of bloods lends itself to such exegesis, nothing in the plain sense of the relevant pentateuchal texts sustains such a reading.

(3) Ancient Semites originally circumcised their male children en masse at an annual spring festival. Scholars hypothesize that this group rite was held at Gilgal, when Shechem was the cult center of what is often termed the Israelite amphictyony.[46]

(4) Circumcision was a rite of dedication, perhaps at its earliest stages, practiced only on firstborn males. The consecration of firstborn animals is integral to the Passover myth in P (Exod 13:2) and non-P texts (13:11–15). Some speculate that the consecration of firstlings and the practice of circumcision began as substitutes for actual firstborn child sacrifice.[47]

The latter two theories can be commended due to plausibility and explanatory value. Group circumcision has been attested among the pre-Islamic Arabs and the ancient Egyptians (Sasson 1966). The origins of Passover as a spring festival of dedication and renewal not only makes sense in the context of the exodus traditions but also fits the shape of the holiday as it is recorded in the nonpentateuchal accounts. Thus, a Passover is celebrated at the covenant

---

44. Propp (1999, 452–54) comprehensively treats the issues and scholarship surrounding the origins of the connection between circumcision and the spring festival. His scope is canonical and his main agenda developmental. Therefore, he does not concentrate directly on the association of Passover and circumcision in the Priestly ideology.

45. Vermes 1958 contains an incisive analysis of the relevant Second Temple and rabbinic texts.

46. See especially Morgenstern 1966, 67–80.

47. On circumcision as a consecratory or sacrificial ritual, see Levenson 1993, 43–52; Cohen 2005, 16–21.

renewals of Josiah (2 Kgs 22:21–23; 2 Chr 35:1–19) and Hezekiah (2 Chr 30) and upon the reconstitution of the Jerusalem community by Ezra (Ezra 6:19–22). It would seem, therefore, that P drew upon an already-existing customary connection between Passover and circumcision and shaped it to his needs. Since P upholds eighth-day circumcision of infants, an individual or communal rite tied to a seasonal festival would be untenable. The Priestly tradent does, however, exploit the Passover-circumcision nexus to fortify and even raise the stakes of the circumcision mandate.

Circumcision and the *Karet* Penalty

Genesis 17:14 contains the penalty clause for failure to circumcise:

וְעָרֵל זָכָר אֲשֶׁר לֹא־יִמּוֹל אֶת־בְּשַׂר עָרְלָתוֹ
וְנִכְרְתָה הַנֶּפֶשׁ הַהִוא מֵעַמֶּיהָ אֶת־בְּרִיתִי הֵפַר

> And an uncircumcised male, who does not circumcise the flesh of his foreskin, that person shall be cut off from his people. He has abrogated my ברית.

The punishment of "cutting off," usually designated the *karet* penalty, is imposed for a wide spectrum of violations in the Priestly literature. The key terminological components of the formula כרת "cut off," נפש "person (soul)," and מעם "from (his) people," occurring in the circumcision verse above, are consistent in all attestations. Since biblical *karet* in general has been studied comprehensively,[48] the focus here will be upon two issues directly germane to circumcision: the nature of the punishment; and the reason why *karet* is imposed for failure to circumcise.

Alienation from God's ברית-Promises

The general consensus is that *karet* is a divinely imposed penalty of some devastating consequence, the nature of which is never specified in the text. Scholars have argued for a range of possibilities from premature death to extirpation of one's line to a harried afterlife.[49] Schwartz (1999, 55–56) takes a more general view. He sees it as a punishment that can come in a variety

---

48. The definitive study remains Wold 1978. For helpful summary treatments, see also Milgrom 1990, 405–7; Schwartz 1999, 52–56.

49. See the scholarship in the note just above.

of forms at no specified occasion. Schwartz's claim is tenable as a start but requires a finer point. As imparted originally to Abraham, every Israelite is a beneficiary of God's threefold ברית-promise: progeny; land; and the relationship entailed in the *Bundesformular*: "I will be your God, and you will be my people [עם]." Israel's access, however, to YHWH's beneficence is contingent on heeding the divine commands. It follows quite simply and logically that if failure to obey entails being cut off from the עם, such excision would entail alienation from God and the ברית-promises. Thus, the *karet* penalty could, as many have theorized, mean premature death or extirpation.

There is one ramification of *karet*, which I consider crucial, that has been overlooked in the scholarship: the notion that the penalty could entail a loss of land tenure.[50] For a number of reasons, forfeiture of one's stake in the land promise would, in the Priestly *Weltanschaung*, constitute a most devastating type of punishment. First, the foundation of the ruling that the daughters of Zelophehad could not marry out of the tribe (Num 36) and of the detailed regulations of Lev 25 is the imperative to preserve the clan stakehold. In the Numbers pericope, the operative term is נחלה, while in Lev 25 אחזה is employed. This imperative, capsulated in Lev 25:23—וְהָאָרֶץ לֹא תִמָּכֵר לִצְמִתֻת, "the land may not be sold irretrievably"—is tethered both to social welfare and theology. Families must not be allowed to descend to such destitution that they become permanently landless. Moreover, all the land is ultimately God's possession. Second, one of the terms in P's lexicon that designates an Israelite "insider," typically used in opposition to גר, is אזרח. Best translated as "native," its root זרח denotes "coming up, rising." The meaning of אזרח is derived from the idea that a native "comes up" from the land. Thus, for the Priestly tradent the semantics of communal identity are connected to rootedness in the land.[51] Consistent with a land-based conception of the penalty and the etymology of אזרח is Levine's observation (1989, 241) that the *karet* image may have at its root the cutting down of trees or pulling them up from the land. Finally, it is worth noting a potential connection, as regards the *karet* penalty, between premature or unnatural death, harried afterlife, and loss of land tenure. Olyan 2005 lays out a hierarchy of burial possibilities based upon desirability and posits a connection between the state of one's interment and the conditions of one's afterlife. The most desirable burial is in the family plot,

---

50. It is notable that, when theorizing about the nature of the *karet* punishment, scholars often turn to rabbinic literature and medieval Jewish exegetes and thus arrive at the extirpation answer. Jubilees, however, is typically neglected. In that work (2:27; 15:26, 34), failure to circumcise and to observe the Sabbath, infractions that in the Bible are punishable by *karet*, cause the sinner to be uprooted from the land.

51. On the גר and אזרח and the connection to Lev 25, see above, chapter 3.

wherein internment suggests an undisturbed "rest." This type of internment is represented in phrases such as "lying down with one's ancestors," as in וַיִּשְׁכַּב דָּוִד עִם־אֲבֹתָיו וַיִּקָּבֵר בְּעִיר דָּוִד "David lay down with his fathers and was buried in the city of David" (1 Kgs 2:10). An Israelite's family plot would have been located on his or her clan land stake. אחזה, which is a *Leitwort* in Lev 25 (25:13, 24, 25, 27, 28,3 2, 33 [2x], 34, 41, 45, 46) is also employed in the phrase אחזת קבר "burial plot" (Gen 25:4, 9).[52]

Abrogation of the ברית

Scholars have searched in vain for a common denominator to all the violations that warrant the *karet* penalty. Wold (1982, 175), however, does observe that in P flagrant violation of God's dictates constitutes an offense against his holiness. This proposition does not fully account for the distinction between transgressions that bring *karet* and those for which other or no penalties attach. However, Wold's holiness thesis does have some explanatory power. The key to understanding the relationship between willful disobedience, insult against God's holy name or precincts, and the *karet* penalty can be found in the motive or explanatory clauses that follow a number of the listings of *karet*-bearing violations. Leviticus 19:8 applies *karet* to one who eats of a שלמים offering on the third day. The reason given for the penalty is כִּי־אֶת־קֹדֶשׁ ה' חִלֵּל "because he profaned what is holy to YHWH." According to Lev 20:3, devoting one's children to Molech has the following consequence: לְמַעַן טַמֵּא אֶת־מִקְדָּשִׁי וּלְחַלֵּל אֶת־שֵׁם קָדְשִׁי "thereby defiling my sanctuary and profaning my holy name." Thus it warrants *karet*. Numbers 19:13 articulates a similar motive for imposing *karet* upon one who acquires corpse contamination but fails to cleanse himself properly: אֶת־מִשְׁכַּן ה' טִמֵּא "He defiled YHWH's tabernacle." Numbers 9:3 provides a different explanatory clause in the case of the *karet* sanction for those who fail to offer the paschal offering: כִּי קָרְבַּן ה' לֹא הִקְרִיב בְּמֹעֲדוֹ "For he did not offer YHWH's offering in its appointed time." The sense that this *karet* penalty addresses direct violation of YHWH's command is underscored by the fact that the explanatory clause echoes the general injunction of Num 28:2:

אֶת־קָרְבָּנִי לַחְמִי לְאִשַּׁי רֵיחַ נִיחֹחִי תִּשְׁמְרוּ לְהַקְרִיב לִי בְּמוֹעֲדוֹ

---

52. אחזה has the etymology of "something one holds tightly," based upon its derivation from the root אחז. While the term most often denotes landholding, it can also refer to other types of property, such as slaves (Lev 25:45–46 per above).

"Be careful that you offer to me my offering, my food, my gifts, my pleasing odor, in its appointed time."

The syntax of each differs slightly. Two employ כי, one למען, and one is asyndetic. Yet all provide an explanation for the severity of the punishment. The common denominator is an offense against God's name, possessions, and domicile, all stemming from deliberate violation of particular commandments.

The telling case of *karet* that most underscores the sense of disobedience and ultimately is most relevant to the relationship of *karet* to circumcision is found in Num 15:30–31. These verses provide a rationale for the *karet* penalty and extend its applicability.[53] Throughout the Priestly corpus the *karet* penalty is imposed for violation of individual commands such as eating sacrificial blood and fat (Lev 7:25–27) or working on the Sabbath (Exod 31:14). In Num 15 it is applied for willful violation of God's commands in general:

30 וְהַנֶּפֶשׁ אֲשֶׁר־תַּעֲשֶׂה בְּיָד רָמָה מִן־הָאֶזְרָח וּמִן־הַגֵּר אֶת־ה' הוּא מְגַדֵּף וְנִכְרְתָה הַנֶּפֶשׁ הַהִוא מִקֶּרֶב עַמָּהּ
31 כִּי דְבַר־ה' בָּזָה וְאֶת־מִצְוָתוֹ[54] הֵפַר

---

53. Scholars are divided regarding the relative dating of this particular chapter, which contains a collection of legal material covering diverse subjects. On the unit of text dealing with inadvertent and intentional sin (15:22–31) the chronology is often viewed with reference to the parallel passage in Lev 4:3–21. Gray (1903, 178–83) and Snaith (1967, 251–52) see the Leviticus pericope as the more recent composition, while Noth (1968, 114), Freidman (1981, 108, 146), Milgrom (1990, 402–5), and Levine (1993, 395–98) view the Numbers passage as late P. Knohl (1995, 105), labels Num 15 as HS, making effectively the same chronological judgment. With regard to inadvertent sins, the most persuasive argument is made by Toeg (1973/74, 1–20). Fishbane neatly digests Toeg's observation with regard to verses 30–31; "one must construe the addendum as invoking כרת for any willful transgression of *any* of the commandments, and not just for the transgression of particular ones, as is the rule elsewhere" (1985, 192). Licht refuses to assign priority to either Lev 4:3–21 or Num 15:22–29. Still, he regards the purpose of Num 15:30–31 as a corrective to a possible misunderstanding arising from both of the former passages: that sacrifice can atone for blatant intentional sin. Thus, while not making an explicit chronological argument, his assertion can only imply that at least verses 30–31 are secondary (1985, 90–93).

54. There is versional support from the LXX (τὰς ἐντολὰς αὐτοῦ) and the Samaritan Pentateuch for the plural מצותיו here. An emendation would be plausible, since our verse is the only instance of מצוה (sing.) in P. Nonetheless, I suspect that MT

הִכָּרֵת תִּכָּרֵת הַנֶּפֶשׁ הַהִוא עֲוֹנָה בָהּ

But the person who does this[55] defiantly, whether native or stranger, it is YHWH whom they revile, and this person will be cut off from among their people. Because they spurned the word of YHWH and abrogated his command, that person will surely be cut off; their sin is upon them.[56]

The use of הפר מצוה/מצות instead of the standard idiom הפר ברית suggests the association of ברית and מצות in P's lexicon by the time of the composition of this unit. Moreover, the combination of בזה and פרר in Num 15:31 is paralleled only in Ezek 16:59 and 17:18–19, where הפר ברית is the operative phrase.[57]

---

preserves the original reading, with singular מצוה parallel to singular דבר in the same verse. Text criticism aside, it is still viable to read מצוה as a collective referring to the aggregate of the divine commands (see Exod 24:12; Deut 26:13; 30:11).

55. The implied direct object of the verb תעשה ("does this") in verse 30 is to be found in verses 22–23, namely, violation of all the commandments. עשה ביד רמה in 30 replaces verse 24's עשה לשגגה and 27's תחטה בשגגה.

56. My interpretation of the text is based upon the assumption that the *karet*-bearing infraction is the deliberate violation of the commands, with את ה' הוא מגדף in verse 30 and כי את דבר ה' בזה ואת מצותו הפר in 31 providing explanatory motive clauses. (On this class of motive clauses, see Gemser 1953.) The legal formulation can be structured as a protasis with a double apodosis: If anyone transgresses any of God's commands (protasis), they have blasphemed God (apodasis 1—explanatory, result clause) and thus incur the *karet* penalty (apodasis 2—sanction). In other words, any deliberate sin warrants the stiffest punishment *because* it dishonors God. There is a tradition of reading this unit otherwise. The rabbis characterize the מגדף as a blasphemer and see that act as a specific violation warranting the *karet* penalty (m. Ker. 1:1; see b. Ker. 7a–b). The talmudic understanding is affirmed by Rashi (glossing Num 15:30) and, more recently, Sonsino, but opposed by Ibn Ezra (ad loc.) and Maimonides (*Guide*, 3:41). Moreover, my contention that את ה' הוא מגדף is a motive clause rather than an articulation of the sin is buttressed by Sonsino's observation that such "asyndetic motive clauses are quite common in P" (1980, 97, 103, 289). Wold contradicts himself on this point. In his article (1979, 25) he classifies blasphemy as an action that warrants *karet*, citing Num 15:30. However, in his dissertation (1978, 55–56) he categorizes the operative parts of Num 15:30–31 as motive clauses. The same inconsistency is evident in Milgrom's JPS Numbers commentary, between the analysis in excursus 35 (1990, 402–5) and the textual commentary to Num 15 (1990, 226).

57. Note Levine's observation (1993, 398 [with the typographical error 10:59 for 16:59]).

CIRCUMCISION AND THE CULT

This pivotal Numbers text illuminates the crucial connection between failure to circumcise and the *karet* penalty. In many instances, *karet* was imposed for violation of individual commands. Numbers 15 interprets the punishment more broadly, for anyone who deliberately flouts the divinely imposed laws. If *karet* was imposed for any defiant transgression, all the more would it be warranted for one who, *ab initio*, completely refused to bear or mark his son and slaves with the sign of commitment to the commandments.

Summary

As laid out in this chapter, scholars, based on evidence from non-P biblical passages (Exod 4; Josh 5), ancient non-Israelite cultures, and postbiblical Jewish traditions, have legitimately attributed numerous valences to circumcision. These include fertility, purification, expiatory or dedicatory sacrifice, and communal, festal celebration. None of these, however, may be viably ascribed to circumcision in the Priestly writings. By setting out the practice in the only command not imparted during the desert epoch and configuring it as almost completely devoid of ritualized elements, P effectively cut off any link between circumcision and cultic practice, infrastructure, and personnel. Consequently, the uniqueness of the practice is underscored and the ברית-driven significance of circumcision highlighted all the more starkly.

General Summary: Actual Genital Circumcision

In the Priestly corpus, circumcision is the only regulation intended for Israel that appears in the pre-Israelite stage of history.[58] As such, it occupies a unique position in P's ideology. The setting of the injunction in tandem with YHWH's inaugural ברית-promises constitutes a powerful statement of P's agenda. The relationship of God and Israel, along with its concomitant benefits, is not unconditional. It is contingent upon the people's attention to YHWH's commands. Circumcision is called אות ברית and is a sign of Israel's responsibility to follow the full battery of YHWH's commands. By the same token, the intact foreskin signifies the rejection of YHWH and his statutes.

Genesis 17 mandates that all slaves be circumcised along with the masters' households. This circumcision does not afford slaves membership in the Israelite קהל, nor does it grant them a share in the ברית-promises. Rather, it highlights their subordinate status. The secondary status of the foreigner

---

58. The prohibition against consuming blood in Gen 9:1–7 is directed to all humanity.

in general is embodied in the semantic ברית/blessing contrast that is set up between Isaac and Ishmael. A similar invidious contrast is evident between Abraham and Sarah, setting the tone for the secondary status of women in P's society. Circumcision does function to demarcate gender-ascribed roles and societal rank. Beyond this, circumcision in the Priestly imagination bears no relationship to the penis or its function.

According to Gen 17:14, the *karet* penalty is imposed for failure to circumcise. What this punishment entails is never clarified in the text, beyond the fact that it is divinely imposed. I maintain that *karet* represents the antithesis of God's ברית-promises: one could be denied progeny, lose a stake in the land, or otherwise be alienated from YHWH's presence. *Karet* penalties devolve upon those who willfully disgregard YHWH's authority. Since circumcision is a sign of Israel's commitment to abide by the divine mandates, imposition of *karet* for failure to incise oneself or one's male dependents with the sign of that commitment follows quite naturally.

Seven is the number in the Priestly system most often used to represent cultically significant discrete units of time and quantity. Most germane to the question of eighth-day circumcision is the fact that sacrificial animals and priestly ordinands must wait seven days before they are ritually viable. In the same manner, the male infant is only ritually viable on the eighth day. Thus, the eighth day has no inherent significance; rather, it is the first day that the circumcision could be performed.

Within the Passover regulations of Exod 12 is the requirement that all who eat of the paschal sacrifice must be circumcised. The statute has a built-in redundancy, since all Israelites and slaves must be circumcised *ab initio*. This legislation therefore forges a special link between circumcision and Passover observance. In P, as in the rest of the pentateuchal sources, Passover is associated with the exodus from Egypt. The exodus is the event whereby Israel was rescued from Egyptian servitude and the ברית-promises realized. The circumcision requirement is thus fully consistent with Passover as the paradigmatic covenant festival. The ברית-centered implications of circumcision are set into relief by the patent lack of ritualization and the decoupling of the rite from P's system of festivals, offerings, and purification.

Part 2
Foreskin Metaphors

5
Introduction

The image of an uncircumcised body part in the Hebrew Bible is typically taken to signify some type of disability due to occlusion. Rashi states the case concisely in his gloss on Exod 6:12, which refers to Moses' uncircumcised lips: "Blocked [אטום] lips. And thus, I understand all usage of ערלה as blockage. 'Their ears are uncircumcised (Jer 6:10),' blocked from hearing; 'uncircumcised of heart,' blocked from understanding; ... uncircumcised of the flesh—because the penis is blocked and covered by it [the foreskin]." Rashi also extends the same assertion to the ערלה of fruit trees mentioned in Lev 19:23–24: "[It is] blocked and covered and separated from consumption."[1] Levine seconds Rashi's observation: "It seems that whenever the image of the foreskin is employed, the physical condition original to the image peers through simile and metaphor" (1987, 18). Modern scholars generally evince similar viewpoints. Regarding the heart, Hartley emphasizes the sense of defect quite prosaically: "The heart has become so hard that it has become encased in a hard growth like the foreskin. This condition requires surgery" (1992, 469). Driver describes the uncircumcised heart as "closed in, and so impervious to good influences and good impressions ... unreceptive of godlike affections" (1895, 125) Hall puts the matter in cognitive terms: "A circumcised mind is a mind of the right kind, one able to participate in God's covenant" (1992, 1026). Levine's characterization, "thickened heart,"[2] is attested as early as the LXX to Deut 10:16, which renders עָרְלַת לְבַבְכֶם as τὴν σκληροκαρδίαν ὑμῶν "your thickened hearts." The scholarly *Tendenz* exemplified above must be reappraised. First, the harmonic interpretation of the aforementioned passages assumes a single and essential meaning for the foreskin metaphor and ignores the possibility of contextual differences.

---

1. Rashbam, Bechor Shor, and Nachmanides adopt Rashi's interpretive tack in their glosses on Lev 19:23–24.

2. Levine avers, "The thickness of heart prevents one from feeling proper emotions or thinking proper thoughts" (1987, 18).

Second, I have demonstrated (50–52) that the Bible and contemporaneous Near Eastern literature impart no information concerning the physiology or utility of the foreskin. In the relevant Priestly texts, circumcision and the foreskin are treated solely as symbols of adherence to or abrogation of God's ברית-commands. Moreover, views about the utility of the foreskin such as those expressed by Rashi are culturally bound and of little probative value as regards the Bible and its milieu.³ Thus a reader lacks any viable means of unpacking a biblical ערלה metaphor, vis-à-vis its implications for a heart, ear, or lip, even if, as Levine (1987, 18) opines, it referred to any concrete physical condition. Finally, the "broad brush" notion of "thickness, or, blockage," where, as Levine asserts, "whenever the image of the foreskin is employed, the physical condition original to the image peers through simile and metaphor," lacks appropriate nuance. Such an overgeneralization does not account for what may be a variegated array of complex symbolic expressions in the respective passages.

A preferred approach would entail close scrutiny of each text on its own terms, drawing contextually anchored conclusions. The ensuing study follows this tack, treating Exod 6 and Lev 19; 26, the P texts in which the foreskin metaphor occurs. I begin with a probe of the meaning and function of the foreskin image in its immediate context. The scope of the inquiry is widened with a look at how the metaphors in each pericope are connected to P's conception of literal, genital circumcision and ערלה. Finally, the individual passages are situated within the broader framework of the Priestly ideological program.

Initially, however, in order to supply a frame of reference for the scriptural exegesis, an examination of the nature and function of metaphors and other symbolic language is required.

Metaphor and Symbolic Language

The term *metaphor* is of Greek origin, deriving from the combination of two words, the preposition μετά "with, toward, over" and the verb φέρω "carry."

---

3. A study of the varying attitudes toward the foreskin across boundaries of time and culture is beyond the scope of the present study. The problem with making any generalization is highlighted humorously by Propp (1987, 362–63), who mentions that Jewish sources from the late Amoraic times onward held "that women find intercourse with circumcised men less satisfying." Propp continues "Curiously, the women of the Ubangi basin, where circumcision is also practiced, report the opposite. One suspects that there is in fact no difference, though the opinion of these women is to be taken more seriously than that of Maimonides."

Thus, metaphor is generally understood as the "carrying over" or "transference" of meaning from one thing to another. In the well-known metaphor "all the world's a stage," meaning from the conceptual field of drama is carried over to the world in general. Using Richards's formulation (1981, 52–53), the world is the "tenor," the main subject of the metaphor, while stage is the "vehicle," by which the world is characterized. Making sense of the metaphor requires a basic understanding of the vehicle, in this case, the field of drama, and more specifically the role played by a stage. Similarly, unpacking the oft-discussed metaphor "YHWH is my shepherd" necessitates a familiarity with Israelite pastoral culture. As regards the present study, the foreskin, a word referring to a piece of skin particular to the penis, has been "carried over" and used with respect to the heart, lips, ear, or fruit tree.[4]

Linguists distinguish between "live" and "dead" metaphors. A "dead" metaphor is one that has become lexicalized, that is, ingrained and routinized in the language to the extent that is treated as a literal expression. As such, the metaphor has also lost any apparent link to its original conceptual field. One example of a dead metaphor would be the phrase "foot of the hill." This is a metaphor inasmuch as "foot," which is specifically a lower extremity of the body, has been carried over for use in descriptions of topography. However, "foot of the hill" has become interchangeable in English with "bottom of the hill." Moreover, "foot of the hill" has been completely severed from its field of commonplace associations. One does not speak of a hill's "toe" or "ankle" as connected to its "foot," nor is the term "knee" ever used in reference to a section of the hill found above the foot.[5] In contradistinction, boxing metaphors are live, for example, when employed to describe human discourse and debate. Their vitality is evidenced by the wide symbolic use of imagery from the semantic and ideational fields of the "sweet science" and of the potential for fluidity and creativity in the use of such metaphors. Thus an unprepared debater may be "pummeled" by an opponent, while an aggressive debater may "land a flurry of blows." Likewise, an unethical debater who levels an *ad hominem* attack is often accused of a "low blow" or of "hitting below the belt."

A second category of symbolic language is *metonymy*. Lakoff and Johnson provide a working definition of metonym as distinguished from metaphor:

---

4. On the use of metaphor in the Hebrew Bible, see especially Brettler 1989; Bisschops and Francis 1999; and Cohen 2003.

5. The "foot of the hill" example is used by Cohen (2003, 24–25) as illustrative of a dead metaphor. Cohen compares the image with Biblical Hebrew רגלי ההר, also a dead metaphor, which he argues is indistinguishable in the language from the expression תחתית הרר. On dead metaphors, see also Cruse 1986, 42; Wellek and Warren 1973, 301.

"Metaphor is principally a way of conceiving of one thing in terms of another, and its primary function is understanding. Metonymy, on the other hand, has primarily a referential function, that is, it allows us to use one entity to *stand for* another" (1980, 36). Soskice offers a similar characterization. Metonymy is when "one uses an adjunct to stand for the whole" (1985, 57). To appropriate Soskice's illustration, when we declare "the White House said today," we are referring to a statement made by the president or one of his representatives. To make sense of this statement, we need not have any information about the physical properties of any types of dwellings. Moreover, according to Soskice, "it would be a failure in comprehension if, on hearing the phrase 'the White House said today' one wondered if shutters and doors opened like mouths" (1985, 57).

Synecdoche is a type of metonym where a part stands in for the whole or vice versa. For example, a person requiring assistance to move furniture could say, "I need the help of some *strong people*." The same idea could be expressed synechdochally with the statements "I need the help of some *strong backs*" or "I need the help of some *strong arms*." Here a part of the body refers to, or stands in for, the whole. However, the choice of the synecdochic part must make sense within the conceptual and linguistic system of the speaker/writer. Thus, in the situation described above, the expression "I need some *strong heads*" would constitute an inappropriate synecdoche. Lakoff and Johnson note that, "like metaphors, metonymies are not random or arbitrary occurrences, to be treated as isolated instances. Metonymic concepts are also systematic" (1980, 139). With these prefatory reflections, a close reading of the Priestly texts that evince foreskin metaphors can proceed.

6
Exodus 6: Moses' Foreskinned Lips

Setting

Exodus 6:2–7:7 is P's rendering of the Mosaic call narrative. It is a doublet of the older JE account found in Exod 3:1–4:17.[1] In its skeletal details, the Priestly version replicates the divine commission and Mosaic demur found in the older tale but is absent a theophany comparable to the burning bush.[2] Beyond the call narrative, Exod 6 contains some important reflections of Priestly ideology. The new, Israelite phase of history is differentiated from the ancestral chapter through the revelation to Moses of the divine name YHWH. In the Priestly imagination, God had been known to the patriarchs only by the appellation El Shaddai (Exod 6:3). The whole exodus narrative is also inaugurated with God's declaration that he remembers his ברית-promises to the patriarchs and will actualize them in favor of the enslaved Israelites (Exod 6:4–5):

וְגַם הֲקִמֹתִי אֶת־בְּרִיתִי אִתָּם לָתֵת לָהֶם אֶת־אֶרֶץ כְּנָעַן ... וָאֶזְכֹּר אֶת־בְּרִיתִי

---

1. Childs (1974, 47–89, 108–20) and Propp (1998, 180–242, 261–85) contain in-depth studies of the texts and comprehensive reviews of the relevant scholarship. Van Seters (1994, 35–63) undertakes a close reading of the older narrative, which he considers Yahwistic.

2. Blenkinsopp (1983, 160) notes the affinity of the exodus narratives to the prophetic commissions, especially that of Jeremiah. See also Van Seters 1994, 44–46, 57–62. The ancients certainly read the Mosaic commission in light of the prophetic calls. This is evident from the haggadah of Moses' infancy in Pharaoh's house, which conflates elements of Exod 4 and Isa 6 (Exod. Rab. 1:26). Similarly, Symmachus understands Moses' uncircumcised lips as "impure." He recasts Exod 6:12 as οὐκ εἰμὶ καθαρός τῷ φθέγματι "I am not pure of voice," influenced, no doubt, by Isaiah's confession (6:5) אִישׁ טְמֵא־שְׂפָתַיִם אָנֹכִי.

"And I will fulfill my ברית with them, to give them the land of Canaan ... and I have remembered my ברית."[3]

The pericope also includes a genealogy that foreshadows a number of pivotal Priestly succession traditions. The list extends from Aaron through Eleazar to Phinehas (6:14–25). In bypassing Nadab and Abihu, Aaron's eldest and expected heirs, it foreshadows their tragic demise recounted in Lev 10. The genealogy also anticipates Phinehas's succession to the priesthood, confirmed by God's ברית-promise in Num 25:10–13. A unique feature of the Exod 6 genealogy is the inclusion of the wives of Amram (Yocheved, 6:20), Aaron (Elisheva, 6:23), and Eleazar (Putiel's daughter, 6:25). Ibn Ezra avers that the women are mentioned to accord special honor to their respective sons. The lineage of Aaron's wife Elisheva is especially important. As the daughter of Amminadab and sister of Nahshon, her marriage to Aaron inextricably links the royal and priestly dynasties.[4]

Cross has shown that a number of P narratives (e.g., Num 20:2–13; 25) seem to undermine Moses and elevate Aaron and his offspring at Moses' expense.[5] To Cross's list can be added the Exod 6 commission account, which deprecates Moses on several fronts.[6] This particular priestly diminution of Moses is perhaps the most insidious, as it is accomplished within the framework of Moses' call to leadership.

---

3. P's periodization of history according to YHWH's ברית-promises is well known in the scholarship. See, e.g.,Wellhausen 1957, 338–40; von Rad 1962, 134–35.

4. P is distinctly amonarchic. The Priestly narrative is set in the desert. Thus its cultic system stands independent of any prevailing political structure, whether it be a monarchy or governorship of the type held by Nehemiah. The highest political officer in P is the נשיא, reflecting a tribal order. The Priestly literature may, however, contain subrosa recognition of the Davidic monarchy. For example, P tradition does acknowledge the preeminence of the Judahites (Num 1:26–27; 2:3–4; 7:12–17). Moreover, the Aaronide genealogy in Exod 6:23 records the intermarriage of the priestly and royal ancestral houses, perhaps anticipating the relationship between David and Zadok (e.g., 1 Kgs 1:8) and the link between the two offices that is manifest most explicitly in the restoration prophecies of Hag 1:1, 12, 14; 2:2; and Zech 2:14.

5. Cross 1973, 195–215. See also Friedman 1987, 197–98. Cross and Friedman utilize their textual observations to construct a scenario of competing Mushite and Aaronide Levitical families who officiate at the shrines of Shiloh and Jerusalem, respectively. While I find their literary observations trenchant, I do not endorse their historical reconstructions, which are highly speculative and based upon scant evidence.

6. Noted by Propp 1998, 284–86.

The anti-Mosaic tendencies in our text are best seen against the background of the earlier call narrative. P appears to know the older tradition and subtly but deliberately recasts it to Aaron's credit and Moses' detriment. P's rewriting of the JE version is evident from the close narrative and linguistic correspondences.[7]

In Exod 4:10, Moses attempts to refuse the divine commission, citing his weak verbal ability.[8] After some give and take, God offers to send Aaron alongside Moses (4:16):

וְדִבֶּר־הוּא לְךָ אֶל־הָעָם וְהָיָה
הוּא יִהְיֶה־לְּךָ לְפֶה וְאַתָּה תִּהְיֶה־לּוֹ לֵאלֹהִים

And he will speak for you to the people, and it shall be.[9] He will be your mouth, and you will be his God.

Exod 7:1 records YHWH's response to Moses in the parallel priestly account:

רְאֵה נְתַתִּיךָ אֱלֹהִים לְפַרְעֹה וְאַהֲרֹן אָחִיךָ יִהְיֶה נְבִיאֶךָ

See, I will make you a God to Pharaoh, and Aaron your brother will be your prophet.

P uses nearly the same terminology but alters the language slightly in order to improve Aaron's position in the exchange. In this case, rather than being God to Aaron, Moses is God to Pharaoh. Aaron is elevated from mere mouthpiece to the more exalted role of prophet.

Moses' Foreskinned Lips

The Priestly *coup de grâce* emerges from Moses' own mouth. P's adaptation of Moses' response to God has Moses protesting that the Israelites never heed Moses, so neither will Pharaoh (Exod 6:12). Moses articulates the reason for this lack of obedience is because וַאֲנִי עֲרַל שְׂפָתָיִם "I am uncircumcised of lips" (Exod 6:12). This demur, repeated in Exod 6:30 (with the syntax of 6:12

---

7. On P's use of older JE material in Exodus, see Propp 1999, 266–70.

8. On the possible medical nature of this affliction, see Tigay 1978.

9. I divide this verse differently from MT. The *etnach* under הָעָם yields a very awkward, nearly untranslatable sequence וְהָיָה הוּא יִהְיֶה־לְּךָ. The use of והיה is singular. However, I believe it is the only way to make sense of the term in context.

inverted), serves as a *Weideraufnahme* enclosing the genealogy.¹⁰ Superficially, Moses' words can be understood, in line with Exod 4:10, as denoting speech defect. In fact, the versions typically coordinate their renditions of Exod 6:12, 30 with 4:10.¹¹ However, as I have underscored throughout this study, ערלה is a heavily laden term in the Priestly lexicon. As such, it must be more thoroughly unpacked. What, then, are the ramifications of this characterization of Moses?

We have seen that literal, genital circumcision and ערלה are inextricably tied to P's covenantal ideology. Moreover, the Priestly conceptions of YHWH's ברית-promises are central to Exod 6. God will uphold (הקם, 6:4) and remember (זכר, 6:5) his responsibility to bestow upon Israel their special land and an exclusive relationship with him. This fulfillment of the promises commences with redemption of the people from Egyptian bondage. Moses is commissioned to be God's instrument in fulfilling the ברית-promises by conveying a divine request to Pharaoh. Thus, on a primary level, the image of Moses' foreskinned lips must be interpreted in light of P's notions of covenant.

Given that possession of a foreskin by an Israelite male explicitly connotes rejection or abrogation (הפר) of the ברית (Gen 17:14), Moses' resistance to YHWH's commission is understandably symbolized and embodied by an ערלה locution. Since Moses' charge is verbal, having God's words to Pharaoh pass his lips, as it were, ערל שפתים is a particularly apt image.

Another layer of meaning for the Exod 6 foreskin image hinges upon the sense of "immaturity," based upon an understanding of the seven days previous to circumcision, when the infant has a foreskin, as representing a lack of viability or readiness. Moses, would, in effect, be declaring his lack of readiness to undertake his mission. This type of reluctance is reminiscent of Jeremiah's balk when confronted with YHWH's presence and the impending prophetic commission. The prophet there declares: אֲהָהּ אֲדֹנָי ה' הִנֵּה לֹא־יָדַעְתִּי דַּבֵּר כִּי־נַעַר אָנֹכִי "Ahah, Lord God, here, I don't know how to speak, for I am a youth."

It could be argued that the foreskinned lips image is a synecdoche, whereby Moses' mouth ערלה signals, pars par toto, his general character. Rejecting the divine charge to execute the covenantal mission would be seen

---

10. See Long 1987 on these types of authorial *Weideraufnahmen*, which function to extract the narrative from its logical progression in time.

11. Ancient harmonizations of Exod 4:10 and 6:12, 30 include Onqelos's יקיר ממלל "heavy of speech," Neofiti's חגר ממלל "constrained speech," and Peshitta's ܠܥܓ ܠܫܢ "stutter."

as representing a wholesale rejection of YHWH's authority.¹² The foreskin expression here is more aptly characterized as metaphoric, whose implications are upon Moses' verbal intransigence. We see in the phrase ערל שפתים the transference of a phallic image to the mouth, conoting a lack of readiness or blatant unwillingness to communicate YHWH's covenantal message to Pharaoh. In any event, the term ערלה is quite weighty in P's lexicon, and the ramifications of its usage with regard to Moses may extend beyond the Exod 6 call narrative.

KARET AND MOSES' LIFE STORY

The presence of a foreskin on an Israelite male brings the penalty of *karet* (Gen 17:14). By labeling Moses an ערל, metaphorically or synecdocally, the text portrays his resistance to God's commission, as with other *karet*-bearing offenses, as an act of treachery against God. Moses' transgression is perhaps all the more flagrant, since it entails an abandonment of God's just recently affirmed ברית-promises to Israel and a profanation of YHWH's holy name, the just-revealed Tetragrammaton. We have seen that *karet* should be understood as the withdrawal of God's ברית-promises: fecundity, exalted descendants, land, and relationship to God (as per Gen 17:4–8). A review of Moses' biblical "life story" would indicate that he was, in effect, sanctioned with *karet* and ultimately denied the aggregate ברית-promises.

The Levite genealogy in 6:16–25, which is framed by Moses' ערלה confession, sheds light on Moses' fate generally by opening a window on Levite and priestly succession episodes throughout the P corpus. In like manner, this localized negative characterization of Moses also presages his fate as envisioned by the Priestly author. This destiny includes future offenses against God and the resultant severe punishments.

First, our passage has affinities to Moses' affront against YHWH at "the waters of Meribah" in Num 20:1–13. The text records God's angry reaction to Moses' striking the rock (Num 20:12).

וַיֹּאמֶר ה' אֶל־מֹשֶׁה וְאֶל־אַהֲרֹן
יַעַן לֹא־הֶאֱמַנְתֶּם בִּי לְהַקְדִּישֵׁנִי לְעֵינֵי בְּנֵי יִשְׂרָאֵל

---

12. This reading could follow, by extension, from Hurowitz's argument (1989), based upon comparative evidence from Akkadian mouth purity rituals, that Isaiah's confession of impure lips should be understood synecdochally, marking the prophet's general state of defilement, cultic and moral, and consequent unsuitability to stand in the divine presence or carry out a divine prophetic commission.

לָכֵן לֹא תָבִיאוּ אֶת־הַקָּהָל הַזֶּה אֶל־הָאָרֶץ אֲשֶׁר־נָתַתִּי לָהֶם

God said to Moses and Aaron, "Since you did not have faith in order to sanctify me in the sight of the Israelites, so you will not lead this congregation into the land that I have given to them."

Here we see that Moses, as in Exod 6, has angered God by refusing to speak when commanded. In the Meribah pericope, the transgression is against YHWH's holiness, which results in Moses being denied the land promise. Further, the fact that the Exod 6 genealogy culminates in the birth of Phinehas calls the reader's attention to Num 25. In the Baal Peor episode, Phinehas's precipitous zealotry on God's behalf בְּקַנְאוֹ אֶת־קִנְאָתִי (Num 25:11) is contrasted to Moses' inaction in the face of Israel's apostasy. As a reward, Phinehas is granted the בְּרִית כְּהֻנַּת עוֹלָם, the ברית-promise of exalted lineage that Moses will not receive. The Levite genealogy also provides the clue to the final dimension of the implicit *karet* penalty that P imputes to Moses. Though Moses and Aaron's birth to Amram and Yocheved are both registered, the genealogy only proceeds through the Aaronide line. Moses on the other hand, has no recorded familial legacy. This is also the case throughout the rest of the Pentateuch. The birth of Moses' son Gershom is noted only in Exod 2:22, a non-P text. He appears again exclusively in the Chronicler's records.[13] Even here the Mosaic line is quite limited. Thus, while even Korah the rebel is provided with offspring, P manages, at least on the literary front, to extirpate the Mosaic line.

The Priestly author makes use of the figurative ערלה imagery to subtly denigrate Moses at the expense of Aaron. This Moses versus Aaron dynamic can be situated within the larger matrix of P narrative. However, P's device here is perhaps the most cleverly subversive because it undercuts Moses' position at the very moment he is called by God to assume his position of leadership and undertake his inaugural mission, the freeing of Israel from Egyptian bondage. It is likely that this particular aspect of the Mosaic call narrative has gone relatively unrecognized because of unchallenged assumptions about the meaning of the ערלה imagery held since antiquity.

One might question the credibility of a thesis that posits such a blatant and pregnant self-denigratory statement on the part of a story's protagonist. Sternberg, however, explains why such dissonance is not uncommon, pointing out that biblical narrative is

---

13. 1 Chr 23:15, 16; 26:24. See also the reference to גֵּרְשֹׁם בֶּן־מְנַשֶּׁה, the Danite priest, in MT Judg 18:20, which the LXX reads as Γερσωμ υἱοῦ Μωυσῆ.

regulated by a set of three principles: ideological, historiographic and aesthetic. How they cooperate is a tricky question ... but that they do operate is beyond question. For at some points—or from some viewpoints—we find each laid bare, as it were, asserting its claims and exerting its particular influence on narrative selection and arrangement. (1985, 41)

Here the ideological program of the Priestly tradent, the denigration of Moses in favor of Aaron, is "laid bare" and seems to have triumphed over the aesthetics of sustaining credible character development.

7
Leviticus 19: Foreskinned Fruit Trees

Setting

Leviticus 19 is a collection of diverse types of legal material, from agricultural to cultic to sexual to ethical. It contains one of the most famous of all the biblical dicta (19:18): וְאָהַבְתָּ לְרֵעֲךָ כָּמוֹךָ "love your fellow as yourself." The laws vary widely in form. Some are staccato apodictic statutes (19:11–15, 26–32), while others are more involved casuistic laws, with penalty and motive clauses (19:5–8, 20–22). A number of the regulations appear only in this chapter (19:11–17, 19–25); others are close parallels of statutes found elsewhere in P (19:5–8, 9–10, 26). The chapter is punctuated frequently by אני ה'/אלהיכם proclamations (19:3, 4, 10, 12, 14, 16, 18, 25, 30, 31, 32, 34, 37) and framed by a holiness injunction (19:2) and an exodus reference (19:36).

Scholarship regarding the structure of the chapter has been fairly uniform.[1] Commentators have treated individual units within the pericope but have been unable to discern an overall organizing principle. Attempts to find structuring devices have only met with partial success. For example, Ibn Ezra (on 19:23) notes that the laws of mixed species (19:19), the female servant (19:20–22), and fruit tree ערלה are linked by the use of the word זרע (19:19, 20) and the idea of planting seeds implied in 19:23. The medieval exegete is not, however, able to apply his associative approach any more extensively. Theories of an organic link to the Decalogue or a foundational decalogue for the chapter (Elliger 1966, 243, 248) have been forced. Affinities between laws in Lev 19 and other pentateuchal corpora suggest an ethical foundation common to various traditions within biblical Israel but need not point to any specific textual dependence. Although some, such as Knohl and Schwartz, see Lev 19 as a whole cloth Holiness composition, one cannot rule out the

---

1. See Sun 1990, 164–219; Schwartz 1999, 241–23; Levine 1989, 124–35; Noth 1965, 136–44; Hartley 1992, 301–27; and Wenham 1979, 261–75.

possibility that some of the laws have ancient, pre-Priestly provenance. No one has, as yet, been able to date parts, or all, of the chapter based upon linguistic or other objective criteria.

Foreskinned Fruit Trees

Leviticus 19:23–25, which Schwartz identifies as legal section 11 (1999, 269),² contains the law of fruit-tree עורלה. It regulates horticultural practices and is designated to be observed when Israel settles the land:

(23) וְכִי־תָבֹאוּ אֶל־הָאָרֶץ וּנְטַעְתֶּם כָּל־עֵץ מַאֲכָל
וַעֲרַלְתֶּם עָרְלָתוֹ אֶת־פִּרְיוֹ
שָׁלֹשׁ שָׁנִים יִהְיֶה לָכֶם עֲרֵלִים לֹא יֵאָכֵל
(24) וּבַשָּׁנָה הָרְבִיעִת יִהְיֶה כָּל־פִּרְיוֹ קֹדֶשׁ הִלּוּלִים לַה'
(25) וּבַשָּׁנָה הַחֲמִישִׁת תֹּאכְלוּ אֶת־פִּרְיוֹ
לְהוֹסִיף לָכֶם תְּבוּאָתוֹ אֲנִי ה' אֱלֹהֵיכֶם

(23) When you come to the land, and you plant any tree for food, you shall *foreskin its foreskin*,⁴ its fruit. Three years it shall be *foreskin* to you, it may not be eaten. (24) And in the fourth year, all its fruit shall be holy, as praise for YHWH. (25) And in the fifth, you may eat its fruit, thus increasing its bounty. I am YHWH your God.

The gist of the law is unambiguous: the first three years of a fruit tree's yield may not be eaten by anyone; in the fourth year, the fruit is dedicated to God; thereafter, it may be consumed at will. Beyond this, the language of the regulation leaves more questions than answers. Most significantly, how are we to understand the figurative use of עורלה here? In this regard, the denomina-

---

2. Schwartz organizes the chapter into eighteen distinct legal sections.

3. The LXX has a plus here, ἣν κύριος ὁ θεὸς ὑμῶν δίδωσιν ὑμῖν "which the Lord your God gives you." The full formula is common in P (Exod 12:25; Lev 14:34; 23:10; 25:2; Num 15:2). Zakovitch (1977, 440) opines that MT is defective, while Schwartz (1999, 338) suggests that the formula is not appropriate to the context. Here, both versions could be "original" owing to a certain amount of fluidity in the early stages of the Pentateuch's formation.

4. The phrase "foreskin its foreskin" makes little sense in English. I let that infelicitous yet accurate translation stand to illustrate the problem that interpreters since antiquity have had with the Hebrew וַעֲרַלְתֶּם עָרְלָתוֹ. A more appropriate English rendering will be offered following my discussion of the relevant issues.

tive וַעֲרַלְתֶּם, unique to this passage, is especially problematic. Moreover, what accounts for the three/four/five pattern in the legislation?

It would seem that the Priestly legislator anticipated the difficulties that his potential readership/audience might encounter, so he provided a series of very helpful explanatory clauses. The ערלה of fruit trees is clearly metaphoric. The fruit is the foreskin; thus, by extension, the tree is the penis. The phrase עָרְלָתוֹ אֶת־פִּרְיוֹ "its ערלה [that is] its fruit" clarifies the issue explicitly. Similarly, the idiosyncratic verb form וַעֲרַלְתֶּם, literally "you shall foreskin," is elucidated in the next verse by the clause יִהְיֶה לָכֶם עֲרֵלִים "it shall be foreskin to you." This clause is then definitively explained by the apodictic conclusion of the verse: לֹא יֵאָכֵל "it shall not be eaten."

The question, then, is why the author resorted to such complex imagery when he could have written a much more straightforward proscription, such as *וְכִי־תָבֹאוּ אֶל־הָאָרֶץ וּנְטַעְתֶּם כָּל־עֵץ מַאֲכָל שָׁלֹשׁ שָׁנִים לֹא תֹאכְלוּ אֶת־פִּרְיוֹ "When you come to the land and you plant any tree for food, you shall not eat its fruit for three years." Eilberg-Schwartz phrases the question aptly: "Of the dozens of other things that the priests declare forbidden, they apply the metaphors of 'uncircumcised' and 'foreskin' to none of them. Why then did they see a metaphoric relationship between this particular forbidden item and the male foreskin?" (1990, 150). While some, such as Eilberg-Schwartz, have suggested a fertility dynamic common to humans and trees, a preferable solution involves P's method of developing legal categories. P has terms that refer to other forbidden edibles, such as טמא, נבלה, טרפה (Lev 11). In fact the LXX translators, seemingly confused by וַעֲרַלְתֶּם עָרְלָתוֹ, render the phrase περικαθαριεῖτε τὴν ἀκαθαρσίαν αὐτοῦ "you shall purge its impurity." With this interpretive move, the Greek translators fold the fruit proscription into the category of forbidden animal products that are labeled טמא. Foods of the above-mentioned classes are all animal products and are categorically off-limits to all Israelites. However, the law of forbidden fruit is time-bound, and a new category label is therefore required.

The choice of the ערלה label is due to a number of factors. Most important, the fruit is proscribed because all firstlings, animal and vegetable, must be sanctified to God. Until that is accomplished, humans may not partake. However, fruit in its first three years was considered immature, unfit for divine consumption, ritually unviable, and thus also off-limits to Israel.[5]

---

5. This factor is treated uniformly in the commentaries (see above). A comprehensive review of the issues and relevant scholarship can be found in Schwartz 1999, 338–42. Josephus's digest of the law (*Ant.* 4.226–227) does not mention foreskin but is an extremely cogent rendition of a complex biblical passage. He explains simply that

Since the foreskin of a child remains until he is ritually viable on the eighth day, there is clear conceptual overlap between the two regulations. Finally, like the foreskin on the end of a penis, fruit hangs off the end (branch) of a tree or vine; thus, the metaphor arises from a common-sense association.

The three/four/five pattern, as opposed to seven/eight of ערלה and circumcision, is the result of the combination of typology and horticultural reality. Though not so pervasive in P, numerical patterns based upon the number three are common in the Bible and the ancient Near East.[6] More important, it is likely that fruit in the first three years of a tree or vine's growth was substandard. The evidence from the biblical period is almost nonexistent. The single datum from Hammurapi's Code (60) suggests that an orchard is viable in the fifth year.

šumma awīlum eqlam ana kirîm zaqāpim ana nukaribbim iddin nukarribum kiriam izqup 4 šanātim kiriam urabba ina ḫamuštim šattim bēl kirîm u nukaribbum mitḫāriš izuzzū bēl kirîm zīttašu inassaq-ma ileqqe

If a man gave a field to a gardener to plant an orchard, and the gardener plants the orchard, he must tend the orchard for four years. In the fifth year, the orchard's owner and the gardener will divide equally. The owner of the field will choose and take his share.

Contemporary viticulture and horticulture confirms what the ancients seemed to have understood, that three to four years is a reasonable wait for viable fruit production. However, the trees and vines during the preliminary period may not be utterly bare. For example, random immature grape clusters may appear on a vine.[7] Thus, a regulation forbidding their consumption is in order.[8]

---

fruit in its first three years is immature and therefore unsuitable for human consumption or sacral offering. The produce, viable in the fourth year, must be donated to God, as with any firstling and agricultural tithes.

6. On three/four/five in Lev 19:23–25, see Zakovitch 1977, 439–42.

7. I am grateful to Fred Frank (Konstantin Frank Vineyards, New York) and Charles Mazza (Cornell University Department of Horticulture) for this information (personal communication).

8. Contra Carmichael 1996, who discounts any real horticultural basis for the law. He argues, "Farmers will know what to do with the fruit of new trees, without needing to be told in a directive." He misses the point completely, that the law is not meant to teach farmers sound orchard and vineyard management. Rather, it is to pro-

Though the force of the law, that fruit is unavailable for consumption in the first three years of a tree's growth, is transparent, translation of the phrase וַעֲרַלְתֶּם עָרְלָתוֹ has divided scholars. Two camps have emerged: one favors translations such as "you shall leave/reject/abhor its fruit";[9] the second group renders the verb וַעֲרַלְתֶּם with "cut" or its equivalent.[10] This split is manifest in the Targumim. Onqelos reads תרחקון "reject," while Pseudo-Jonathan has תגזרון "cut." The biblical regulation might allow for both alternatives in practice, as long as the fruit is not used. Still, the second option is untenable as a translation. The Targum may have favored the rendition "cut" because in rabbinic practice ערלה fruit was removed.[11] Moderns who favor "cut" or "trim" do so based upon the rationale that to treat something as foreskin would be to cut it off. Additionally, they may be motivated by a desire to find within the law the practical means to carry it out. This reading, however, totally disregards the language of the text. Had the Priestly legislator intended the fruit to be cut as a foreskin is cut, a form of מול would have been employed, or another verb that denoted cutting, such as גזר, כרת, or בתר. The verbal *hapax* וַעֲרַלְתֶּם must have a meaning that is the opposite of cut. Moreover, it is not unusual for the P and other Torah legislators to articulate a principle without providing explicit direction as to how the principle must be operationalized. One example is the leaven prohibition in Exod 12 and Deut 16. The respective regulations read: בַּיּוֹם הָרִאשׁוֹן תַּשְׁבִּיתוּ שְּׂאֹר מִבָּתֵּיכֶם "on the first day you shall eliminate leaven from your homes" (Exod 12:15), and שִׁבְעַת יָמִים שְׂאֹר לֹא יִמָּצֵא בְּבָתֵּיכֶם "for seven days no leaven shall be found in your homes" and וְלֹא־יֵרָאֶה לְךָ שְׂאֹר בְּכָל־גְּבֻלְךָ שִׁבְעַת יָמִים "no leaven shall be seen by you, in all your borders, for seven days" (Deut 16:4). Though they articulate a principle clearly, there is no indication in any of these formulations as to how to the leaven should be eliminated.[12]

---

tect God's *sancta*, including his *prima fructi* prerogative. Additionally, the connection Carmichael makes to the Judges narrative is tenuous, based primarily upon the use of the term הלולים and the three years of Abimelech's rule. On the general flaws in Carmichael's methodology, see Levinson 1990; Stackert 2008.

9. NJPS; Noth 1965, 137; Hartley 1992, 307.

10. Levine 1989, 131; Eilberg-Schwartz 1990, 151–52; Milgrom 2000, 1678–80.

11. Much of the Mishnaic tractate 'Orlah deals with the disposal of ערלה fruit, which would imply its removal from the tree. This would be sound horticultural and viticultural practice, since fruit that was left would drain the resources of the tree or the vine.

12. This "halakic" issue is addressed for the first time within the biblical period in the famous Elephantine Passover Papyrus, Cowley 30. While most of it seems to replicate scriptural regulation, albeit in Aramaic, the conclusion contains the following

Though "leave" is a reasonable rendition of וַעֲרַלְתֶּם, "reject" is to be favored for two reasons. First, the fruit is, in a sense, rejected by God until the fourth year. Moreover, since the foreskin is a symbol of the rejection of God's commands, that nuance should be factored into the reading of the verse. Consequently, the operative phrase can be rendered in intelligable English, "You shall reject its foreskin, its fruit."

The law of the fruit tree ערלה shows a fairly idiosyncratic use of foreskin imagery on the part of the Priestly tradent. This imagery has confounded translators and exegetes since antiquity. Nonetheless, P's use of the metaphor is quite coherent. The legislator needed to create a legal category that reflected the idea of time-bound prohibition and nonviability. The practice of circumcision provided the legislator with a suitable vehicle.

---

innovation regarding the disposition of the leaven. הנעלו בתוניכם וחתמו בין יומיא [אלה] "lock it up in your chambers and seal it during [these] days."

8
Leviticus 26: Israel's Foreskinned Heart

Setting

Leviticus 26 has been studied in the commentaries and other publications.[1] Despite the extensive treatment of the pericope, the uncircumcised heart image in Lev 26:41 has thus far evaded scholarly scrutiny. Two factors may have contributed to this neglect: (1) interpreters come to the text with preconceived notions and thus have not found a close examination of the metonym necessary (on the nature of these assumptions, see above); (2) the image of the uncircumcised heart is generally regarded as "prophetic," while Leviticus is typed as "legalistic." Consequently, the uncircumcised heart tends to be addressed more enthusiastically in studies of Deuteronomy and Jeremiah. For instance, Mayer (1997, 158–62) includes attestations of the image in Deuteronomy, Jeremiah, and Ezekiel but only mentions circumcision in P in connection with the legal and covenant issues in Gen 17. A similar bias can be found in Hoffman 1996. The thesis of his first chapter, "Bible and Birth," depends upon a disjuncture between prophetic (preexilic and exilic) and priestly (postexilic) religion, and thus he ignores circumcision of the heart in Leviticus. Le Déaut's generally perceptive study evidences a similar oversight. He presents a synoptic analysis of the Targumim to Deut 10:16 and 30:6 but omits discussion of the Aramaic versions of Lev 26:41 (1981, 199–200). This lacuna is all the more glaring given the fact that Pseudo-Jonathan and Neofiti's renditions there, ליב זדנא "willful, wicked heart," diverge from the standard targumic "translation" of ערל לבב/לב as ליב טפשא "foolish heart."

---

1. See, for example, Hoffman (1953:240–68), Noth (1965:193–201), Elliger (1966:360–379), Wenham (1979:32–34), Hartley (1992:451–475), Levine (1989:182–192), and Milgrom (2001:2272–2364). Notable are those of Grünwaldt (1999:112–120, 348–374), Sun (1990:439–559) and Baumgart (1999). In my view, Levine (1987) remains the most important contribution to the scholarship.

P's עֲרְלָה of the heart image bears scrutiny in its own right. I begin with an introduction to Lev 26, focusing on setting, structure, and compositional history. I then turn to a close analysis of the circumcision of the heart image, examining it within its immediate context as well as within the larger matrix of Priestly ideology.

Leviticus 26:3–46 has been labeled "the epilogue to the Holiness Code." This appellation was given because the blessings and curses following the book's legal material resemble the epilogue to law collections such as Hammurapi's Code.[2] Throughout the ancient Near East, these types of formulae, especially the imprecations, are also attached to treaties, boundary markers, and monuments. "Epilogue" may not be the most apt designation here, because, unlike epilogues in cognate cultures, Lev 26 and its parallels in D and the prophets concludes with provisions for the people's restoration. Levine's title (1987; 1989, 275–81), "A Priestly Statement on the Destiny of Israel," is more fitting.

The pericope begins with ten verses of blessings (26:3–12) appertaining to those who follow God's dictates: אִם־בְּחֻקֹּתַי תֵּלֵכוּ (26:3). What follows is a much more extensive execratory portion (26:14–39). The blessing and curse units are separated by an אני ה' proclamation (26:13).[3] The maledictory section is comprised of five subsections, each of which details increased levels of punishment for Israel's continued refusal to "toe the line." These passages are delineated by formulaic statements such as וְאִם־לֹא תִשְׁמְעוּ לִי (26:14) and וְאִם־עַד־אֵלֶּה לֹא תִשְׁמְעוּ לִי (26:18; see also 26:21, 23, 27). Scholars have noted a similar trope of escalating disaster in the וְלֹא־שַׁבְתֶּם עָדַי oracle in Amos 4:6–11 and in the plagues heaped upon Pharaoh for his continued refusal to set the people free.

The final unit (26:40–45) signals Israel's redeemability. The possibility exists for a return from exile to the land and conditions of bounty described in 26:3–12. God will remember his בְּרִית-promises to the patriarchs (26:42) and to the רִאשֹׁנִים, the generation taken out of Egypt (26:45). The divinely granted salvation is conditioned on a two-step penitential process: confession of the peoples' and their ancestors' iniquities (וְהִתְוַדּוּ אֶת־עֲוֹנָם וְאֶת־עֲוֹן אֲבֹתָם, 26:40); and humbling of their uncircumcised heart (אוֹ־אָז יִכָּנַע לְבָבָם הֶעָרֵל), 26:41bα).[4] Consequently, the people will have compensated for their sins (וְאָז יִרְצוּ אֶת־עֲוֹנָם, 26:41bβ).

---

2. A similar "epilogue" appears in Deut 28–30 following its law collection in 12–26.

3. אני ה' also punctuates the penultimate verse in the chapter.

4. On the syntagma אוֹ־אָז, see below.

Leviticus 26 manifests distinct semantic and conceptual affinities to the preceding chapter. The escalating divine punishments are reminiscent of the successively worsening economic straits to which an Israelite might be subjected. In Lev 25, the units are similarly delineated by recurrent language: וְ/כִּי־יָמוּךְ אָחִיךָ "If your fellow is degraded" (25:25, 35, 39); and finally, וְכִי תַשִּׂיג יַד גֵּר ... וּמָךְ אָחִיךָ עִמּוֹ "If the גר gains power ... and your fellow is degraded in relation to him" (25:47). The motif of a "Sabbath for the land" also frames the two contiguous chapters (וְשָׁבְתָה הָאָרֶץ שַׁבָּת לַיהוָה [25:2]; אָז תִּשְׁבַּת הָאָרֶץ וְהִרְצָת אֶת־שַׁבְּתֹתֶיהָ and אָז תִּרְצֶה הָאָרֶץ אֶת־שַׁבְּתֹתֶיהָ [26:34]; וְתִרֶץ אֶת־שַׁבְּתֹתֶיהָ [26:43]).

Our pericope is tightly structured through the use of linguistic symmetry where language from the blessing unit is echoed by phraseology in the curse section. For example, God's blessing, such as

וְנָתְנָה הָאָרֶץ יְבוּלָהּ וְעֵץ הַשָּׂדֶה יִתֵּן פִּרְיוֹ

"the land will provide its bounty and the tree of the field will yield its fruit" (26:4),

has a corresponding curse:

וְלֹא־תִתֵּן אַרְצְכֶם אֶת־יְבוּלָהּ וְעֵץ הָאָרֶץ לֹא יִתֵּן פִּרְיוֹ

"the land will not provide its bounty and the tree of the land will not yield its fruit" (26:20).

Israel's action, וַהֲלַכְתֶּם עִמִּי קֶרִי "you [Israel] are hostile to me" (26:15), has a corresponding divine reaction: וְהָלַכְתִּי אַף־אֲנִי עִמָּכֶם בְּקֶרִי "I [God] in turn will be hostile to you" (26:24). Similarly, Israel's apostasy,

וְאִם־בְּחֻקֹּתַי תִּמְאָסוּ וְאִם אֶת־מִשְׁפָּטַי תִּגְעַל נַפְשְׁכֶם
לְבִלְתִּי עֲשׂוֹת אֶת־כָּל־מִצְוֹתַי לְהַפְרְכֶם אֶת־בְּרִיתִי

"If you reject my laws and spurn my statutes, so that you do not do all my commands, thereby abrogating my ברית" (26:15),

is contrasted to God's loyalty:

לֹא־מְאַסְתִּים וְלֹא־גְעַלְתִּים לְכַלֹּתָם לְהָפֵר בְּרִיתִי אִתָּם

"I will not reject them, and I will not spurn them, so as to destroy them, thereby abrogating my ברית with them" (26:44).

This literary mirroring serves two purposes. It highlights the divine "measure for measure" retribution and, at the same time, foregrounds YHWH's beneficence. While up to a point Israel is paid back in full for every instance of apostasy, YHWH stops short of destroying the people utterly, even though they abandon him entirely.

Leviticus 26:39–43

Leviticus 26:39–43, which contains the foreskinned heart metaphor, constitutes both the crux unit in the pericope and the section most germane to the present study. The text of the section, along with a translation, is provided here:

(39) וְהַנִּשְׁאָרִים בָּכֶם יִמַּקּוּ בַּעֲוֹנָם בְּאַרְצֹת אֹיְבֵיכֶם
וְאַף בַּעֲוֹנֹת אֲבֹתָם אִתָּם יִמָּקּוּ
(40) וְהִתְוַדּוּ אֶת־עֲוֹנָם וְאֶת־עֲוֹן אֲבֹתָם בְּמַעֲלָם אֲשֶׁר מָעֲלוּ־בִי
וְאַף אֲשֶׁר־הָלְכוּ עִמִּי בְּקֶרִי
(41) אַף־אֲנִי אֵלֵךְ עִמָּם בְּקֶרִי וְהֵבֵאתִי אֹתָם בְּאֶרֶץ אֹיְבֵיהֶם
אוֹ־אָז יִכָּנַע לְבָבָם הֶעָרֵל וְאָז יִרְצוּ אֶת־עֲוֹנָם
(42) וְזָכַרְתִּי אֶת־בְּרִיתִי יַעֲקוֹב וְאַף אֶת־בְּרִיתִי יִצְחָק
וְאַף אֶת־בְּרִיתִי אַבְרָהָם אֶזְכֹּר וְהָאָרֶץ אֶזְכֹּר
(43) וְהָאָרֶץ תֵּעָזֵב מֵהֶם וְתִרֶץ אֶת־שַׁבְּתֹתֶיהָ בָּהְשַׁמָּה מֵהֶם
וְהֵם יִרְצוּ אֶת־עֲוֹנָם יַעַן וּבְיַעַן בְּמִשְׁפָּטַי מָאָסוּ
וְאֶת־חֻקֹּתַי גָּעֲלָה נַפְשָׁם

(39) The remnants among you will languish, from their iniquity, in the land of your enemies. And more, they will also languish from the iniquity of their ancestors. (40) And they will confess their iniquity and the iniquity of their ancestors, the treachery that they committed against me, and more, how they were hostile to me. (41) Since I have been hostile to them and brought them to the land of their enemies, and if then[5] their uncircumcised hearts are humbled, then they will

---

5. The syntagma אוֹ־אָז has challenged exegetes. The most common use of אוֹ denotes an either/or alternative (GKC 162). However, this usage does not fit the context. Israel's submission and God's sending them to the land of their enemies are not presented as alternatives. At this point in our pericope, Israel's presence in the land of its enemies is already a fact (26:33–39). Rather, Israel's submission is a result of the exile and leads to the forgiveness of their sins. Two equally plausible interpretations of the syntax have been proposed, both of which lend themselves to essentially the same

compensate for their iniquity. (42) I will remember my ברית with Jacob, and my ברית with Isaac, and my ברית with Abraham I will also remember, and I will remember the land. (43) And the land will be rid of them and will compensate for its Sabbaths by being desolate from them, and they will compensate for their iniquity, for the very reason that spurned my statutes and despised my rules.

A two-pronged approach to the image of the foreskinned heart in Lev 26 is in order. The first component is a treatment of the metaphor and its relationship to P's conceptions of actual circumcision and ערלה. The second is a study of the verb יכנע (*niphal* third masculine singular of כנע), which, as will be demonstrated, holds the key to understanding the metaphor and the passage as a whole.

Circumcision and Leviticus 26

Genital circumcision in P is a mark of Israel's obligation to follow God's commands. The benefits to compliance with YHWH's dictates are detailed in the ברית-promises to Abraham: offspring; land; and relationship to God. The foreskin is a sign of the rejection of divine mastery. As a consequence of this rejection, the ערל receives the divinely imposed *karet* penalty, an ostensible withdrawal of the ברית-promises. In the Priestly law and practice reviewed thus far, the circumcision/ערלה-ברית/*karet* dichotomy is manifest on the level of the individual (see above, 70–75). Leviticus 26 concerns Israel as a

---

reading of the unit. My translation, "and if then," picks up the nuances of both alternatives. (1) The LXX's καὶ τότε could attest to an original Hebrew ואז, with MT's או "a corrupt dittograph of אז" (Wevers 1997, 461). Alternatively, the Greek translator could have been smoothing out a rough syntactic edge. Reading או אז as equivalent to ואז would allow for a simple sequence, "I will bring ... and then they will submit ... and then they will be forgiven." There is strong support for following LXX and treating או here as a simple conjunction. Hoffman (1953, 256) cites the medieval grammarian Ibn Janah, who adduces numerous scriptural examples: Lev 4:23; 13:16; 19:20; Num 15:6; Deut 13:2. However, Lev 4:23 supports both a conjunctive and a conditional reading of או. Deut 13:2 is not the best illustration, as או in that verse is better translated as "or." (2) Rashi (echoed by Nachmanides), using Exod 20:26 as his prooftext, asserts that או here should be read with an implicit אם (on או in conditional sentences, see GKC 159cc). Our sequence would be rendered, "I will bring.... If, they then submit ... then they will be forgiven." (3) Levine (1989, 181) suggests a third option. He equates או אז with כי אז in Josh 1:8. His analysis falls short because he brings no other examples of this usage of או.

corporate entity.[6] The use of the heart metonymy allows the Priestly tradent to extend the circumcision/ברית ideology to the group level. The people can be labeled, communally, as circumcised or foreskinned, regardless of the gender of any individual or the state of their penises.

A look at Lev 26 will show the distinct imprint of P's circumcision/ברית ideology. The initial blessing section of the pericope (26:3–13) details Israel's rewards for observing God's laws faithfully. The passage basically elaborates upon the key ברית-promises enumerated originally to Abraham. Verses 4–8 describe a bounteous land, free from enemy domination. Verse 9 echoes the פרו ורבו motif that permeates the Priestly corpus and reiterates God's commitment to Israel:

וּפָנִיתִי אֲלֵיכֶם וְהִפְרֵיתִי אֶתְכֶם וְהִרְבֵּיתִי אֶתְכֶם וַהֲקִימֹתִי אֶת־בְּרִיתִי אִתְּכֶם
"I will turn toward you and make you fruitful and multiply you and and fulfill my ברית with you."

Verses 11–12 articulate God's commitment to maintain his relationship with Israel and include the *Bundesformular* וְהָיִיתִי לָכֶם לֵאלֹהִים וְאַתֶּם תִּהְיוּ־לִי לְעָם "I will be your God and you will be my people." The short, positive unit concludes with a reference to God's redemption of Israel from Egyptian slavery:

אֲנִי ה' אֱלֹהֵיכֶם אֲשֶׁר הוֹצֵאתִי אֶתְכֶם מֵאֶרֶץ מִצְרַיִם מִהְיֹת לָהֶם עֲבָדִים
"I am YHWH your God who brought you out of the land of Egypt, from being slaves to them."

The use of לָהֶם underscores the fact that they are now YHWH's special possession. In sum, the first ten verses of our chapter describe a circumcised corporate Israel.

Leviticus 26:14–38 is a significantly enlarged negative image of 26:3–13. It lays out a corporate *karet* penalty for deliberate rejection of God's commands and abrogation of his ברית. The passage opens:

(14) וְאִם־לֹא תִשְׁמְעוּ לִי וְלֹא תַעֲשׂוּ אֵת כָּל־הַמִּצְוֺת הָאֵלֶּה
(15) וְאִם־בְּחֻקֹּתַי תִּמְאָסוּ וְאִם אֶת־מִשְׁפָּטַי תִּגְעַל נַפְשְׁכֶם
לְבִלְתִּי עֲשׂוֹת אֶת־כָּל־מִצְוֺתַי לְהַפְרְכֶם אֶת־בְּרִיתִי

---

6. On ideas of biblical Israel as a corporate entity, see Kaminsky 1995, 30–54.

(14) And if you do not heed me and do not do all these commands, (15) and if you spurn my laws and despise my statutes, so as not to do all my commands, thereby abrogating my ברית.

These verses are reminiscent of the passage in Num 15 that treats the deliberate violator of God's rules (see my discussion of this passage above, ch. 4):

(30) וְהַנֶּפֶשׁ אֲשֶׁר־תַּעֲשֶׂה בְּיָד רָמָה מִן־הָאֶזְרָח וּמִן־הַגֵּר אֶת־ה' הוּא מְגַדֵּף וְנִכְרְתָה הַנֶּפֶשׁ הַהִוא מִקֶּרֶב עַמָּהּ:
(31) כִּי דְבַר־ה' בָּזָה וְאֶת־מִצְוָתוֹ הֵפַר הִכָּרֵת תִּכָּרֵת הַנֶּפֶשׁ הַהִוא עֲוֺנָה בָהּ:

(30) But the person who does this defiantly, whether native or stranger, it is YHWH whom they revile, and this person will be cut off from among their people. (31) Because they spurned the word of YHWH and abrogated his command, that person will surely be cut off; their sin is upon them.

Leviticus 26 takes the principle spelled out in Num 15 regarding the individual Israelite, and applies it communally.

The implications of the corporate *karet* penalty, the withdrawal of God's ברית-promises, are spelled out dramatically in the extended execratory passage. Israel is alienated from the land and its bounty and spurned by God. The antithesis of the offspring promise is most horrifying:

וַאֲכַלְתֶּם בְּשַׂר בְּנֵיכֶם וּבְשַׂר בְּנֹתֵיכֶם תֹּאכֵלוּ

"You will eat the flesh of your sons, and the flesh of your daughters you will eat."

The chapter ends with the reversal of Israel's fortune. The redactor's employment of the circumcision image in the denouement of the chapter speaks to the stress placed on the conditional nature of Israel's relationship with God. The communal "circumcision" signals Israel's renewed commitment to serve God and follow his commands. Only then will God reaffirm his devotion to his people. The explicit linkage of circumcision, ברית, and מצות in our pericope underscores the P tradent's commandment-centered view of the relationship between God and Israel.

Goldingay (2000) asserts that the figurative circumcision imagery speaks to the denigration of the practice of circumcision in biblical tradition. He uses a very Pauline argument to show that genital circumcision is empty of any power when the people's heart needs to be circumcised.⁷ Hermisson (1973, 76) more aptly asserts that Lev 26 and the comparable passages in D and Jeremiah testify to the centrality of the rite. Only a practice of such moment would be employed to symbolize Israel's transgression and salvation on a communal level. Figurative circumcision of the heart does not undermine genital circumcision. Rather, the two function in tandem. Circumcision of the flesh is a sign of every individual Israelite's obligation to follow YHWH's commands, while circumcision of the heart connotes the communal actualization of the commitment.

The Priestly narrative takes Israel no farther than the other side of the Jordan. However, Lev 26 encapsulates the cycle of sin, exile, and restoration that is recounted at length in the Deuteronomist's and Chronicler's histories. One might assert that the זכר ברית statements in Lev 26:42, 44–45 are P's equivalent to the Chronicler's Cyrus proclamation, which concludes the entire Hebrew canon (2 Chr 36:22–23). Circumcision, then, should be viewed as a linchpin of the Priestly *Heilsgeschichte*. In P's account, God's relationship with Israel begins with Abraham. The relationship is inaugurated in Gen 17 with a juxtaposition of God's promises and the circumcision mandate imposed upon the Patriarch. This practice is a sign of Israel's future obligation to the full spectrum of God's commands. Leviticus 26 details Israel's breech of its obligations and God's withdrawal of his ברית-promises. The relationship is repaired by the elimination, or neutralization, of the communal foreskin. This process is juxtaposed to God's affirmation of his promises to the patriarchs. These texts show circumcision to be the pivotal act in Israel's ongoing relationship to God. In effect, Israel's life story, in the words of the Priestly tradent, commencing with Abraham and concluding with the nation's restoration to the land, is book-ended by circumcision and YHWH's ברית-promises.⁸

MEANING AND USE OF כנע

כנע, a *hapax* in the Priestly corpus, is, at first glance, out of place in our unit. Instead, one would expect a form of מול.⁹ Since כנע "humbling, self-abase-

---

7. See Rom 2:28–29; Phil 3:2–3; Col 2:11–12; and Justin, *Dial.* 19.92.113. The early church had a supersessionist agenda, while Goldingay resurrects the argument in service of his feminist rhetoric.

8. Although the restoration passage concluding Lev 26 represents the endpoint in Israel's history according to P, it is found near the center of the Torah. This is a further example of the type of anachrony discussed above (39–41).

9. The fully articulated image of the alteration or correction of a foreskinned heart would be either מול + לבב (ערל לבב + מול (verb + two nouns in construct) or ערל + לבב + מול

ment" replaces מול as the action that solves the problem of the uncircumcised heart, it provides the exegetical key to our metonym. Absent any other occurrences of כנע in the P corpus, a survey of the verb throughout the canon is warranted.¹⁰

Two basic usages of the verb can be discerned: political and military; and penitential.¹¹ The first category is applicable to human actors and to God. Examples include the following: (1) Led by a judge or king, the Israelites subdue an enemy power in battle. That nation then becomes subservient, usually carrying a tributary obligation:

וַתִּכָּנַע מוֹאָב בַּיּוֹם הַהוּא תַּחַת יַד יִשְׂרָאֵל וַתִּשְׁקֹט הָאָרֶץ שְׁמוֹנִים שָׁנָה

"The Moabites were humbled before Israel [under the leadership of Ehud], and the land was quiet for eighty years" (Judg 3:30).¹²

(2) God destroys Israel's enemies, generally Canaanites:

וְיָדַעְתָּ הַיּוֹם כִּי ה' אֱלֹהֶיךָ הוּא־הָעֹבֵר לְפָנֶיךָ אֵשׁ אֹכְלָה

(verb + noun + adjective). The basic form is attested in Deut 10:16: "circumcise the foreskin of your hearts" וּמַלְתֶּם אֵת עָרְלַת לְבַבְכֶם. Deut 30:6, "YHWH will circumcise your heart and your offspring's heart" וּמָל ה' אֱלֹהֶיךָ אֶת־לְבָבְךָ וְאֶת־לְבַב זַרְעֶךָ is an elliptical form of the metonym, with ערל being assumed by the author/reader. On the significance of God as the circumciser, see Brettler 1999. Jer 4:4, "circumcise yourselves to YHWH and remove the foreskins of your hearts" הִמֹּלוּ לַה' וְהָסִרוּ עָרְלוֹת לְבַבְכֶם fills out the basic image. Though there might be nuances to the inclusion of לה', I suspect that its presence is a matter of poetic rather than theological concern. The composer broke up the basic image in order to form a bicolon, the standard poetic building block.

הִמֹּלוּ לַה' **Circumcise** yourselves to YHWH
וְהָסִרוּ עָרְלוֹת לְבַבְכֶם and remove **the foreskins of your hearts**.

On the break-up of stereotyped phrases as a stylistic feature of biblical poetry, see Melamed 1961; Watson 1995, 328–32.

10. כנע is attested only in *hiphil* and *niphal*. A review of the word and its usage can be found in Wagner 1997. I include my own synthesis to give clear and explicit context for my arguments regarding the use of the verb.

11. Note the semantic equivalence of the Akkadian verb *kanāšu*, which is used in military contexts to indicate the submission of an enemy to military might and conquest or as a proper posture of respect to a superior or deity (see *CAD* s.v. *kanāšu*).

12. Judg 8:28 (Gideon-Midian); 11:33 (Jepthah-Ammon); 1 Sam 7:13 (Samuel-Philistines); 2 Sam 8:1 = 1 Chr 18:1 (David-Philistines); 1 Chr 20:4 (David-Philistines); 2 Chr 13:18 is an exceptional case: Judah subdues Israel after a war between Abijah and Jeroboam.

> הוּא יַשְׁמִידֵם וְהוּא יַכְנִיעֵם לְפָנֶיךָ
> וְהוֹרַשְׁתָּם וְהַאֲבַדְתָּם מַהֵר כַּאֲשֶׁר דִּבֶּר ה' לָךְ

Know this day that it is YHWH your God who moves before you, a devouring fire; he will vanquish them, and he will humble them before you so that you may dispossess them and destroy them quickly, as YHWH indicated to you. (Deut 9:3)[13]

In the penitential usage, Israelite individuals, typically kings,[14] or groups[15] sin against God and then humble themselves penitentially. As a consequence, divine punishment is abated or averted.

> הֲרָאִיתָ כִּי־נִכְנַע אַחְאָב מִלְּפָנָי
> יַעַן כִּי־נִכְנַע מִפָּנַי לֹא־אביא[16] הָרָעָה בְּיָמָיו
> בִּימֵי בְנוֹ אָבִיא הָרָעָה עַל־בֵּיתוֹ

"Did you see how Ahab humbled himself before me? Only because he humbled himself before me, I will not bring about the harm in his time. In the time of his son, I will bring the harm on his house" (1 Kgs 21:29).

Three occurrences of כנע do not fit squarely into the above categories. Psalms 106:42 and 107:12 recount Israel's humbling, at the hand of God or its enemies, because of its rebellious actions. They are reminiscent of the penitential usage, especially since the humbling leads to reconciliation. However, the abnegation is not self-imposed, as with the penitential category.[17] Job 40:12 is close to the YHWH warrior class of usage, although those who are humbled are not Israel's Canaanite enemies: רְאֵה כָל־גֵּאֶה הַכְנִיעֵהוּ וַהֲדֹךְ רְשָׁעִים תַּחְתָּם "View every proud man, and humble him, trample down the wicked."

---

13. These all occur in the *hiphil,* with God as agent. Judg 4:23; Isa 25:5; Ps 81:15; Neh 9:24; 1 Chr 17:10. On YHWH as warrior, see Brettler 1993; Kang 1989; Miller 1973; and Dozeman 1996.

14. 2 Kgs 22:19 = 2 Chr 34:27 (Josiah); 2 Chr 32:26 (Hezekiah); 33:12, 19 (Manasseh). The term is also used of kings who failed to humble themselves: 2 Chr 33:23 (Amon); 36:12 (Zedekiah).

15. 2 Chr 7:14 (Israelites in general); 12:1–12 (Rehoboam and his leadership); 30:11 (members of the tribes of Asher, Manasseh, and Zebulun).

16. Qere אָבִיא.

17. These psalms are probably late; see Hurvitz 1972, 173.

LEVITICUS 26: ISRAEL'S FORESKINNED HEART

Examples of כנע as a verbal marker of penitence are found in Kings (1 Kgs 21:29; 2 Kgs 22:19), yet the image of "self-abasement" leading to divine mercy comes to fruition in the work of the Chronicler.[18] The penitential use of כנע in Chronicles sheds light on Lev 26:41 and thus will be explored in greater depth. As noted above, it is employed with Israelite kings or groups who deliberately defy God and incur punishment. The offenders see the error of their ways and humble themselves before God, seeking forgiveness. God's clemency is always forthcoming. One trenchant example is God's dream-revelation to Solomon following the building of the temple (2 Chr 13–14). It is an extremely compact parallel to Lev 26:

(13) הֵן אֶעֱצֹר הַשָּׁמַיִם וְלֹא־יִהְיֶה מָטָר
וְהֵן־אֲצַוֶּה עַל־חָגָב לֶאֱכוֹל הָאָרֶץ וְאִם־אֲשַׁלַּח דֶּבֶר בְּעַמִּי
(14) וְיִכָּנְעוּ עַמִּי אֲשֶׁר נִקְרָא־שְׁמִי עֲלֵיהֶ
וְיִתְפַּלְלוּ וִיבַקְשׁוּ פָנַי וְיָשֻׁבוּ מִדַּרְכֵיהֶם הָרָעִים
וַאֲנִי אֶשְׁמַע מִן־הַשָּׁמַיִם וְאֶסְלַח לְחַטָּאתָם וְאֶרְפָּא אֶת־אַרְצָם

(13) If I stop the heavens and there is not rain, and if I command the locust to consume the land, and if I send disease among my people— (14) and my people, who bear my name, humble themselves and pray and seek me out and turn from their evil ways—then I will hear from the heavens and forgive their sins and heal their land.

Another brief account of Israel's fate brought on by sin is 2 Chr 12:1–12. Rehoboam ascends to the Judean throne and along with the people abandons God's teaching (12:1). This abandonment is characterized in the next verse as מעל. As a result, King Shishak of Egypt launches a successful campaign against Judah and advances on Jerusalem. In a statement that reflects a measure-for-measure ideology, the prophet Shemaiah indicates to the king and his officers the reason for their ill-fate (12:5):

כֹּה־אָמַר ה' אַתֶּם עֲזַבְתֶּם אֹתִי וְאַף־אֲנִי עָזַבְתִּי אֶתְכֶם

"Thus said YHWH 'You have abandoned me so I have abandoned you.'"

---

18. On כנע as a key ideological term in Chronicles, see Driver 1956, 536; Japhet 1989, 260–61; and Kelly 1996, 55–56.

The people humble themselves, and although they suffer some conquest and humiliation at the hands of the Egyptian king, they are ultimately saved. The pericope concludes (12:12):

וּבְהִכָּנְעוֹ שָׁב מִמֶּנּוּ אַף־ה' וְלֹא לְהַשְׁחִית לְכָלָה וְגַם בִּיהוּדָה הָיָה דְּבָרִים טוֹבִים

When he [Rehoboam] had humbled himself, YHWH's anger was averted, and he did not utterly destroy, and in Judah, there were positive things.

That the theme of penitence pervades the episode is indicated by the fourfold occurrence of the verb כנע (12: 6, 7 [2x], 12).

A final noteworthy example involves Hezekiah (2 Chr 32:24–26), who becomes sick and prays to God. He is informed that his arrogance גבה לב is the cause of his illness. The king repents immediately (32:26):

וַיִּכָּנַע יְחִזְקִיָּהוּ בְּגֹבַהּ לִבּוֹ הוּא וְיֹשְׁבֵי יְרוּשָׁלָם
וְלֹא־בָא עֲלֵיהֶם קֶצֶף ה' בִּימֵי יְחִזְקִיָּהוּ

And Hezekiah humbled himself because of his arrogance, along with the inhabitants of Jerusalem. And God's wrath did not come upon them during the time of Hezekiah.

The semantic and conceptual affinities between Lev 26 and the Chronicler's work are numerous. The people defy God deliberately. In part of the punishment section, Lev 26:19, וְשָׁבַרְתִּי אֶת־גְּאוֹן עֻזְּכֶם, shows that, as with the case of Hezekiah, Israel's pride, which God shatters, figures into the equation. According to Lev 26:40, מעל "treachery against God" is the offense that precipitates the cycle of punishment and penitence. In Chronicles, the collocation of מעל and כנע occurs on five occasions (2 Chr 12:1–12; 28:19; 30:1–11; 33:10–20; 36:11–14).

In the Chronicler's ideology of sin and penitence, pride, treachery, and deliberate offense are offset by self-abasement, כנע. In Lev 26, since כנע corrects the ערלה, then Israel's uncircumcised heart is a symbol of its pride, מעל, and intransigence. Interpreters have long read ערלה of the heart as a metaphor connoting defect, an inability to turn toward God. However, the clear sense of *deliberate* sin in Lev 26 and the relevant Chronicles passages cannot be overemphasized. One might object that the distinction between disability and unwillingness is a fine one, yet the difference is crucial in the Priestly view. P makes much of the distinction between זדון "intentionality" and שגגה

"unintentionality." Sins of the former class are unredeemable, while a highly developed complex of rituals is in place for unintentional infractions.[19]

It is not unreasonable to inquire as to why P employed the term כנע in place of מול in this "new heart" passage. A review of contemporary scholarship has shown that the meaning of the standard phrase ערל לב + מול has been elusive. The same opacity and/or ambiguity may have obtained in the biblical period. P's use of כנע served to elucidate the figurative language and to place the foreskinned heart symbolism more clearly within the framework of sin and penitence appropriate to the larger pericope.

Metaphor, Metonym, and Synecdoche

Foreskinned heart expressions are certainly metaphors, as they "carry over" phallic imagery for use as cardiac imagery. The expression in Lev 26:41 must be classified as a dead metaphor. I have argued that literal circumcision and ערלה in P have been effectively severed from any functional connection to the penis and explicitly have a symbolic quality. All the more, then, has the metaphor been decoupled from its original field of commonplaces. P's association of the verb כנע with the foreskin, where one might have expected a form of מול, is particularly telling in this regard. As has just been elucidated, etymologically כנע refers to the physical act of "bending" and is used commonly to indicate submission or subjugation. One does not, by any means, eliminate or correct a foreskin by subjugation or even bending. It seems, therefore, that at least in the Priestly mindset the expression "foreskinned heart" has been lexicalized, frozen as a theological idiom indicating intransigence, rebellion, or resistance. This is likely the case in non-P material, since, as shown above, the usage of ערל לב, with or without מול, is consistent throughout the canon.

While foreskinned heart expressions are metaphors, they operate as metonyms or synecdoches. They are not meant to describe, actually, the condition of a person's heart. Rather, the heart stands in, *pars par toto*, for the character of the person in question. In the case of Lev 26:41, the image does not even refer to the personality of a single individual. Rather, the idiom encapsulates the wholesale intransigence of the nation of Israel, portrayed in the texts as a corporate entity.

---

19. Lev 4–5; 19:20–22; 22:14–16; Num 5:5–10; 15:22–31. On P's ideology of repentance, see especially Milgrom 1976. On Num 15, perhaps the key passage on the distinction between unwitting and deliberate sin, see further Toeg 1974.

In the Bible, לב/לבב[20] "heart" images are typically synecdochal, with the heart standing for the whole person. This "part for the whole" relationship operates systematically and dovetails with the general biblical understanding of the heart as the emotive, volitive, and cognitive center of the human being.[21] The synecdochal use of "heart" obtains in English usage. For example, there is no substantive difference between the expressions "win them over" and "win their *hearts*." A survey of biblical usage of לב yields the same type of equivalency. Some apropos illustrations from the biblical canon follow.

Psalm 33:11 praises YHWH's cognitive processes:

עֲצַת ה' לְעוֹלָם תַּעֲמֹד מַחְשְׁבוֹת לִבּוֹ לְדֹר וָדֹר

YHWH's counsel abides forever, the thoughts *of his heart* for all generations.

Micah 4:12 similarly refers to the impenetrability of God's thoughts:

וְהֵמָּה לֹא יָדְעוּ מַחְשְׁבוֹת ה' וְלֹא הֵבִינוּ עֲצָתוֹ

They did not know YHWH's thoughts or understand his counsel.

The two characterizations are interchangeable and even employ the same word pair מחשבה/עצה. In the first instance, לב functions as a synecdoche.

A positional description of the heart is often used to denote attitude and emotion. A "straight" heart is "honest," and a "bowed" heart is "subdued or humbled." These images are all synecdochic. The following pairs of verses show the interchangeability of an image with or without לב.

(Ps 97:11) אוֹר זָרֻעַ לַצַּדִּיק וּלְיִשְׁרֵי־לֵב שִׂמְחָה
(Job 1:1) וְהָיָה הָאִישׁ הַהוּא תָּם וְיָשָׁר

Light is sown for the righteous and happiness for the *straight of heart*.[22]
And that man was *straight* and without fault.

---

20. Hereinafter, לב will be employed to represent both לב and לבב, as no semantic distinction between the two can be discerned (Fabry 1997).

21. Fabry (1997) identifies the לב as the locus of vital, affective, noetic, and voluntative activity. Carasick (1996, 124–49) studies biblical images of the heart as the cognitive center. He labels this usage of לב as metaphor, without exploring the distinction between metaphor, metonym and synechdoche.

22. Further attestations of ישר לב are 1 Kgs 3:6; Pss 94:15; 119:7.

וַיִּלְחָצוּם אוֹיְבֵיהֶם וַיִּכָּנְעוּ תַּחַת יָדָם (Ps 106:42)
וַיַּכְנַע בֶּעָמָל לִבָּם כָּשְׁלוּ וְאֵין עֹזֵר (Ps 107:12)

Their enemies oppressed them [Israel], and they were *humbled* by them.
He [God] *humbled their* [Israel's] *hearts* through suffering; they faltered with no one to help.

In Soskice's words, it would be "a failure in comprehension" if the reader looked for an actual straight or bent internal organ underlying these images. The heart in these cases stands in for the whole individual.[23] The foreskinned heart image in Lev 26:41 is similarly synecdochic.

As a dead metaphor, functioning synecdochally, the foreskinned heart in Lev 26:41 is at a great remove from any connection to the penis. Thus, in this case "the physical condition original to the image" is unlikely to appear. Moreover, interpreting the expression in concrete terms, as indicating an actual hardened, thickened, or blocked heart, represents in Soskice's terms "a failure in comprehension." Instead, the subjugation of the heart's ערלה constitutes a potent image of penitence, at the core of P's theology of covenant and restoration.

Leviticus 26 and Penitence

Leviticus 26:40, וְהִתְוַדּוּ אֶת־עֲוֺנָם וְאֶת־עֲוֺן אֲבֹתָם, emphasizes that, along with humbling the ערלה of the heart, the other step toward the restoration of divine favor is confession. Milgrom has shown (1976, 104–28; 1991, 301–3, 1042–44) that confession is an essential feature in P's theology and juridical system. In order to take advantage of the חטאת for unwitting cultic infractions (Lev 5:5), the wrongdoer must confess his or her sins. Similarly in the case of fraud (Num 5:5–9), the offender must confess as a precursor to restitution. In this instance, as in Lev 26:40, the offense is termed מעל. Finally, one element of the Day of Atonement ceremony is the priest's confession (Lev 16:21). The verb התודה is used in each instance.

The Day of Atonement ritual is, in fact, mirrored in Lev 26. Along with the confession of the priest and the sacrificial complex, the people are commanded (Lev 16:29):

---

23. The biblical canon contains myriad examples of "heart" synechdoches, such as טהר לב "pure heart" (Ps 51:12; Prov 22:11), חכם לב "wise heart" (Exod 28:3), אביר לב "heroic heart" (Ps 76:6), and נדב לב "giving heart" (2 Chr 29:21).

בַּחֹדֶשׁ הַשְּׁבִיעִי בֶּעָשׂוֹר לַחֹדֶשׁ תְּעַנּוּ אֶת־נַפְשֹׁתֵיכֶם
On the tenth day of the seventh month you must afflict yourselves.

The same injunction is repeated in Lev 16:31 and 23:27, 29, 32. How this self-affliction is to be accomplished is not specified in the text. Non-P biblical evidence, noted by Ibn Ezra (glossing Lev 16:29), points to fasting (Isa 58:3, 10; Ps 35:13), whereas m. Yoma 8:1 (see Bechor Shor on Lev 16:29) specifies a broader range of abstention, mirroring typical rites of mourning.[24] נכנע can carry the same meaning as ענה נפש.

In 2 Kgs 21:27–29, Ahab's self-abasement is described as follows:

(27) וַיְהִי כִשְׁמֹעַ אַחְאָב אֶת־הַדְּבָרִים הָאֵלֶּה
וַיִּקְרַע בְּגָדָיו וַיָּשֶׂם־שַׂק עַל־בְּשָׂרוֹ וַיָּצוֹם וַיִּשְׁכַּב בַּשָּׂק וַיְהַלֵּךְ אַט
(28) וַיְהִי דְּבַר־ה׳ אֶל־אֵלִיָּהוּ הַתִּשְׁבִּי לֵאמֹר
(29) הֲרָאִיתָ כִּי־נִכְנַע אַחְאָב מִלְּפָנָי

(27) When Ahab heard these words [Elijah's prophecy of doom], he tore his clothes and put sackcloth on his body and fasted and slept in the sackcloth and went about in quietude. (28) Then God spoke to Elijah the Tishbite, saying (29) "Have you seen how Ahab humbled himself before me?"

Josiah's posture of self-humiliation is recounted similarly (2 Chr 34:27):

יַעַן רַךְ־לְבָבְךָ וַתִּכָּנַע מִלִּפְנֵי אֱלֹהִים
בְּשָׁמְעֲךָ אֶת־דְּבָרָיו עַל־הַמָּקוֹם הַזֶּה וְעַל־יֹשְׁבָיו
וַתִּכָּנַע לְפָנַי וַתִּקְרַע אֶת־בְּגָדֶיךָ וַתֵּבְךְּ לְפָנָי
וְגַם־אֲנִי שָׁמַעְתִּי נְאֻם־ה׳

Since your heart was softened and you humbled yourself before God when you heard his words regarding this place and its inhabitants.

---

24. The Mishnah delineates abstention from food, drink, baths, anointment with oil, wearing leather shoes, and sex. Note also the self-denial practiced by the Elephantine Jews after the destruction of their temple: ועד זנה יומא אנחנה שקקן לבשן וציׄמין נשיא זילן כארמלה עבידין משח לא משחין וחמר לא שתין "Until this day we have worn sackcloth and fasted, our women have acted like widows, we have not anointed ourselves, nor have we drunk wine" (Cowley 30:20–21).

You humbled yourself before me and tore your clothes and wept before me and I have heard, oracle of YHWH.

Thus, Lev 26:40–41, describing Israel's communal atonement, replicates standard elements of P's penitential repertoire while diverging from P's typical penitential lexicon. The particular use of כנע serves to illuminate what might otherwise have been an opaque or ambiguous figurative image, that of the foreskinned heart.

Summary

Leviticus 26 is a pivotal kerygmatic passage for the Priestly ideologue. In its canonical setting, the pericope represents a predictive look at Israel's potential destiny. The *Sitz im Leben* of the final redaction is the historical memory of the Judean exile and restoration. The pericope frames the nation's fate in terms of the consequences of acceding to God's will or rebelling against it. Finally, it shows that YHWH does not fully forsake his people. In our Priestly restoration pericope, Israel must make the first and definitive reparatory move. Confession is required, along with humbling of the people's collectively uncircumcised heart. The image is metonymic, referring to the Israelite community, who are willfully rejecting God's ברית-commands. P's vision is largely consistent with that of Zech 1:3 and Mal 3:7, where the initiative is in the nation's hands. In contradistinction, according to Ezek 36:22–31 and Lam 5:21, Israel's repentance is the result of her deliverance.[25] Deuteronomy 30 finds a middle ground. In verses 2–3, the return to God must be initiated by Israel before God restores their fortune. However, in 30:6 God circumcises Israel's heart, taking responsibility for the ultimate corrective measure.

The menu for restoration in Lev 26 constitutes the convergence of two of P's core ideological constructs. The first involves circumcision, which marks Israel's commitment to honor YHWH's dictates and indicates the conditional nature of God's favor. The second is P's penitential theology, the combination of confession and self-abasement that constitutes two of the three pillars of the Day of Atonement ritual panoply.

---

25. The tension within the Hebrew canon to which I have alluded, over divine versus human initiative in repentance and restoration, is captured brilliantly in Lam. Rab. 5:1. The rabbis project a debate on the matter between God and Israel, wherein both parties cast the above-cited scriptural verses at each other like chords from "Dueling Banjos."

General Summary: Foreskin Metaphors

The Priestly tradent employs ערלה imagery in a diverse set of contexts with maximum rhetorical impact. This multiplicity reflects the centrality of circumcision and its image field in P's thought-world. In Lev 19, P has recourse to the concept of ערלה in order to invent a new legal category. The Priestly tradent extends the idea of time-bound ritual viability from the world of human interaction with the sacred to the sphere of horticulture. In a completely different type of interpretive move, P applies the ערלה label to Moses as a means of undermining his position as founding leader of the Israelite nation. Moreover, with the use of a single powerful epithet, ערל שפתים, the author hints at the unfolding of Moses' destiny throughout the Pentateuch. This multifaceted denigration of Moses is skillfully integrated into the actor's commission tradition. Additionally, P constructs the narrative edifice on the foundation of the older JE call tradition. Leviticus 26 is P's microcosm of Israel's *Heilsgeschichte*. In this pivotal pericope, the Priestly author employs the symbol of Israel's uncircumcised heart as a mark of the nation's wholesale rejection of God and his commandments. As literal ערלה incurs a *karet* penalty, Israel's intransigence results in the withdrawal of YHWH's ברית-promises of land, progeny, and unique relationship. It is only the elimination of the figurative foreskin, engendered by confession and self-abasement, that restores divine favor and returns Israel to its land. Circumcision, both actual and figurative, is employed in the Priestly Torah to book-end the account of Israel's destiny from Abraham to the restoration of Zion.

Epilogue: Circumcision and the Exile

The notion that circumcision gained significance during the Babylonian exile has long been an article of faith among many scholars.[1] The standard contention is that, since the Mesopotamians did not practice circumcision, the rite became a prime signifier of Israelite identity and faith in Babylon. Moreover, circumcision was crucial to a people bereft of their temple, since observance of the rite was not dependent upon either land or cult center. The Sabbath and Passover are similarly treated in the scholarship.[2] Smith (1989, 139–149) articulates the theory, calling such practices "rituals of resistance." The following statements are characteristic of the school of thought:

> This basic structure of the P narrative is related in some way to the project of rebuilding the temple and restoring the cult in the land of Israel, reduced to a small and impoverished province after the Babylonian conquest. Consistent with this historical connection is the care in which P notes the establishment of circumcision, Passover and sabbath, *all of which assumed great importance from the time of the Babylonian exile.* (Blenkinsopp 1992, 218–19, emphasis added)

> As has long been recognized, too, a particularly important factor for the dating of the Priestly Document is the prominence which it gives to the Sabbath and to circumcision. Both institutions had certainly been long observed in Israel. But we have no evidence whatsoever for assuming that, in their inner meaning, these customs stood in a specially close connexion with Jahwism. But from the time of the exile, and especially for those exiled in Babylon, this was changed. Living as the exiles did amongst a people who did not practice circumcision, the good old usage here became all at once a token of the difference.... Thus it was in the Exile that the Sabbath and

---

1. The view has held sway at least since Wellhausen (1957, 340–42).
2. Grünwaldt (1992) mounts a full-blown defense of the circumcision-Sabbath-Passover axiom but adds no new data or syntheses to the discussion. See also Wyatt 1990.

circumcision won a *status confessionis* which they afterwards preserved for all time. (von Rad 1962, 79)

As this argument is typically advanced by those who assert the late date of P, the reasoning is somewhat circular. Since P wrote in the exilic and/or restoration periods, circumcision as a "sign of the covenant" made sense in those eras. Since circumcision as an identity marker only made sense during and after the Babylonian exile, the Priestly literature must have emerged in or after the sixth century B.C.E.

My goal is not to prove that the Priestly conceptualization of circumcision had a logical place in the religion and social world of preexilic Judah.[3] Consistent with my assertion of the ahistorical character of the Priestly writings (8) I contend that there is no viable connection to be made between P's vision of circumcision and any particular period in biblical history. Therefore, I wish simply to demonstrate the weakness of the arguments connecting an increased emphasis upon circumcision due to the Babylonian captivity. This topic is broached because it is, as noted above, all too often treated as "gospel." The biblical and extrabiblical evidence will be evaluated with the recognition that the major problem is the absence of substantial data.[4]

Scholars have maintained that the centrality of the Sabbath was a phenomenon of the exile. The biblical evidence, from incontrovertibly exilic and postexilic sources, lends some credibility to this assertion. Nehemiah 13:15–22 recounts the enactment of strict measures by the leaders of the restoration community to prevent the transaction of business on the Sabbath. Deutero-Isaiah (Isa 58:13–14), Jeremiah (Jer 17:19–27), and Ezekiel (Ezek 20), all trumpet the import of the Sabbath and inveigh against its profanation.[5] More significantly, Isa 51:1–8 upholds Sabbath observance as a main requirement

---

3. For this approach, see Weinfeld 1968. Such a claim is not unreasonable, only difficult, if not impossible, to substantiate. It is also made much less often than assertion of a link between circumcision and the exile. Those who assert an early date for P generally do not reference circumcision as a key element of their arguments.

4. My contention here was anticipated by Ackroyd, who, against the trend described above, asserts: "whether it [circumcision] became especially prominent in the exilic period is unknown." Without going into any depth, he simply notes that "the whole theme is one of obscurity, and the evidence insufficiently secure" (1968, 36).

5. Weinfeld (1968, 127–28) asserts that these traditions address the fact that Israel became increasingly lax in its Sabbath observance, not that the practice gained new import. His reading is possible, but no more so than the above interpretation of the data. Also, Weinfeld does not account for Second Isaiah's prioritization of the Sabbath in 51:1–8.

for Israelites who wish to benefit from God's imminent salvation, as well as for foreigners and eunuchs who wish to join the community and worship on the Temple Mount.

In contrast, there is not a single comparable attestation in the Prophets or Writings of a circumcision command or exhortation.[6] This silence could be construed as a sign that circumcision was not a primary concern of any exilic or postexilic biblical authors.[7]

The exilic and postexilic prophetic texts that do mention circumcision take its observance by the Israelite community for granted. The following texts, for example, deal with the inappropriate presence of the alien, labeled ערל "uncircumcised," in the temple and in Jerusalem:

---

6. Jer 4:4, which calls for circumcision of the heart, is not included. Sperling (1989, 70–72) suggests that ברית in Isa 51:4, 6 refers specifically to circumcision. He cites Radak but fails to note that this interpretation is an afterthought, appended to Kimchi's primary reading of the phrase מחזיקים בבריתי. Sperling's assertion of terminological correspondence to Gen 17 is less than decisive, especially since P in that chapter and elsewhere uses the phrase שמר ברית, never מחזיק ברית. Moreover, Sperling is inconsistent with regard to his own view on the dating of biblical traditions. If, as he asserts, the Priestly Pentateuch is a product of the Persian period (1999), he would have a hard time arguing that Second Isaiah could have had a stable version of Gen 17 before him. Two understandings of ברית in Isa 56 are viable. (1) The most likely alternative is that ברית indicates broadly the correct divinely ordained path. Joseph Kara and Radak prefer this reading, suggesting that ברית here refers to the מצוות, the totality of God's commands. This interpretation dovetails with 56:2, which contains the charge to Judeans who await YHWH's deliverance: שֹׁמֵר שַׁבָּת מֵחַלְּלוֹ וְשֹׁמֵר יָדוֹ מֵעֲשׂוֹת כָּל־רָע "Observe the Sabbath [specific] and desist from evil [general]." Additionally, ברית in Isa 24:5 (כִּי־עָבְרוּ תוֹרֹת חָלְפוּ חֹק הֵפֵרוּ בְּרִית עוֹלָם "because they transgressed teachings, overturned laws, and abrogated the eternal covenant") clearly has this more general connotation. (Most usages of ברית in Isaiah refer to God's promises and thus are not relevant to the present inquiry.) (2) ברית could also refer directly to the Sabbath, as understood in Exod 31:16. Thus the verses can be read as examples of synonymous parallelism. Isa 56:4 would be a tricolon with the parallel elements שמר שבת, בחר חפץ, and מחזיק ברית, while 56:6 is the more compact unit, containing the parallel members שמר שבת and מחזיק ברית.

7. Hoffman (1996, 41) views P's circumcision mandate in light of the emphasis upon lineage and the repudiation of exogamy found in Ezra and Nehemiah. In doing so, he glosses over some important issues: (1) the books of Ezra and Nehemiah never mention circumcision; (2) in P, it is only the high priest who is constrained to endogamy, but he must marry from within the priestly clan (Lev 21:14). The Priestly writings never broach the subject of intermarriage, either to promote or to prohibit it.

כִּי לֹא יוֹסִיף יָבֹא־בָךְ עוֹד עָרֵל וְטָמֵא

for the uncircumcised and the defiled will never enter you again (Isa 52:1);

בַּהֲבִיאֲכֶם בְּנֵי־נֵכָר עַרְלֵי־לֵב וְעַרְלֵי בָשָׂר לִהְיוֹת בְּמִקְדָּשִׁי לְחַלְּלוֹ אֶת־בֵּיתִי

When you brought the aliens, uncircumcised of heart and uncircumcised of flesh, to be in my sanctuary and to profane my house (Ezek 44:7);

and the parralel verse:

כָּל־בֶּן־נֵכָר עֶרֶל לֵב וְעֶרֶל בָּשָׂר לֹא יָבוֹא אֶל־מִקְדָּשִׁי

No alien, uncircumcised of heart or flesh, may enter my sanctuary (Ezek 44:9).

The equation of foreskin and foreignness implies that circumcision is an established mark of Israelite identity. Jeremiah 9:24–25 similarly links the alien and the ערל:

(24) הִנֵּה יָמִים בָּאִים נְאֻם־ה' וּפָקַדְתִּי עַל־כָּל־מוּל בְּעָרְלָה
(25) עַל־מִצְרַיִם וְעַל־יְהוּדָה וְעַל־אֱדוֹם וְעַל־בְּנֵי עַמּוֹן וְעַל־מוֹאָב
וְעַל כָּל־קְצוּצֵי פֵאָה הַיֹּשְׁבִים בַּמִּדְבָּר
כִּי כָל־הַגּוֹיִם עֲרֵלִים וְכָל־בֵּית יִשְׂרָאֵל עַרְלֵי־לֵב

(24) Behold, the time is coming, oracle of YHWH, when I shall take notice of all who are circumcised of the foreskin, (25) of Egypt and of Judah and of Edom and of the Ammonites and of all those desert dwellers who cut their forelocks. Because all the nations are uncircumcised and all the house of Israel is uncircumcised of the heart.

Moreover, a fundamental assumption of the Jeremiad is Israel's adherence to the custom. The problem, according to the prophet, is that, despite their circumcised genitalia, the peoples' hearts remain uncircumcised. In other words, though they bear the sign of devotion to God, their actions and attitudes belie their commitment.[8] It is evident, then, that no indisputably late

---

8. On the ideological issues raised in Jer 9:24–25, see Steiner 1999; Blank 1961, 193–207). Scholars (see discussion in Holladay 1986, 319–20) date this passage to the late monarchy or early exile. The chronological setting does not affect the argu-

biblical source either promotes the practice of circumcision or bemoans its neglect. This is in contrast to Sabbath observance, which seems to be considered quite important by a variety of exilic and postexilic tradents.

Another approach to the question of P's circumcision law as a phenomenon of the exile involves an investigation into the social, religious, and demographic realities of the eastern diaspora. How would the Jews have maintained a distinct identity in Chaldean and Achemenid Babylonia? Is there any indication that circumcision was a decisive practice in this regard? For guidance in this area, we can look to biblical and Babylonian sources regarding the Judean communities. Additionally, evidence about other exiled peoples is instructive.[9]

Jews, along with other Semites (Arameans, Phoenicians, and Arabs) and Egyptians, were defeated and deported eastward by the Neo-Babylonians. Unlike the Assyrian Sargonids, who dispersed conquered peoples among various Mesopotamian population centers, the Babylonians transferred the communities relatively intact and settled them in an underpopulated area of the Nippur region near the Chebar River.[10] These ethnic/national groups were able to preserve their own leadership hierarchies[11] and develop distinct administrative associations, called *ḥad/ṭru*.[12] Akkadian records also attest to toponyms in the Nippur region that correspond to town and regional designations of the various exiled peoples. Ephal notes the possibility that "an organized community of *emigres* from a Syrian town flourished in Babylonia, and it returned to its home-town somewhat in the manner of the Jews 'who came up out of the captivity of those exiles… (and) returned to Jerusalem and Judah, *each to his own town*' (Ezra 2:1; Neh. 7:6; cf. also Ezra 2:21–35; Neh. 7:25–37)" (1978, 87).

---

ment that Jeremiah assumes observance of circumcision rather than militating in favor of it.

9. For the Babylonian data, I rely on Zadok 1977; 1979; Ephal 1978. I credit Ziony Zevit for suggesting that I look into the "realia" and for directing me to the Ephal article.

10. The Babylonian towns of Tel Abib (Ezek 3:15) and Tel-melah, Tel-harsha, Cherub, Addan, and Immer (Ezra 2:59) are mentioned in the Bible. See the map in Aharoni and Avi-Yonah 1993:125.

11. Ephal (1978, 76–79) notes the Akkadian institutional designation *puḫur šībūtu ša miṣiraia* "assembly of the elders of Egypt" and the equivalent biblical references from exilic and postexilic sources, זקני הגולה, "elders of the diaspora" (Jer 29:1); זקני יהודה and שבי יהודיא, "Judean elders" (Ezek 8:1; Ezra 5:5, 9; 6:7, 8, 14); and זקני ישראל, "Israelite elders" (Ezek 14:1; 20:1, 3).

12. These are attested for many exiled people but not for the Judeans.

Zadok collected and analyzed onomastic evidence, principally from the business archives of the Murashu family banking concern. A few of his conclusions are germane. He finds evidence of continued use of Yahwistic names among Jews of the second and third generations in Nippur. Moreover, the Akkadian names of Jews contain common Babylonian theophoric elements rather than distinctively Nippurean characteristics. Zadok, therefore, concludes "that there was no influence of the Enlil temple at Nippur on the Jews" (1979, 86). He asserts, similarly, that the Nippur temple "does not seem to have exercised any cultic influence on most of the tribal people." Zadok's work also indicates that Jews were as likely to assimilate with other exiled peoples as they were to intermix with and be influenced by Babylonians. There are no extrabiblical sources that indicate the religious practices of the Jews in Babylonia. However, the Akkadian texts, which are consistent with scriptural traditions, suggest that the exiles were not constrained to develop "counter-traditions" to distinguish themselves from their Babylonian hosts. Rather, the demographics of the exile allowed for the maintenance of group cohesion and identity.

Daniel is the only biblical narrative work set in Babylon during the period of captivity. According to the text, it was publicly apparent to King Nebuchanezzar (or his courtiers) that the Judeans had a distinctive language (Dan 1:4), maintained distinctive names (1:6–7), and observed a set of dietary restrictions (1:8–16).[13] They also openly revered a single deity, identified generically as אלה שמיא "God of Heaven" (2:17, 36, 47), and עליא חי עלמא[14] "most-high, ever-living" (4:31). The text also recounts that Daniel prayed privately thrice daily, facing Jerusalem (6:11). Most agree that even the oldest portions of Daniel were written at least two hundred years after the events and personages described in them.[15] Whether or not the author of Daniel was a credible witness about the religious traditions of the Jews under Neo-Babylonian rule is not germane to the present inquiry. The key point is that circumcision is *not* mentioned as the, or even a, custom practiced by the exiles that would have set them apart from their hosts. Finally, it should be noted that the Elephantine documents, which constitute the major repository of evidence concerning Jewish communities in the Persian period, have no mention of circumcision.

---

13. The motif of the "kosher Jew in the foreign court" is also found in Greek Esth 5:28; Jdt 12:1–9; Tob 1:10–11; and 'Abot R. Nat. A 17. On the literary traditions about Jews in foreign courts, see Wills 1990.

14. Reading with the Kethib.

15. On the dating of Daniel, see Hartman and Di Lella 1978, 9–18; Collins 1993, 24–38.

There is no evidence whatsoever that circumcision gained significance during the sojourn in Babylon. The little data available identify other possible factors as crucial in the maintenance of Judean distinctiveness, and the biblical evidence points to other observances, such as the Sabbath, as attaining greater import during and after the sixth century B.C.E. These indicators therefore support the argument that P's circumcision regulations and ideology cannot be linked to any identifiable historical event or circumstance. Thus, any effort to date these traditions cannot be separated from one's general view of the date of P. Moreover, textual evidence is only of real value in charting the innerbiblical development of attitudes about circumcision. There is no viable means of measuring the extent to which the Priestly legislation and ideology was actualized in the "real-life" practice of Israel during the biblical epoch.

Conclusion

Synthesis

The circumcision traditions considered in this work resonate with several key components of Priestly thought: the command-centered significance of ברית; the regimented stratification of society; and the theology of restoration. The Priestly literature evinces a distinctive use of the word ברית. It can denote divinely imposed commands as well as promises issued by YHWH. The ברית-commands can refer to individual obligations incumbent upon Israel or the aggregation of God's precepts, the חקים, מצות, and משפטים (Lev 26:15). The thirteen-fold occurrence of the word ברית in Gen 17 underscores the essential connection of circumcision and ברית in the Priestly *Weltanschaung*. The very pointed employment of the term in the pericope allows for a number of conclusions regarding P's ideology. The initial twenty-two verses of Gen 17 are occupied with a dialogue between YHWH and Abraham. That dialogue can be divided into five distinct units. The first two units (17:1–3a, 3b–8) and the last two (17:15–18, 19–22) concern God's promises to Abraham, Sarah, Isaac, and Ishmael. The key components of the ברית-promise are great and numerous progeny, the land of Canaan, and a unique relationship with YHWH. However, by setting up a semantic distinction between ברית and blessing, the Priestly tradent distinguishes between Israelite males and females, and Israelites and foreigners. While Isaac is a beneficiary of God's ברית, Ishmael, the paradigmatic foreigner, despite the fact that he is also circumcised, receives a blessing but no ברית. His blessing includes only the offspring component; the land and relationship elements of the ברית are strictly reserved for Abraham and Isaac. Those two fundamental promises are the ones that are later to be fulfilled with the Israelite nation, as stated in Exod 6:4, 7: "And I will fulfill my ברית with them, to give them the land of Canaan," and "I will take them as my own nation, and I will be God to them." Like Ishmael, Sarah is only granted the blessing of offspring, although it is announced to Abraham. Thus, the text articulates the proxy nature of her relationship to YHWH and the ברית-promises.

The core section of Gen 17, verses 9–14, which is comprised of the circumcision laws, contains only the command type of ברית. The embedding of a command and its fulfillment within a larger group of promissory passages suggests that in P the patriarchal covenant is not unconditional. God's beneficence is contingent upon compliance with his dictates. The pivotal verse in the circumcision pericope, Gen 17:11, provides the rationale for the practice: "And you must circumcise the flesh of your foreskins, and it shall be a sign of the ברית between me and you." Here ברית has as its referent the totality of the divine commands, consistent with the use of the term in Lev 26:15. Thus, circumcision is understood as a sign of Abraham's, and subsequently Israel's, obligation to observe all of YHWH's dictates. A sense of *anachrony* inheres in the passage, as the unit defies the strict bounds of the narrative's chronological framework. Abraham, by circumcising himself and his male dependents, signals a commitment to a battery of laws that have not been disclosed to him. While the immediate context of the chapter is God's interaction with Abraham, the circumcision command is intended for Israelites in future generations. The Priestly author, therefore, can retroject to the ancestral era the obligation to a set of commands that are not actually imparted until later in Israel's history.

P inaugurates Israel's history by bestowing a set of promises upon Abraham, the first patriarch. These promises are linked to the observance of a single command, circumcision. The promises will ultimately be put into effect when Israel becomes a nation after their departure from Egypt. Similarly, the practice of circumcision signals every individual Israelite's duty to comply with the full complement of מצות. These commands will also be imposed when Israel achieves national status. Just as the ברית-promises to Abraham are inextricably linked to the practice of circumcision, so will Israel's ability to receive YHWH's grace be bound to its observance of YHWH's commands. As a corrolary to the ברית-centered import of circumcision, the *karet* penalty devolves upon those who fail to bear the sign or affix it on their male dependents. *Karet*, a divinely initiated punishment whose nature is not apparent in the text, is inflicted upon those who violate certain specific statues or, as articulated in Num 15, willfully abrogate God's commands generally. I claim that *karet* entails a withdrawal of YHWH's ברית-promises: progeny; relationship with God; and stake in the land. In any event, with circumcision constructed as a sign of one's obligation to God's commands, failure to circumcise does not only represent an unwillingness to perform this one act. Rather, it can symbolize a wholesale rejection of divine authority. Thus, in the Priestly worldview, *karet* would be a fitting sanction. The idea of circumcision as a sign of the ברית-commands also undergirds the special link between the marking rite and Passover. According to Exod 12:43–49, anyone with a foreskin is precluded from partaking of the paschal sacrifice, and Passover is the only observance with this stipulation. In P and throughout the canon, the exodus is the paradigmatic salvific episode in Israel's early history. The manumission from Egyptian servitude leads to the realization of God's promises conveyed to Abraham and reiterated to Moses. Passover, which commemorates the exodus, is thus the archetypal ברית-focused festival. Thus, bearing the ברית-sign would be by extension a requisite for participating in the celebration, more so than any other in the seasonal cycle.

All slaves are to be circumcised, and a circumcised גר may eat the paschal offering alongside a native Israelite. However, these foreigners do not, upon circumcision, become part of the Israelite community, attain equal status to the אזרח, or gain a stake in the ברית-promises. The foreign slave is circumcised because he is completely subordinated to his master. Consequently, he must submit to the authority of the master's God. The גר occupies an intermediate position between the slave and the Israelite. He enjoys certain rights on a par with his Israelite hosts and is bound to some of the same strictures. For example, though he may not possess leaven during Passover, a גר is not constrained to perform the festal offering. He does have the option of eating the paschal sacrifice, but if he wishes to exercise that choice, he is also enjoined to circumcise himself and all his male charges. As mentioned above, circumcision here is a prerequisite for participation in the Passover, which is the paradigmatic celebration of the ברית-promises. While it affords the alien eligibility, just for this one ceremony, it does not effectuate his entry into the community of Israel.

Circumcision also functions as one among several indices of women's secondary status in the Priestly social order. Since a female cannot be circumcised, she cannot herself bear the ברית-sign. Women are clearly obligated to the commands laid out in the Torah and, as members of the Israelite קהל, also benefit from the ברית-promises. Still, they take on the obligations and entitlements as legal and social extensions of their fathers or husbands.

The uniqueness of circumcision is conspicuous when the rite is surveyed against the background of P's detailed and complex matrix of cultic practice. First, it is the only decree intended for Israel that is issued in the ancestral period, to an individual figure, rather than in the desert milieu, to the Israelite nation. More remarkable is the almost complete absence of ritualization or processual specificity in the circumcision instruction. This lack of detail underscores the instrumental nature of the practice. Only the sign is of moment, not how it is affixed. The lack of ritual dimension also seems to strategically highlight the explicit ברית-sign meaning by denying circumcision any of the implications it carries in some non-P biblical traditions (Exod 4; Josh 5) and non-Israelite cultures. These potential valences include purification, expiation, dedication, or fertility.

The impact of circumcision on P's ideological and rhetorical landscape is also quite potent relative to many other cultic practices, due to its metaphoric reverberations. The Priestly tradent uses circumcision imagery creatively and in diverse settings. Consistent with an agenda of elevating Aaron at Moses' expense, P composes a version of the Mosaic call narrative wherein the protagonist declares himself to be ערל שפתים "foreskinned of lips." This characterization is exploited to point up Moses' immaturity or to paint his initial rejection of the commission as a rejection of God's ברית and an offense against YHWH's holy name. This rejection hints at further infractions on Moses' part, such as the striking of the rock at the waters of Meribah. Moses' self-proclaimed ערלה foreshadows what may be an implicit *karet* penalty, the withdrawal of God's ברית-promises. The desert leader and lawgiver never sets foot in the promised land, and his line is effectively extirpated, at least as far as the text is concerned.

The Priestly legislator also uses ערלה imagery to innovate a legal category. In Lev 19:23–25, consumption of fruit from the first three years of a tree's growth is completely off-limits. The eighth-day component of the circumcision mandate, which implies a seven-day "foreskinned" period before an infant is circumcised, provides a vehicle to characterize the underdeveloped produce as ritually nonviable. In P's system, all firstlings, whether human, animal, or vegetable, must be dedicated to God. Since the immature fruit would be unsuitable for divine consumption, humans must wait as well. In the fourth year, the fruit is sacred, and in the fifth and thereafter, its use and consumption is at the discretion of the landowner. The three/four/five pattern, though common in the Bible and ancient Near Eastern literature, is rare in the Priestly corpus. This duration represents the convergence of theology and agricultural reality.

The weightiest foreskin metaphor is that of corporate Israel's heart in Lev 26. This chapter, often labeled the "epilogue" to the Holiness Code, projects the future destiny of Israel. If the people obey God's will, they will be blessed with the land's bounty. If they reject YHWH's statutes and abrogate his ברית, God will withdraw his grace from them. The escalating punishments heaped upon the people for their sins, which culminate in exile from the land and alienation from God, represent a communal *karet* penalty. Israel's repudiation of the ברית commands is symbolized by their foreskinned heart. The remedy, therefore, that would restore Israel to the land and YHWH's favor is confession and removal of the foreskin from the people's corporate heart. God will then remember and fulfill the ברית-promises he originally imparted to Abraham. The restoration passage highlights the significance of circumcision in Priestly thought. Just as circumcision and the ברית-promises to Abraham in Gen 17 inaugurate YHWH's relationship with Israel, so they signal the climactic moment in the nation's *Heilsgeschichte*. In P's view, actual and cardiac circumcision are complementary. The former operates on the level of the individual, while the latter appertains to the Israelite nation. As genital circumcision signifies Israel's obligation to do YHWH's will, circumcision of the heart represents a collective actualization of this commitment. By the same token, as an Israelite's foreskin signifies a rejection of his devotion to YHWH, so does the foreskinned heart stand for Israel's alienation from God and the promised land. The relationship between Israel and YHWH, governed by the lattice of ברית-commands and promises, is initiated in Gen 17 with Abraham, the first patriarch. The breach of that relationship, followed by its repair and restoration, is capsulized in Lev 26 with the Israelite collective. Thus in the Priestly Torah, circumcision, actual and metaphorical, operates as a crucial literary device, framing Israel's sacred story.

Circumcision in Canonical Perspective

Priestly circumcision traditions have heuristic value for the study of circumcision in the entire Hebrew canon. In particular, the circumcision-ברית relationship resonates in passages beyond the Pentateuch. Joshua 5:2–9 recounts the circumcision (or recircumcision) of every Israelite male at Gilgal upon arrival in Canaan. Crossing the Jordan represent the nation's actualization of the land promise, the last in the triad of YHWH's ברית-promises (Gen 17:8; Exod 6:4). Attainment of this privilege must be accompanied by a communal acceptance of the ברית-obligations, signaled by the mass enactment of the circumcision rite. By analogy, corporate Israel is circumcised en masse almost immediately upon entering the land, as a newborn must be circumcised on the eighth day, upon his first moment of ritual viability, marking his entry into the Israelite community.

A few diverse texts configure the foreskin of the penis and/or of the heart as a sign of foreignness (Isa 52:1; Jer 9:25–26, Ezek 44:7, 9). This foreskin-foreignness equation is not a matter of ethnicity.[1] Rather, it is tied to the notion that an alien is one who is not privy to the ברית-promises of land and special relationship with YHWH or bound by the concomitant obligations.

Circumcision of the heart images appear three times in the Hebrew Bible outside the Priestly corpus; Deut 10:16; 30:6; and Jer 4:4. Though there are a

---

1. The exceptions in this context are the Philistines, who are labeled distinctively as הערלים "the foreskinned people" (e.g., Judg 1:3; 15:18; 1 Sam 14:6; 17:26; 31:4; 2 Sam 1:20; 1 Chr 10:4), no doubt because as original Hellenes, like all the Sea Peoples, they would not have practiced circumcision.

number of substantive differences both stylistic and conceptual between each occurrence, they are all illuminated by our understanding of Lev 26:41. The passages are remarkably consistent in the way they understand circumcision. In every case the foreskinned heart signifies the Israelite nation's unwillingness or inability to adhere to YHWH's commandments. Disobedience produces divine anger and alienation, with consequent collective punishment, which, in the pentateuchal texts, leads ultimately to exile from the land. Metaphorical circumcision, or otherwise removal of the foreskin, symbolizes a communal recommitment to God and his precepts, resulting in reinstatement of divine favor and return to the land. Such a cause-and-effect cycle of obedience and grace versus waywardness and castigation is the integral dynamic of a ברית-based relationship between YHWH and Israel. This dynamic is reiterated throughout the canon and is not unique to any particular authorial tradition. In Lev 26 a command-centered representation of figurative circumcision and foreskin linked to a complex of divine promises is fully explicable in view of P's conceptualization of literal, genital circumcision, as articulated in Gen 17, Exod 12 and Lev 12. On the other hand, Deuteronomy has no laws or narratives that touch upon genital circumcision, nor does it or Jeremiah record any statements as to the practical or ideological implications of the rite. Therefore, the exegete is harder pressed to unpack the circumcision-of-the-heart metaphors in Deuteronomy and Jeremiah. Yet the consistent employment of the circumcised heart as a restoration trope strongly suggests that the framers of Deuteronomy, Jeremiah, and the Priestly corpus shared some fundamental notions about the actual practice of circumcision.

Circumcision in Jewish Tradition

Circumcision as presented in the Priestly pentateuchal corpus provides an indispensable baseline for tracking the development of the ritual in ancient Jewish literature. In relation to the Priestly Torah, early Jewish circumcision traditions evince continuities, disjunctures, and innovations.

Continuity

The centrality of circumcision with regard to the Torah's notion of covenant becomes so embedded in Jewish consciousness that ברית and διαθήκη are often used as a technical term for circumcision. The first instances of such a direct terminological equation appear in 1 Maccabees (e.g., 1:15, 63), and the usage pattern becomes conventional in later Jewish writings. For example, in the Tannaitic corpus (m. Avot 3:11), circumcision is given the label בריתו של אברהם אבינו "the covenant of Abraham our father," while

CONCLUSION 129

the traditional circumcision liturgy repeatedly refers to the rite simply as "the ברית." Similarly, the phrase "blood of the covenant," which in the Hebrew Bible indicates sacrificial blood (Exod 24:8; Zech 9:11; see also Ps 50:5), is in Amoraic literature and after an idiom for circumcision blood (see y. Ned. 3:9; Cohen 2003).

The circumcised heart as restoration motif, found in P and throughout the Hebrew canon, gains traction in early Jewish writings. For instance, it is employed analogously in Jub. 1:22–24, in the Dead Sea Scrolls (*Barkhi Nafshi* 4Q434 1 I, 4: *Dibre Hame'orot* 4Q 504 4, 11), and in the Babylonian Talmud (b. Ber. 29a, the Havineinu prayer). Finally, we can see that in Jewish law the foreskin metaphor of Lev 19:23–25 loses any symbolic resonance or connection to circumcision. The term ערלה in the halakah (see the mishnaic and talmudic tractates of that name) is an economic and agricultural rubric, having the solely technical connotation of fruit in its initial three years.

DISJUNCTURE

Circumcision represents a parting of the ways between Judaism and nascent Christianity, as the New Testament's program serves to obviate the significance of the rite. As regards praxis, though Jesus and John are circumcised (Luke 1:59; 2:21), the Jerusalem council determines that Gentile members of the church community need not be. Rather, one's heart is fully purified through belief in God (Acts 15:1–11; 21:25). This ideology is fully voiced in the Pauline writings. Circumcision of the flesh is, at best, superficial and made redundant by circumcision of the heart, brought about through faith in and relationship with Jesus. This relationship is salvific in and of itself (Rom 2:25–5:5; 1 Cor 7:17–20; Gal 5:1–15; 6:11–18; Eph 2:11–12; Phil 3). As such, circumcision is likened to baptism (Col 2:6–19). Justin Martyr (*Dial.* 18–19, 24, 27–29, 92, 113–114) and the Epistle of Barnabas (9; 10:12) affirm the Pauline ethos while evincing a harsh anti-Jewish tenor. Barnabas declares that the circumcision mandate is evil and false (9:3–4), and Justin reads circumcision as signaling the Jews' rejection of, and by, God, justifying their persecution at the hands of Rome (*Dial.* 16, 19).

INNOVATION

While emergent Christianity devalued and ultimately discarded circumcision, Jewish tradition upholds the centrality and import of the rite. The P writings, the Torah, and the Tanak in its entirety concentrate upon the "why" of circumcision, and, as we have seen, there is little indication beyond the eighth-day command as to the "how." However, in early Jewish literature, increasing attention is paid to the process. Jubilees 15 condemns those who circumcise yet retain a portion of the foreskin. Further, m. Šab. 18:3–19:6, the most extensive piece of circumcision legislation in the tannaitic writings, nominally pertains to the decision that the timely performance of a circumcision overrides the command against labor on the Sabbath (see m. Šab. 9:3). In addition, the unit lays out in some detail the key subrituals of the circumcision practice. Timing is underscored: an infant may not be circumcised before the eighth day or after the twelfth (see m. ʿArak. 2:2), but circumcision may be postponed indefinitely when the infant's health is at risk (see m. Neg. 7:5). At the core of the circumcision ritual are three elements: מילה (cutting); פריעה (peeling back the foreskin to expose the corona); and מציצה (blood drawing). The פריעה requirements are quite stringent, presumably to prevent the appearance of uncircumcision (see Jub. 15, per above) and to deter reversal through epispasm (see m. Yebam. 8:1; Mek. R. Shimon b. Yohai Boʾ 12:45). Anyone may perform a circumcision save a deaf person, a minor, or one who is mentally defective (m. Meg. 2:4). Finally, m. Pesaḥ. 3:7; 5:3; 8:8 (= m. ʿEd. 5:2) treat the intricacies of circumcising non-Jews as a prerequisite to their partaking of the paschal offering.

Jewish texts also ascribe new meanings to circumcision and raise the stakes for the rite's observance. The most scathing criticism in the books of Maccabees is leveled at Jewish apostates who abandon "the sacred covenant" (1 Macc 1:13–15; see also Josephus, *Ant.* 12.241). Jubilees 15 notes that the angels were created circumcised, and Jews who spurn the practice are labeled "sons of destruction" or "sons of Beliar." An apocalyptic Qumran fragment (4Q 458 2 II, 4) speaks of the swallowing up of the uncircumcised in the eschaton. In the same vein, m. ʾAvot 3:11 affirms that anyone who "abrogates the covenant of Abraham" forfeits his share in the world to come. Finally, 2 Bar 66:5 revises the account of Josiah's reform (per 2 Kgs 23:1–27; 2 Chr 34:29–33) by allowing that the king saw to it that every Israelite was circumcised.

In a few select passages in the Greek versions, circumcision is treated as a rite of purification, and the foreskin is regarded as an impurity (LXX Lev 19:23; Deut 30:6; Josh 5:4; Symmachus Exod 6:12, 30; Jer 4:4). Postbiblical interpretations of the "bloody bridegroom" episode (Exod 4:24–26) speak to the power of circumcision blood. The LXX states that circumcision blood averted the death of Moses, while several Targumim attribute a sacrificial valence to circumcision, averring that circumcision blood has atoning and salvific power (Onqelos, Neofiti, Pseudo-Jonathan Exod 4:24–26; Pseudo-Jonathan Exod 12:13; and Tg. Ezek. 16:6). Rabbinic tradition holds the foreskin to be a מום, a physical defect, citing as a prooftext Gen 17:1, God's charge to Abraham: "walk before me and be whole" (תמים, Gen. Rab. 46). While the "plain sense" of the verse refers to moral blamelessness, the midrash, playing on the semantic range of תמים, rereads the image as physical. A particularly dramatic testament to the weight given to circumcision by the rabbis is attested in m. Ned. 3:11, in a sequence of declarations commencing with the phrase "Great is circumcision...." The climactic statement is "Great is circumcision because if not for it, the Holy One Blessed Be He would not have created the world."

In early Judaism, circumcision evolved into a ritual of conversion, and the foreskin became a paradigmatic and consistently employed sign of foreignness. The Hasmoneans conquered and converted non-Jewish peoples such as the Idumeans, compelling them to be circumcised (1 Macc 2:46; Josephus, *Ant.* 12.278; 13.257-258, 318-319). Esther (Gk. Add. C) complains that "she loathes the bed of the uncircumcised," while LXX Esth 8:17 and Jdt 14:10 allude to the circumcision of all converts. Similarly, Josephus's account of the Judaization of the Adiabenian royals (*Ant.* 20.17-96) affirms the necessity of circumcision for male proselytes, and in rabbinic tradition circumcision, along with immersion, is mandated for conversion (Sipre Num. 108).

The heightened importance of circumcision must be understood in its historical and cultural contexts. In the biblical epoch, Egyptians and many Semitic peoples practiced circumcision. Thus, in their world at large, biblical Israelites were not unique because of their circumcision. In the Greco-Roman world, however, circumcision was regarded as a barbaric act of mutilation. Attitudes toward circumcision range from mockery (Horace, *Sat.* 1.9.68-74; Petronius, *Sat.* 68.8; 102.14; Martial, *Epig.* 7.30, 55, 82; 11.94; Juvenal, *Sat.* 14.99) to blunt condemnation (Strabo, *Geog.* 16.2.37; Tacitus, *Hist.* 5.2). Circumcision was especially noticeable in a culture where public nakedness in bath and sport was the norm and a well-formed but uncut physique was the desired masculine aesthetic. Medical writings suggest that Gentiles with less than prominent foreskins would undergo corrective surgeries (Celcus, *Med.* 7.25.1-2). After the first Jewish revolt (73 C.E.), genital examination was employed in collection of the *fiscus Judaicus* ("Jewish tax"; Suetonius, *Dom.* 12.2; Martial, *Epig.* 7.55). Against this background, circumcision emerged as a distinctive mark of Jewish identity, to be maintained despite the high cost of social alienation and ostracism.[2]

---

2. On circumcision as an identity marker in postbiblical Judaism, see Collins 1985; Barth 1990; Cohen 1999; 2005; Neihoff 2003; and Bernat 2009.

Conclusion

Circumcision as presented in the Priestly corpus is certainly a distinctive ritual and a powerful symbol. Although, as noted by Cohen, circumcision "figures prominently in only a few sections of the bible" (1987, 52), those few passages within P's Torah have a resonance and weight that is disproportionate to their word count. However, assertions such as "it is one of the most important commandments of the law" and "it is of equal weight to all the commandments of the Torah" should be regarded as hyperbole. The Priestly tradent deliberately restricted the potential meanings of circumcision; thus the implications of the rite are minimal for P's all-important cultic system. Most significantly, the dynamics of circumcision in the Priestly literature are exclusively internal, and its ramifications are solely upon the relationship between Israel and her deity. Nowhere in the P document is circumcision configured as mark of ethnic identity or communal boundaries that distinguished Israel from the surrounding nations. While select non-P texts do highlight the foreskin as a symbol of foreignness, they are somewhat diffuse, and their identity dynamic can be viewed as a function of a covenant ideology akin to that of the Priestly tradent. It is only in the postbiblical Greco-Roman era that circumcision attains a significance that is both internal and external, as a defining mark of Jewish identity and a sign of the covenant between God and Israel.

Works Cited

Aaron, D. 2001. *Biblical Ambiguities: Metaphor, Semantics and Divine Imagery*. Leiden: Brill.
Aharoni, Y., and M. Avi-Yonah. 1993. *The Macmillan Bible Atlas*. 3rd ed. Rev. A. Rainey and Z. Safrai. New York: Macmillan.
Ackroyd, P. 1968. *Exile and Restoration*. OTL. Philadelphia: Westminster.
———. 1991. *The Chronicler and His Age*. JSOTSup 101. Sheffield: Sheffield Academic Press.
Albertz, R. 1994. *A History of Israelite Religion in the Old Testament Period*. Translated by J. Bowden. OTL. Louisville: Westminster John Knox.
Alexander, T. 1983. Genesis 22 and the Covenant of Circumcision. *JSOT* 25:17–22.
Alexander, B. C. 1991. *Victor Turner Revisited: Ritual as Social Change*. Atlanta: Scholars Press.
Althann, R. 1981. MWL, "Circumcise" with the Lamedh of Agency. *Bib* 62:239–40.
Amit, Y. 1997. Creation and the Calendar of Holiness [Hebrew]. Pages 13–29 in *Tehilla le Moshe: Biblical and Judaic Studies in Honor of Moshe Greenberg*. Edited by M. Cogan and B. Eichler. Winona Lake, Ind.: Eisenbrauns.
Appiah, K. 2006. The Case for Contamination. *New York Times Magazine* January 1.
Baker, D. 1979. Division Markers and the Structure of Leviticus 1–7. *SB* 1:9–15.
Baltzer, K. 1971. *The Covenant Formulary*. Translated by D. Green. Philadelphia: Fortress.
Barnes, W. H. 1997. Non-synoptic Chronological References in the Books of Chronicles. Pages 106–31 in *The Chronicler as Historian*. Edited by M. P. Graham, K. G. Hoglund, and S. L. McKenzie. JSOTSup 238. Sheffield: Sheffield Academic Press.
Barr, J. 1961. *The Semantics of Biblical Language*. Oxford: Oxford University Press.
———. 1974. *Language and Meaning*. Leiden: Brill.
———. 1989. *The Variable Spellings of the Hebrew Bible*. Oxford: Oxford University Press.
———. 1997. Some Semantic Notes on the Covenant. Pages 22–38 in *Beitrage zur Alttestamintlichen Theologie: Festschrift für Walther Zimmerli zum 70. Geburtstag*. Göttingen: Vandenhoeck & Ruprecht.
Barth, L., ed. 1990. *Berit Mila in the Reform Context*. Los Angeles: Berit Mila Board.
Baumgart, N. 1999. Überkommene Traditionen neu Aufgearbeitet und Angeeignet: Lev 26, 3–45. *BZ* 43:1–25.

Bechtel, L. 1994. What If Dina Is Not Raped. *JSOT* 62:19–36.
Bell, C. 1992. *Ritual Theory, Ritual Practice.* New York: Oxford University Press.
———. 1997. *Ritual: Perspectives and Dimensions.* New York: Oxford University Press.
Berlin, A. 1979. Grammatical Aspects of Biblical Parallelism. *HUCA* 50:17–43.
Bernat, D. 2004. Biblical *Waṣfs* beyond Song of Songs. *JSOT* 28:327–49.
———. 2009. Circumcision. *Dictionary of Early Judaism.* Grand Rapids: Eerdmans.
Bickerman, E. 1976. Couper une Alliance. Pages 67–93 in idem, *Studies in Jewish and Christian History I.* Leiden: Brill.
Bienkovski, P. 2000. Slavery. Pages 274–75 in *Dictionary of the Ancient Near East.* Edited by Piotr Bienkowski and A. R. Millard. Philadelphia: University of Pennsylvania Press.
Bird, P. 1987. The Place of Women in the Israelite Corpus. Pages 397–419 in *Ancient Israelite Religion: Essays in Honor of Frank Moore Cross.* Edited by P. D. Miller; P. D. Hanson and S. D. McBride. Philadelphia: Fortress.
Bisschops, R. and Francis, J. 1999. *Metaphor, Canon, and Community: Jewish, Christian, and Islamic Approaches.* New York: Lang.
Black, M. 1962. *Models and Metaphors.* Ithaca, N.Y.: Cornell University Press.
Blank, S. 1961. *Jeremiah: Man and Prophet.* Cincinnati: Hebrew Union College Press.
Blau, J. 1956/57. Bloody Bridegroom [Hebrew]. *Tarbiz* 26: 1–3.
Blenkinsopp, J. 1983. *A History of Prophecy in Israel.* Philadelphia: Westminster.
———. 1992. *The Pentateuch: An Introduction to the First Five Books of the Bible.* New York: Doubleday.
———. 1996. An Assessment of the Alleged Pre-Exilic Date of the Priestly Material of the Pentateuch. *ZAW* 108:495–518.
Boling, R. 1975. *Judges.* AB 6A. Garden City, N.Y.: Doubleday.
———. 1982. *Joshua.* AB 6. Garden City, N.Y.: Doubleday.
Brettler, M. 1978/79. The Promise of the Land of Israel to the Patriarchs in the Pentateuch. *Shnaton* 5/6:7–24.
———. 1989 *God Is King: Understanding an Israelite Metaphor.* JSOTSup 76. Sheffield: Sheffield Academic Press.
———. 1993. Images of YHWH the Warrior in Psalms. *Semeia* 61:135–65.
———. 1999. Predestination in Deut 30:1–10. Pages 171–88 in *Those Elusive Deuteronomists: The Phenomenon of Pan-Deuteronomism.* Edited by L. Schearing and S. McKenzie. JSOTSup 268. Sheffield: Sheffield Academic Press.
Bright, J. 1977. *Covenant and Promise.* London: Cambridge University Press.
Breugemann, W. 1991. Genesis 17:1–22. *Int* 45:55–59.
Budge, E., and L. King. 1902. *Annals of the Kings of Assyria.* London: British Museum.
Callender, D. 1998. Servants of God(s) and Servants of Kings in Israel and the Ancient Near East. *Semeia* 83/84:67–82.
Carasik, M. 1996. Theologies of the Mind in Biblical Israel. Ph.D. diss. Brandeis University.

Carmichael, C. 1996. A Strange Sequence of Rules: Leviticus 19.20–26. Pages 182–205 in *Reading Leviticus: A Conversation with Mary Douglas*. Edited by J. F. A. Sawyer. JSOTSup 227. Sheffield: Sheffield Academic Press.

Carver, N. 1996. Philosophy as Grammer. Pages 139–71 in *The Cambridge Companion to Wittgenstein*. Edited by H. Sluga and D. Stern. Cambridge: Cambridge University Press.

Childs, B. 1974. *The Book of Exodus: A Critical and Theological Commentary*. OTL. Philadelphia: Westminster.

———. 1986. *Old Testament Theology in a Canonical Context*. Philadelphia: Fortress.

Chirichigno, G. 1993. *Debt Slavery in Israel and the Ancient Near East*. JSOTSup 141. Sheffield: Sheffield Academic Press.

Clements, R. 1967. *Abraham and David: Genesis XV and Its Meaning for Israelite Tradition*. SBT 2/5. Naperville, Ill.: Allenson.

Cohen, S. J. D. 1999. *The Beginnings of Jewishness*. Berkeley and Los Angeles: University of California Press.

———. 2005. *Why Aren't Jewish Women Circumcised? Gender and Covenant in Judaism*. Berkeley and Los Angeles: University of California Press.

Collins, J. 1985. A Symbol of Otherness: Circumcision and Salvation in the First Century. Pages 163–86 in *To See Ourselves as Others See Us: Christians, Jews and "Others" in Late Antiquity*. Edited by J. Neusner and E. Frerichs. Chico, Calif.: Scholars Press.

———. 1993. *Book of Daniel*. Hermeneia. Minneapolis: Fortress.

Combes, I. 1998. *The Metaphor of Slavery in the Writings of the Early Church*. JSNTSup 156. Sheffield: Sheffield Academic Press.

Coppens, J. 1941. La Pretendue Aggression Nocturne de Jahve Contre Moise, Sephorah et leur Fils. *ETL* 18:68–73.

Cross, F. M. 1973. *Canaanite Myth and Hebrew Epic*. Cambridge: Harvard University Press.

Crüsemann, F. 1996. *The Torah*. Translated by A. Mahnke. Minneapolis: Fortress.

Cunningham, G., N. Gant, et al., eds. 2000. *Williams Obstetrics 21st Edition*. New York: McGraw-Hill.

Dandamayev, S. 1984. *Slavery in Babylonia from Nabopollasar to Alexander the Great*. De Kalb: Northern Illinois University.

Daube, D. 1963. *The Exodus Pattern in the Bible*. London: Faber & Faber.

Davidson, R. 1979. *Genesis*. CBC. London: Cambridge University Press.

Davies, P. R. 1992. *In Search of 'Ancient Israel'*. JSOTSup 148. Sheffield: Sheffield Academic Press.

Diakonoff, I. 1987. Slave-Labor vs. Non-slave Labor: The Problem of Definition. Pages 1–3 in *Labor in the Ancient Near East*. Edited by M. Powell. New Haven: Yale University Press.

Donner, H., and W. Röllig. 1971. *Kanaanaische un Aramäische Inschriften*. Vol. 1: *Texte*. Wiesbaden: Harrassowitz.

Douglas, M. 1966. *Purity and Danger: An Analysis of the Concepts of Pollution and Taboo*. London: Routledge & Kegan Paul.

Dozeman, T. B. 1996. *God at War: Power in the Exodus Tradition.* Oxford: Oxford University Press.
Driver, S. R. 1895. *A Critical and Exegetical Commentary on Deuteronomy.* ICC. Edinburgh: T&T Clark.
———. 1956. *An Introduction to the Literature of the Old Testament.* 10th ed. New York: Meridian.
Eilberg-Schwartz, H. 1990. *The Savage in Judaism.* Bloomington: Indiana University Press.
Elliger, K. 1966. *Leviticus.* Tübingen: Mohr Siebeck.
Ephal, I. 1978. The Western Minorities in Babylonia in the 6th–5th Centuries B.C.: Maintenance and Cohesion. *Orientalia* 47:74–90.
Fabry, H.-J. 1997. לֵב. *TDOT* 7:399–437.
Fohrer, G. 1972. *History of Israelite Religion.* Translated by D. Green. Nashville: Abingdon.
Fox, M. 1974. Sign of the Covenant: Circumcision in Light of Priestly ʾot Etiologies. *RB* 81:537–96.
Fox, N. S. 2000. *In the Service of the King: Officialdom in Ancient Israel and Judah.* Detroit: Hebrew Union College Press.
Fishbane, M. 1985. *Biblical Interpretation in Ancient Israel.* Oxford: Clarendon.
Flusser, D., and S. Safrai. 1980. Who Sanctified the Beloved in the Womb. *Imm* 11:46–55.
Freedman, D. N. 1964. Divine Commitment and Human Obligation: The Covenant Theme. *Int* 18:419–31.
Friedman, R. E. 1981. *The Exile and the Biblical Narrative.* HSM 22. Chico, Calif.: Scholars Press.
———. 1987. *Who Wrote the Bible?* New York: Summit.
Gane, R. 2005. *Cult and Character: Purification Offerings, Day of Atonement, and Theodicy.* Winona Lake, Ind.: Eisenbrauns.
Garnsey, P. 1996. *Ideas of Slavery from Aristotle to Augustine.* Cambridge: Cambridge University Press.
Geertz, C. 1973. *The Interpretation of Cultures: Selected Essays.* New York: Basic Books.
Gelb, I. 1979. Definition and Discussion of Slavery and Serfdom. *UF* 11:283–97.
Geller, S. A. 1985. Wellhausen and Kaufmann. *Midstream* 39–48.
———. 1990. The Sack of Shechem: The Use of Typology in Biblical Covenant Religion. *Prooftexts* 10:1–15.
———. 1992. Blood Cult: Toward a Literary Theology of the Priestly Work of the Pentateuch. *Prooftexts* 12:97–124.
———. 1996. *Sacred Enigmas: Literary Religion in the Hebrew Bible.* London: Routledge.
Gemser, B. 1953. The Importance of the Motive Clause in Old Testament Law. Pages 50–66 in *Congress Volume: Copenhagen, 1953.* VTSup 1. Leiden: Brill.
Gerstenberger, E. S. 1993. *Leviticus.* ATD 6. Göttingen: Vandenhoeck & Ruprecht.
Gesenius, W. 1910. *Gesenius' Hebrew Grammar.* Edited by E. Kautsch. Translated by A. Cowley. Oxford: Clarendon.

Gevirtz, S. 1990. Circumcision in the Biblical Period. Pages 93–103 in Barth 1990.

Gibson, J. 1998. *Language and Imagery in the Old Testament.* Peabody, Mass.: Hendrickson.

Gilders, W. K. *Blood Ritual in the Hebrew Bible: Meaning and Power.* Baltimore: Johns Hopkins University Press.

Ginsberg, H. L. 1982. *The Israelian Heritage of Judaism.* New York: Jewish Theological Seminary.

Glatt, D. A. 1993. *Chronological Displacement in Biblical and Related Literature.* SBLDS 139. Atlanta: Scholars Press.

Glick, L. B. 2005. *Marked in Your Flesh: Circumcision from Ancient Judea to Modern America.* New York: Oxford University Press.

Goldingay, J. 2000. The Significance of Circumcision. *JSOT* 88:3–18.

Goody, J. 1977. Against Ritual. Pages 25–35 in *Secular Ritual.* Edited by S. F. Moore and B. G. Meyerhoff. Assen: Van Gorcum.

Gorman, F. 1990. *The Ideology of Ritual: Space, Time and Status in the Priestly Theology.* JSOTSup 91. Sheffield: Sheffield Academic Press.

———. 1994. Ritual Studies and Biblical Studies: Assessment of the Past, Prospects for the Future. *Semeia* 67:13–36.

Gray, G. B. 1903. *A Critical and Exegetical Commentary on Numbers.* ICC. Edinburgh: T&T Clark.

Gray, J. 1976. *I and II Kings.* OTL. Philadelphia: Westminster.

Greenberg, M. 1983. *Ezekiel 1–20.* AB 22. New York: Doubleday.

———. 1984. The Design and Themes of Ezekiel's Program of Restoration. *Int* 38:181–208.

———. 1997. *Ezekiel 21–37.* AB 22A. New York. Doubleday.

Greenspahn, F. E., ed. 1991. *Essential Papers on Israel and the Ancient Near East.* New York: New York University Press.

Groot, J. de. 1943. The Story of the Bloody Husband (Exodus IV 24–26) *OtSt* 2:10–17.

Gruber, M. 1987. Women in the Cult according to the Priestly Code. Pages 35–48 in *Judaic Perspectives on Ancient Israel.* Edited by J. Neusner, B. Levine, and E. Frerichs. Philadelphia: Fortress.

Gruenwald, I. 2003. *Rituals and Ritual Theory in Ancient Israel.* Brill Reference Library of Judaism 10. Leiden: Brill.

Grünwaldt, K. 1992. *Exil und Identitat: Beschneidung, Passa und Sabbat in der Priesterschrift.* Frankfurt am Main: Hain.

———. 1999. *Das Heiligkeitgesetz: Leviticus 17–26.* BZAW 271. Berlin: de Gruyter.

Gunkel, H. 1997. *Genesis.* Translated by M. Biddle. Macon, Ga.: Mercer University Press.

Hall, R. G. 1992. Circumcision. *ABD* 1:1025–31.

Hallet, G. 1967. *Wittgenstein's Definition of Meaning as Use.* New York: Fordham University Press.

———. 1977. *A Companion to Wittgenstein's "Philosophical Investigations."* Ithaca, N.Y.: Cornell University Press.

Haran, M. 1979. The Law Code of Ezekiel XL–XLVIII and Its Relation to the Priestly School. *HUCA* 50:45–71.
———. 1985. *Temples and Temple Service in Ancient Israel: An Inquiry into the Character of Cult Phenomena and the Historical Setting of the Priestly School.* Winona Lake, Ind.: Eisenbrauns.
———. 1997. The *Berit* "Covenant": Its Nature and Ceremonial Background. Pages 203–19 in *Tehillah le-Moshe: Biblical and Judaic Studies in Honor of Moshe Greenberg.* Edited by Mordechai Cogan, Barry L Eichler, and Jeffrey H Tigay. Winona Lake, Ind.: Eisenbrauns.
Hartley, J. 1992. *Leviticus.* WBC 4. Waco, Tex.: Word.
Hartman, L. F., and A. A. Di Lella. 1978. *The Book of Daniel.* AB 23. Garden City, N.Y.: Doubleday.
Heger, P. 1999. *The Three Biblical Altar Laws: Developments in the Sacrificial Cult in Practice and Theology: Political and Economic Background.* BZAW 279. Berlin: de Gruyter.
Hendel, R. 1989. Sacrifice as a Cultural System. *ZAW* 101:366–90.
Hermission, H. 1965. *Sprach und Ritus im Altisraelitische Kult: Zur "Spiritualisierung" der Kultbegriffe im Alten Testament.* Neukirchen-Vluyn: Neukirchener.
Hillers, D. 1964a. *Covenant: The History of a Biblical Idea.* Baltimore: Johns Hopkins University Press.
———. 1964b. *Treaty-Curses and the Old Testament Prophets.* Rome: Pontifical Biblical Institute.
Hoffmann, D. 1953. *Leviticus* [Hebrew]. Translated by A. Leiberman. 2 vols. Jerusalem: Mossad Harav Kook.
———. 1969. *Genesis* [Hebrew]. Translated by A. Wasserteil. Bnei Brak: Nezach.
Hoffman, L. 1993. How Ritual Means: Ritual Circumcision in Rabbinic Culture and Today. *SL* 23:78–97.
———. 1996. *Covenant of Blood: Circumcision and Gender in Rabbinic Judaism.* Chicago: University of Chicago Press.
Hoffman, Y. 1986. The Lexicography of the P Document and the Problem Concerning Dating [Hebrew]. *Te'uda* 4:13–22.
Holladay, W. 1986. *Jeremiah 1.* Hermeneia. Philadelphia: Fortress.
Houtman, C. 1983. Exodus 4:24–26 and Its Interpretation. *JNSL* 11:81–103.
Hurowitz, V. 1989. Isaiah's Impure Lips and Their Purification in Light of Mouth Purification and Mouth Purity in Akkadian Sources. *HUCA* 60:39–90.
———. 1992. "His Master Shall Pierce His Ear with an Awl [Exodus 21:6]": Marking Slaves in the Bible in Light of Akkadian Sources. *PAAJR* 58:47–77.
Hurvitz, A. 1972. *Transition Period in Biblical Hebrew* [Hebrew]. Jerusalem: Mossad Bialik.
———. 1982. *A Linguistic Study of the Relationship between the Priestly Source and the Book of Ezekiel.* Paris: Gabalda.
Hyatt, J. P. 1962. Circumcision. *IDB* 1:629–31.
Isaac, E. 1965. Circumcision as a Covenant Rite. *Anthropos* 59:444–56.
Japhet, S. 1989. *The Ideology of the Book of Chronicles.* Translated by A. Barber. Frankfurt am Main: Lang.

Jay, N. 1988. Sacrifice, Descent and the Patriarchs. *VT* 38:52–70.
———. 1992 *Throughout Your Generations Forever: Sacrifice, Religion, and Paternity.* Chicago: University of Chicago Press.
Jensen, P. 1992. *Graded Holiness: A Key to the Priestly Conception of the World.* JSOTSup 106. Sheffield: Sheffield Academic Press.
Johnstone, W. 1998. *Chronicles and Exodus: An Analogy and Its Application.* JSOTSup 275. Sheffield: Sheffield Academic Press.
Joosten, J. 1996. *People and Land in the Holiness Code: An Exegetical Study of the Ideational Framework of the Law in Leviticus 17–26.* VTSup 67. Leiden: Brill.
Joüon, P., and T. Muraoka. 1993. *A Grammar of Biblical Hebrew.* Rome: Pontifical Biblical Institute.
Kalluveettil, P. 1982. *Declaration and Covenant: A Comprehensive Review of Covenant Formula from the Old Testament and the Ancient Near East.* AnBib 88. Rome: Pontifical Biblical Institute.
Kaminsky, J. 1995. *Corporate Responsibility in the Hebrew Bible.* JSOTSup 196. Sheffield: Sheffield Academic Press.
Kang, S. 1989. *Divine War in the Old Testament and in the Ancient Near East.* BZAW 177. Berlin: de Gruyter.
Kaplan, L. 1981. "And the Lord Sought To Kill Him" (Exod 4:24) Yet Once Again. *HAR* 5:65–74.
Kataja, L., and R. Whiting. 1995. *Grants, Decrees and Gifts of the Neo-Assyrian Period.* SAA 12. Helsinki: Helsinki University Press.
Kaufman, S. 1982. The Temple Scroll and Higher Criticism. *HUCA* 53:29–43.
———. 1985. Deuteronomy 14 and Recent Research on the Dating of P. Pages 273–76 in *Das Deuteronomium: Entstehung, Gestalt und Botschaft.* Edited by N. Lohfink. Leuven: Leuven University Press.
Kaufman, Y. 1937–56. *History of Israelite Religion* [Hebrew]. 8 vols. Jerusalem: Mossad Bialik.
Keil, Y. 1997. *Genesis.* Da'at Miqra. Jerusalem: Mossad Harav Kook.
Kelly, B. E. 1996. *Retribution and Eschatology in Chronicles.* JSOTSup 211. Sheffield: Sheffield Academic Press.
Kiuchi, N. 1987. *The Purification Offering in the Priestly Literature: Its Meaning and Function.* JSOTSup 56. Sheffield: Sheffield Academic Press.
Klawans, J. 2003. Rethinking Leviticus and Rereading *Purity and Danger. AJS Review* 27:89–102.
Kline, M. 1968. *By Oath Consigned: A Reinterpretation of the Covenant Signs of Circumcision and Baptism.* Philadelphia: Westminster.
Knohl, I. 1983/84. The Priestly Torah vesus the Holiness School: Sabbath and Festivals [Hebrew]. *Shnaton* 7/8:109–46.
———. 1995. *The Sanctuary of Silence: The Priestly Torah and the Holiness School.* Translated by J. Feldman and P. Rodman. Philadelphia: Fortress.
Kondo, H. 1996. *The Book of Sake.* New York: Kodansha International.
Korpel, M. 1993. The Epilogue to the Holiness Code. Pages 107–22 in *Verse in Ancient Near Eastern Prose.* Edited by J. de Moor and W. Watson. Neukirchen-Vluyn: Neukirchener.

Kosmala, H. 1962. The Bloody Husband. *VT* 12:14–28.
Kraemer, D. 1993. On the Relationship of the Books of Ezra and Nehemiah. *JSOT* 59:73–92.
Kropat, A. 1909. *Die Syntax des Autors der Chronik verglichen mit der seiner Quellen: Ein Beitrag zur historischen Syntax des hebräischen.* Weimar: Hof-Buchdruckerei.
Kugler, R. 1997. Holiness, Purity, the Body and Society: Evidence for Theological Conflict in Leviticus. *JSOT* 76:3–27.
Kutsch, E. 1973. *Verheissung und Gesetz: Untersuchungen zum sogenannten Bund im Alten Testament.* BZAW 131. Berlin: de Gruyter.
Lakoff, G., and M. Johnson. 1980. *Metaphors We Live By.* Chicago: University of Chicago Press.
Le Déaut, R. 1981. Le Thème de la Circoncision du Coeur (Deut XXX 6; Jér IV 4) dans les Versions Anciennes (LXX et Targum) et à Qumran. Pages 178–205 in *Congress Volume: Vienna, 1980.* Edited by J. A. Emerton. VTSup 32. Leiden: Brill.
Lemche, N. P. 1993. The Old Testament—A Hellenistic Book? *SJOT* 7:163–93.
———. 1998. *The Israelites in History and Tradition.* Louisville: Westminster John Knox.
Lesêtre, H. 1926. Circoncision. Pages 772–780 in vol. 3 of *Dictionnaire de la Bible.* Edited by F. Vigouroux. Paris: Librairie Letuouzey.
Levenson, J. 1993. *The Death and Resurrection of the Beloved Son.* New Haven: Yale University Press.
Levine, B. 1971. Prolegomenon. Pages vii–xliv in G. B. Gray, *Sacrifice in the Old Testament.* LBS. New York: Ktav.
———. 1982. Research in the Priestly Source: The Linguistic Factor [Hebrew]. *ErIsr* 16:124–31.
———. 1983. Late Language in the Priestly Source: Some Literary and Historical Observations. Pages 127–35 in *Proceedings of the Eighth World Congress of Jewish Studies.* Jerusalem: World Union.
———. 1987. The Epilogue to the Holiness Code: A Priestly Statement on the Destiny of Israel. Pages 9–34 in *Judaic Perspectives on Ancient Israel.* Edited by J. Neusner, B. Levine, and E. Frerichs. Philadelphia: Fortress.
———. 1989. *Leviticus.* Philadelphia: Jewish Publication Society.
———. 1993. *Numbers 1–20.* AB 4. New York: Doubleday.
———. 2000. *Numbers 21–36.* AB 4A. New York: Doubleday.
———. 2003. Leviticus: Its Literary History and Location in Biblical Literature. Pages 11–23 in Rendtorff and Kugler 2003.
Levinson, B. M. 1989. Calum M. Carmichael's Approach to the Laws of Deuteronomy. *HTR* 83:227–57.
Levy-Bruhl, L. 1937. *L'experience mystique et les symboles chez les primitifs.* Paris: Alcan.
Licht, J. 1962. Milah. Pages 894–901 in vol. 4 of *Encyclopedia Miqra'it.* Jerusalem: Mossad Bialik.
———. 1985. *Commentary on the Book of Numbers* [Hebrew]. 3 vols. Jerusalem: Magnes.

Lindars, B. 1995. *Judges 1–5: A New Translation and Commentary*. Edinburgh: T&T Clark.
Lods, A. 1943. La Mort des Incirconcis. *CRAIBL* 271–83.
Loewenstamm, S. 1980. A Covenant between the Pieces: A Traditio-Historical Investigation. Pages 273–80 in idem, *Comparative Studies in Biblical and Ancient Oriental Literatures*. Neukirchen-Vluyn: Neukirchener.
Lohfink, N. 1994. *Theology of the Pentateuch: Themes of the Priestly Narrative and Deuteronomy*. Translated by L. M. Maloney. Minneapolis: Fortress.
Long, B. 1987. Framing Repetitions in Biblical Historiography. *JBL* 106:385–99.
Luckenbill, D. 1924. *The Annals of Sennacherib*. Chicago: Oriental Institute Press.
Magonet, J. 1996. "But If It Is a Girl, She Is Unclean for Twice Seven Days...": The Riddle of Leviticus 12.5. Pages 144–52 in *Reading Leviticus: A Conversation with Mary Douglas*. Edited by J. F. A. Sawyer. JSOTSup 227. Sheffield: Sheffield Academic Press.
Mayer, G. 1989. מול. *TDOT* 8:158–62.
Mayes, A. D. H. 1981. *Deuteronomy*. NCB. Grand Rapids: Eerdmans.
McCarter, P. K. 1980. *1 Samuel: A New Translation with Introduction, Notes and Commentary*. AB 8. New York: Doubleday.
McCarthy, D. J. 1963. *Treaty and Covenant: A Study in Form in the Ancient Oriental Documents and in the Old Testament*. AnBib 21. Rome: Pontifical Biblical Institute.
McEvenue, S. 1971. *The Narrative Style of the Priestly Writer*. AnBib 50. Rome: Pontifical Biblical Institute.
McKenzie, S. 1991. *The Trouble with Kings: The Composition of the Book of Kings in the Deuteronomistic History*. VTSup 42. Leiden: Brill.
Melamed, E. 1961. Break-Up of Stereotype Phrases as an Artistic Device in Biblical Poetry. *Scripta* 8:115–53.
———. 1975. *Bible Commentators* [Hebrew]. Jerusalem: Magnes.
Mendelsohn, I. 1949. *Slavery in the Ancient Near East: A Comparative Study of Slavery in Babylonia, Assyria, Syria, and Palestine, from the Middle of the Third Millennium to the End of the First Millennium*. New York: Oxford University Press.
Mendenhall, G. E. 1954. Covenant Forms in Israelite Tradition. *BA* 17:49–76.
Milgrom, J. 1967. The Cultic שגגה and Its Influence in the Psalms and Job. *JQR* 58:115–25.
———. 1970. *Studies in Levitical Terminology*. Vol. 1. Berkeley and Los Angeles: University of California Press.
———. 1976. *Cult and Conscience: The Asham and the Priestly Doctrine of Repentance*. SJLA 18. Leiden: Brill.
———. 1990. *Numbers*. Philadelphia: Jewish Publication Society.
———. 1991. *Leviticus 1–16*. AB 3. New York: Doubleday.
———. 1993. Response to Rolf Rendtorff. *JSOT* 60:83–85.
———. 1997. Leviticus 26 and Ezekiel. Pages 57–62 in *The Quest for Context and Meaning: Studies in Biblical Interpretation in Honor of James Sanders*. Edited by C. Evans and S. Talmon. BibInt 88. Leiden: Brill.
———. 1999. The Antiquity of the Priestly Source. *ZAW* 111:10–22.

———. 2000. *Leviticus 17–22*. AB 3A. New York: Doubleday.
———. 2001. *Leviticus 23–27*. AB 3B. New York: Doubleday.
Miller, P. 1973. *The Divine Warrior in Ancient Israel*. HSM 5. Cambridge: Harvard University Press.
Moor, J. de, ed. 1995. *Synchronic or Diachronic: A Debate on Method in Old Testament Exegesis*. OTS 34. Leiden: Brill.
Moore, G. F. 1895. *A Critical and Exegetical Commentary on Judges*. ICC. New York: Scribners.
Morgenstern, J. 1963. The "Bloody Husband" (?) Exod. 4:24–26 Once Again. *HUCA* 34:35–70.
———. 1966. *Rites of Birth, Marriage, Death and Kindred Occasions among the Semites*. Cincinnati: Hebrew Union College Press.
Nelson, R. 1981. *The Double Redaction of the Deuteronomistic History*. JSOTSup 18. Sheffield: Sheffield Academic Press.
———. 1997. *Joshua*. OTL. Louisville: Westminster John Knox.
Nicholson, E. 1986. *God and His People: Covenant and Covenant Theology in the Old Testament*. Oxford: Clarendon.
———. 1998. *The Pentateuch in the Twentieth Century: The Legacy of Julius Wellhausen*. Oxford: Clarendon.
Neihoff, M. 2003. Circumcision as a Marker of Identity: Philo, Origen and the Rabbis on Gen. 17:1–14. *JSQ* 10:89–123.
Noth, M. 1962. *Exodus: A Commentary*. Translated by J. S. Bowden. OTL. Philadelphia: Westminster.
———. 1965. *Leviticus*. Translated by J. E. Anderson. OTL. Philadelphia: Westminster.
———. 1968. *Numbers*. Translated by J. D. Martin. OTL. Philadelphia: Westminster.
———. 1972. *A History of Pentateuchal Traditions*. Translated by B. Anderson. Englewood Cliffs, N.J.: Prentice Hall.
———. 1981 *The Deuteronomistic History*. Translated by D. Green. JSOTSup 15. Sheffield: Sheffield Academic Press.
Olyan, S. 2000. *Rites and Rank: Hierarchy in Biblical Representations of Cult*. Princeton: Princeton University Press.
———. 2005. Some Neglected Aspects of Israelite Interment Ideology. *JBL* 124:601–16.
Paran, M. 1989. *Forms of the Priestly Style in the Pentateuch* [Hebrew]. Jerusalem: Magnes.
Patrick, D. 1994. Is the Truth of the First Commandment Known by Reason? *CBQ* 56:423–41.
Polak, F. 1997. Development and Periodization of Biblical Prose Narrative (I) [Hebrew]. *Bet Miqra* 152:30–52.
1998. Development and Periodization of Biblical Prose Narrative (II) [Hebrew]. *Bet Miqra* 153:142–60.
Polzin, R. 1976. *Late Biblical Hebrew: Toward an Historical Typology of Biblical Hebrew Prose*. HSM 12. Missoula, Mont.: Scholars Press.
Propp, W. 1987. The Origins of Infant Circumcision in Israel. *HAR* 11:355–70.

———. 1993. That Bloody Bridegroom. *VT* 43:495–518.

———. 1999. *Exodus 1–18: A New Translation with Introduction and Commentary.* AB 2. New York: Doubleday.

Prosic, T. 1999. Passover in Biblical Narratives. *JSOT* 82:45–55.

Rad, G. von. 1962. *Old Testament Theology.* Vol. 1. Translated by D. M. G. Stalker. New York: Harper & Row.

———. 1972. *Genesis.* Translated by J. H. Marks. OTL. Philadelphia: Westminster.

Radday, Y., and H. Shore. 1985. *Genesis: An Authorship Study.* AnBib 103. Rome: Pontifical Biblical Institute.

Rainey, A. 1970. Compulsory Labor Gangs in Ancient Israel. *IEJ* 20:191–202.

Ramirez Kidd, J. 1999. *Alterity and Identity in Israel: The גר in the Old Testament.* BZAW 283. Berlin: de Gruyter.

Regev, E. 2001. Priestly Dynamic Holiness and Deuteronomic Static Holiness. *VT* 51:242–61.

Rendsburg, G. 1980. Late Biblical Hebrew and the Date of P. *JANESCU* 12:65–80.

———. 1986 *The Redaction of Genesis.* Winona Lake, Ind.: Eisenbrauns.

———. 1999. Review of Sperling 1998. *AJS Review* 24:359–62.

Rendtorff, R. 1977. *Das überlieferungsgeschichtliche Problem des Pentateuch.* BZAW 147. Göttingen: Vandenhoeck & Ruprecht. ET: *The Problem of the Process of Transmission in the Pentateuch.* Translated by J. J. Scullion. JSOTSup 89. Sheffield: JSOT Press, 1990.

———. 1996. Chronicles and the Priestly Torah. Pages 259–66 in *Texts, Temples and Traditions: A Tribute to Menachem Haran.* Edited by M. Fox et al. Winona Lake, Ind.: Eisenbrauns.

———. 1998 *The Covenant Formula: An Exegetical and Theological Investigation.* Translated by M. Kohl. Edinburgh: T&T Clark.

Rendtorff, R., and R. Kugler, eds. 2003. *The Book of Leviticus: Composition and Reception.* VTSup 93. Leiden: Brill. Repr., Atlanta: Society of Biblical Literature, 2006.

Richards, I. 1981. Philosophy of Rhetoric. Pages 65–91 in *Philosophical Perspectives on Metaphor.* Edited by E. Johnson. Minneapolis: University of Minnesota Press.

Rofé, A. 1987. The Battle of David and Goliath: Folklore, Theology, Eschatology. Pages 28–41 in *Judaic Perspectives on Ancient Israel.* Edited by J. Neusner, E. Frerichs, and B. Levine. Philadelphia: Fortress.

Rooker, M. F. 1990. *Biblical Hebrew in Transition: The Language of the Book of Ezekiel.* JSOTSup 90. Sheffield: Sheffield Academic Press.

Ruwe, A. 1999. *"Heiligkeitsgesetz" und "Priesterschrift": Literaturgeschichtliche und rechtssystematische Untersuchungen zu Leviticus 17,1–26,2.* FAT 26. Tubingen: Mohr Siebeck.

———. 2003. The Structure of the Book of Leviticus in the Narrative Outline of the Priestly Sinai Story. Pages 55–78 in Rendtorff and Kugler 2003.

Sarna, N. 1966. *Understanding Genesis.* New York: Jewish Theological Seminary of America.

———. 1981. The Anticipatory Use of Information as a Literary Feature of the Genesis Narrative. Pages 76–84 In *Creation of Sacred Literature.* Edited by R. Friedman. Berkeley and Los Angeles: University of California Press.

———. 1989. *Genesis*. Philadelphia: Jewish Publication Society.
———. 1991. *Exodus*. Philadelphia: Jewish Publication Society.
Sasson, J. 1966. Cirucmicison in the Ancient Near East. *JBL* 5:473–76.
Sawyer, J. F. A. 1996. The Language of Leviticus. Pages 15–20 in idem, ed., *Reading Leviticus: A Conversation with Mary Douglas*. JSOTSup 227. Sheffield: Sheffield Academic Press.
Schmid, H. 1931. Mose, Der Blutbrautigan. *Judaica* 21:113–18.
Schwartz, B. 1991. The Prohibition Concerning the "Eating" of Blood in Leviticus 17. Pages 34–66 in *Priesthood and Cult in Ancient Israel*. Edited by G. A. Anderson and S. M. Olyan. JSOTSup 125. Sheffield: Sheffield Academic Press.
———. 1996a. The Priestly Account of the Theophany and Lawgiving at Sinai. Pages 103–34 in *Texts, Temples and Traditions: A Tribute to Menahem Haran*. Edited by M. Fox et al. Winona Lake, Ind.: Eisenbrauns.
———. 1996b. "Profane" Slaughter and the Integrity of the Priestly Code. *HUCA* 67:15–42.
———. 1999. *Holiness Legislation: Studies in the Priestly Code* [Hebrew]. Jerusalem: Magnes.
Shields, M. 1995. Circumcision of the Prostitute: Gender, Sexuality, and the Call to Repentance in Jeremiah 3:1–44. *BibInt* 3:61–74.
Ska, J. 1990. *"Our Fathers Have Told Us": Introduction to the Analysis of Hebrew Narratives*. SubBi 13. Rome: Pontifical Biblical Institute.
Skinner, J. 1910. *A Critical and Exegetical Commentary on Genesis*. ICC. Edinburgh: T&T Clark.
Sklar, J. 2005. *Sin, Impurity, Sacrifice, Atonement: The Priestly Conceptions*. HBM 2. Sheffield: Sheffield Phoenix Press.
Smith, D. L. 1989. *The Religion of the Landless: The Social Context of the Babylonian Exile*. Bloomington, Ind.: Meyer Stone.
Snaith, N. H. 1967. *Leviticus and Numbers*. NCB. London: Nelson.
Soggin, A. 1972. *Joshua*. Translated by J. Wilson. OTL. Philadelphia: Westminster.
Sommer, B. 1996. Exegesis, Allusion and Intertextuality in the Hebrew Bible: A Response to Lyle Eslinger. *VT* 46:479–89.
———. 1998. *A Prophet Reads Scripture: Allusion in Isaiah 40–66*. Palo Alto: Stanford University Press.
Sonsino, R. 1980. *Motive Clauses in Hebrew Law: Biblical Forms and Near Eastern Parallels*. SBLDS 45. Chico, Calif.: Scholars Press.
Soskice, J. 1985. *Metaphor and Religious Language*. Oxford: Clarendon.
Sperling, S. D. 1989. Rethinking Covenant in Late Biblical Books. *Bib* 70:50–73.
———. 1998. *The Original Torah: The Political Intent of the Bible's Writers*. New York: New York University Press.
———. 1999. Pants, Persians and the Priestly Source. In *Ki Baruch Hu: Ancient Near Eastern, Biblical and Judaic Studies in Honor of Baruch A. Levine*. Edited by R. Chazan, W. Hallo, and L. Schiffman. Winona Lake, Ind.: Eisenbrauns.
Staal, F. 1975. The Meaninglessness of Ritual. *Numen* 26:2–22.
Steiner, R. 1999. Incomplete Circumcision in Egypt and Edom: Jeremiah (9:24–25) in the Light of Josephus and Jonckheere. *JBL* 118:497–505.

Sternberg, M. 1985. *The Poetics of Biblical Narrative: Ideological Literature and the Drama of Reading*. Bloomington: Indiana University Press.

Sun, H. 1990. An Investigation into the Compositional Integrity of the So-Called Holiness Code (Leviticus 17–26). Ph.D. diss., Claremont Graduate School.

Syren, R. 1993. *The Forsaken First Born: A Study of a Recurrent Motif in the Patriarchal Narratives*. JSOTSup 133. Sheffield: Sheffield Academic Press.

Talmon, S. 1954. Bloody Bridegroom [Hebrew]. *ErIsr* 3:93–96.

Talshir, Z. 1999. Textual and Literary Criticism of the Bible in Post-modern Times: The Untimely Demise of Classical Biblical Philology. *Henoch* 21:235–52.

Tigay, J. 1978. "Heavy of Mouth" and "Heavy of Tongue": On Moses' Speech Difficulty. *BASOR* 231:57–67.

———. 1996. *Deuteronomy: The Traditional Hebrew Text with the New JPS Translation*. JPS Torah Commentary. Philadelphia: Jewish Publication Society.

Toeg, A. 1973/74. A Halakhic Midrash in Num. 15:22–31 [Hebrew]. *Tarbiz* 43:1–20.

Turner, V. 1969. *The Ritual Process: Structure and Anti-structure*. Chicago: Aldine.

Van Seters, J. 1994. *The Life of Moses*. Louisville: Westminster John Knox.

———. 1996a. Cultic Laws in the Covenant Code (Exodus 20,22–23,33) and Their Relationship to Deuteronomy and the Holiness Code. Pages 319–46 in *Studies in the Book of Exodus: Redaction-Reception-Interpretation*. Edited by M. Vervenne. Leuven: Leuven University Press.

———. 1996b. The Law of the Hebrew Slave. *ZAW* 108:534–546.

Vaux, R. de. 1961 *Ancient Israel: Its Life and Institutions*. Translated by John McHugh. New York: McGraw-Hill.

Vawter, B. 1977. *Genesis: A New Reading*. Garden City, N.Y.: Doubleday.

Vermes, G. 1957/58. Baptism and Jewish Exegesis: New Light from Ancient Sources. *NTS* 4:308–19.

Vervenne, M. 1990. The "P" Tradition in the Pentateuch: Document and/or Redaction? Pages 67–90 in *Pentateuchal and Deuteronomistic Studies: Papers Read at the XIIIth IOSOT Congress, Leuven 1989*. Edited by C. Brekelmans and J. Lust. Leuven: Leuven University Press.

Viberg, A. 1992. *Symbols of Law: A Contextual Analysis of Legal Symbolic Acts in the Old Testament*. ConBOT 34. Stockholm: Almquist & Wiksell.

Vink, J. G. 1969. The Date and Origin of the Priestly Code in the Old Testament. Pages 1–144 in idem, *The Priestly Code and Seven Other Studies*. OtSt 15. Leiden: Brill.

Vriezen, T. C. 1967. *The Religion of Ancient Israel*. Philadelphia: Westminster.

Wagner, S. 1997. כנע. *TDOT* 7:204–10.

Warning, W. 1999. *Literary Artistry in Leviticus*. BibInt 35. Leiden: Brill.

Watson, W. G. E. 1984. *Classical Hebrew Poetry: A Guide to Its Techniques*. JSOTSup 26. Sheffield: Sheffield Academic Press.

Watts, J. W. 1999. *Reading Law: The Rhetorical Shaping of the Pentateuch*. Biblical Seminar 59. Sheffield: Sheffield Academic Press.

———. 2006. Review of M. Modeus, *Sacrifice and Symbol: Biblical S0elamim in a Ritual Perspective*. RBL Online: http://www.bookreviews.org/pdf/5079_5353.pdf.

———. 2007. *Ritual and Rhetoric in Leviticus*. Cambridge: Cambridge University Press.
Weber, M. 1952. *Ancient Judaism*. Translated by H. Gerth and D. Martindale. Glencoe, Ill.: Free Press.
Wegner, J. R. 1988. *Chattel or Person? The Status of Women in the Mishnah*. New York: Oxford University Press.
———. 1998. "Coming before the Lord": לפני יהוה and the Exclusion of Women from the Divine Presence. Pages 81–91 in *Hesed Ve-Emet: Studies in Honor of Ernest S. Frerichs*. Edited by J. Magness and S. Gitin. BJS 320. Atlanta: Scholars Press.
Weinfeld, M. 1968. God the Creator in Gen. I and in the Prophecy of Second Isaiah [Hebrew]. *Tarbiz* 37:105–32. (English summary i–ii)
———. 1970. The Covenant of Grant in the Old Testament and in the Ancient Near East. *JAOS* 90:184–203.
———. 1975. Bᵉrith-Covenant vs. Obligation. *Bib* 56:120–28.
———. 1991. *Deuteronomy 1–11: A New Translation with Introduction and Commentary*. AB 5. New York: Doubleday.
———. 1993. *The Promise of the Land: The Inheritance of the Land of Canaan by the Israelites*. Berkeley and Los Angeles: University of California Press.
Wellhausen, J. 1957. *Prolegomena to the History of Ancient Israel: With a Reprint of the Article Israel from the Encyclopaedia Britannica*. Translated by J. S. Black and A. Menzies. New York: Meridian.
Wenham, G. 1979. *The Book of Leviticus*. NICOT. Grand Rapids: Eerdmans.
———. 1994. *Genesis 16–50*. WBC 2. Dallas: Word.
———. 1999. The Priority of P. *VT* 49:240–58.
Westermann, C. 1980. *The Promises to the Fathers*. Translated by D. Green. Philadelphia: Fortress.
———. 1985. *Genesis 12–36: A Commentary*. Translated by J. J. Scullion. CC. Minneapolis: Augsburg.
Wevers, J. 1997. *Notes on the Greek Text of Leviticus*. SBLSCS 44. Atlanta: Scholars Press.
Whybray, N. 1987. *The Making of the Pentateuch: A Methodological Study*. JSOTSup 53. Sheffield: Sheffield Academic Press.
Williamson, P. R. 2000. *Abraham, Israel and the Nations: The Patriarchal Promise and Its Covenantal Development in Genesis*. JSOTSup 315. Sheffield: Sheffield Academic Press.
Wills, L. M. 1990. *The Jew in the Court of the Foreign King: Ancient Jewish Court Legends*. HDR 26. Minneapolis: Fortress.
Wittgenstein, L. 2001. *Philosophical Investigations*. Translated by G. E. M. Anscombe. Oxford: Blackwell.
Wold, D. J. 1978. The Biblical Penalty of *Kareth*. Ph.D. diss., University of California, Berkeley.
———. 1979. The Kareth Penalty in P: Rationale and Cases. Pages 1–46 in *Society of Biblical Literature 1979 Seminar Papers*. SBLSP 18. Missoula, Mont.: Scholars Press.

Wright, D. 1987. *The Disposal of Impurity: Elimination Rites in the Bible and in Hittite and Mesopotamian Literature.* SBLDS 101. Atlanta: Scholars Press.

———. 1991. The Spectrum of Priestly Impurity. Pages 150–81 in *Priesthood and Cult in Ancient Israel.* Edited by G. Anderson and S. Olyan. JSOTSup 125. Sheffield: Sheffield Academic Press.

———. 1999. Holiness in Leviticus and Beyond. *Int* 53:351–65.

———. 2001a Introduction to Leviticus. Pages 142–43 in *The New Oxford Annotated Bible.* 3rd ed. Edited by M. Coogan. New York: Oxford University Press.

———. 2001b. *Ritual in Narrative: The Dynamics of Feasting, Mourning, and Retaliation Rites in the Ugaritic Tale of Aqhat.* Winona Lake, Ind.: Eisenbrauns.

Wuthnow, R. 1987. *Meaning and Moral Order: Explorations in Cultural Analysis.* Berkeley and Los Angeles: University of California Press.

Zakovitch, Y. 1977. The Pattern of the Numerical Sequence Three-Four in the Bible [Hebrew]. Ph.D. diss., Hebrew University.

Zadok, R. 1977. *On West Semites in Babylonia during the Chaldean and Achaemenian Periods: An Onomastic Study.* Jerusalem: Wanaarta/Tel Aviv University.

———. 1979. *The Jews in Babylonia during the Chaldean and Achaemenian Periods: according to the Babylonian Sources.* Haifa: University of Haifa.

Zeusse, E. M. 1987. Ritual. Pages 405–22 in vol. 12 of *Encyclopedia of Religion.* Edited by M. Eliade. New York: MacMillan.

Zevit, Z. 1969. Use of 'bd as a Diplomatic Term in Jeremiah. *JBL* 88:74–77.

———. 1982. Converging Lines of Evidence Bearing on the Date of P. *ZAW* 94:481–511.

———. 2001a. *The Religions of Ancient Israel: A Synthesis of Parallactic Approaches.* London: Continuum.

———. 2001b. Review of S. Gogel, *A Grammar of Epigraphic Hebrew. JBL* 120: 347–48.

Zimmerli, W. 1979. *Ezekiel: A Commentary on the Book of the Prophet Ezekiel.* Vol. 1. Translated by R. Clements. Hermeneia. Philadelphia: Fortress.

Index of Primary Sources

Hebrew Bible

Genesis
- 1–2:4a   60 n. 19
- 1:28   15
- 5:12   60 n. 18
- 6:18   28, 28 n. 5
- 7:2   30 n. 15
- 8:20–22   31 n. 15
- 9   14 n. 4
- 9:1–7   75 n. 58
- 9:9–17   28
- 9:9   28
- 9:11   28
- 9:12   29
- 9:12–17   37
- 9:13   37
- 9:15–16   29, 37
- 9:17   28, 37
- 11:26   60 n. 18
- 15   35, 40
- 15:1   35
- 15:4–5   35
- 15:7   35
- 15:18   35
- 15:9–10   27
- 17–21   9
- 17   2 n. 5, 7 n. 20, 13, 13 n. 1, 14, 16, 20 n. 18, 22, 24, 25, 27, 32, 32 n. 1, 33, 34, 35, 37, 38 n. 34, 39, 40, 43, 50, 55, 67, 75, 97, 104, 117 n. 6, 123, 126, 127, 128
- 17:1   130
- 17:1–3a   14, 15, 123
- 17:1–22   14, 123
- 17:1–27   13
- 17:2   27, 32
- 17:3b–8   14, 16, 123
- 17:4   16, 27, 32
- 17:4–8   87
- 17:5   16
- 17:6   16
- 17:7   16, 19, 27, 32
- 17:7–8   7 n. 20
- 17:8   16, 127
- 17:9   17, 27, 35
- 17:9–10   36, 38
- 17:9–14   1 n. 4, 14, 16, 20, 24, 32, 37, 39, 47, 66, 124
- 17:10   8 n. 24, 17, 18, 27
- 17:10–14   45
- 17:11   3, 8 n. 24, 17, 18, 18 n. 14, 18 n. 14, 24, 27, 36, 37, 38, 39, 51, 124
- 17:11–12   43
- 17:11–14   36, 38, 39
- 17:12   8 n. 24, 17, 18, 61
- 17:13   8 n. 24, 17, 18, 24, 27, 38, 46
- 17:14   7 n. 20, 8 n. 24, 17, 18, 27, 37 n. 33, 70, 76, 86, 87
- 17:15   19
- 17:15–18   14, 19, 34, 123
- 17:16   19
- 17:17   19
- 17:18   19
- 17:19   19, 27, 33
- 17:19–22   14, 19, 123
- 17:20   15, 19, 33
- 17:21   19, 20, 27, 33
- 17:22   20
- 17:23   8 n. 24, 20, 55

17:23–27	1 n. 4, 14, 20, 47	6:30	1 n. 4, 2 n. 5, 8 n. 24, 85, 86, 86 n. 11
17:24	8 n. 24, 20		
17:25	8 n. 24, 20	7:1	85
21:1–5	13, 13 n. 1, 14, 20, 24	12	9, 13, 21, 22, 25, 26, 30 n. 12, 76, 95, 128
21:3	19		
21:4	1 n. 4, 8 n. 24, 55	12:1–13:16	21
21:5	20	12:7	67
22	2 n. 5	12:8	67
24:30	58	12:8–9	66
25:4	72	12:11	67 n. 40
25:9	72	12:13	67 n. 40
25:12–16	33 n. 20	12:15	60 n. 15, 95
26:3–4	40 n. 41	12:19	44 n. 5, 60 n. 15
26:5	40 n. 41	12:19–20	47
31:44–54	27	12:25	92 n. 3
33:17	67 n. 41	12:37	67 n. 41
34	1 n. 4, 2 n. 5	12:43	21
35:4	58	12:43–49	7 n. 20, 13, 21, 25, 45, 48, 59, 66, 124
46:27	60 n. 18		
		12:44	21, 43
Exodus		12:44–49	1 n. 4
2:22	88	12:45	21, 44
2:24	28, 29	12:46	21
2:26	37	12:47	21, 47
3:1–4:17	83	12:48	21, 44, 44 n. 4, 44 n. 5, 46 n. 7, 47
4	75, 83 n. 2, 125		
4:10	85, 86, 86 n. 11	12:49	21, 22, 44 n. 5
4:16	85	13:2	69
4:24–26	1 n. 4, 2 n. 5, 64 n. 30, 69, 130	13:11–15	69
		19	31
4:25	55 n. 5	19:8	28, 31 n. 16
6	9, 80, 83, 84, 86, 87, 88	20:17	34, 48
6:2–7:7	83	20:26	101 n. 5
6:3	83	21	57, 59
6:4	28, 28 n. 5, 86, 123, 127	21:2–6	56
6:4–5	83	21:5	57
6:5	29, 37, 86	21:6	57
6:7	123	21:7	34, 48
6:12	1 n. 4, 2 n. 5, 8 n. 24, 79, 83 n. 2, 85, 86, 86 n. 11	22:29	61
		23:14–19	21 n. 19
6:14–25	84	23:15–17	67 n. 39
6:16–25	87	24	31
6:20	84	24:3	28, 31 n. 16
6:23	84, 84 n. 4	24:3–8	27
6:25	84	24:7	31 n. 16

24:8	64 n. 30, 129	15:14	23 n. 23
24:12	74	15:19	60 n. 15
25:37	60 n. 15	15:19–24	22
28:3	111 n. 23	15:28	60 n. 15
28:41	62 n. 26	15:29	23 n. 23
30:33	51	16	5 n. 17
30:38	51	16:4	60 n. 15
31:12–17	60 n. 19	16:21	111
31:14	51, 73	16:29	44 n. 5, 111, 112
31:16	29, 117 n. 6	16:31	112
32:2	58	17	14, 67 n. 37, 122 (83)
34:18	67 n. 39	17–27	6 n. 20
34:18–26	21 n. 19	17:1–9	30 n. 12
34:22–23	67 n. 39	17:3–9	67
35:22	58	17:8	44 n. 4, 44 n. 5
37:23	60 n. 15	17:10	44 n. 4, 44 n. 5, 46 n. 7
		17:10–14	51
Leviticus		17:11	19
2:13	29	17:12	44 n. 5
4–5	109 n. 19	17:13	44 n. 4, 44 n. 5, 46 n. 7
4:3–21	73 n. 53	17:15	44 n. 4, 44 n. 5
4:6	60 n. 15	18	50, 52
4:17	60 n. 15	18:26	44 n. 5
4:23	101 n. 5	19	9, 64, 80, 91, 114
5:5	111	19:2	91
6:21	66	19:3	91
7:19–21	66	19:4	91
7:25–27	73	19:5–8	91
8:33–9:24	61	19:8	72
9:1	23 n. 23	19:9–10	24 n. 24, 91
10	55 n. 7, 84	19:10	44 n. 5, 91
11	7, 93	19:10a	24 n. 24
12	7 n. 20, 9, 13, 22, 25, 26, 55, 63, 63 n. 29, 65, 65 n. 32, 128	19:10–11	24 n. 24
		19:11–15	91
12–15	22	19:11–17	91
12:2	22, 23, 64	19:12	91
12:2–3	61	19:13	21 n. 20
12:3	1 n. 4, 8 n. 24, 13, 23, 61	19:13b	44 n. 3
12:5	22	19:14	91
13–14	60, 64	19:16	91
13:16	101 n. 5	19:18	91
14:1	23 n. 23	19:19	91
14:34	92 n. 3	19:19–25	91
15	60	19:20	91, 101 n. 5
15:13	64	19:20–22	91, 109 n. 19

19:23	8 n. 24, 91, 92	24:22	44 n. 5
19:23–24	79, 79 n. 1	25	44 n. 3, 71, 71 n. 51, 72, 99
19:23–25	1 n. 4, 92, 94 n. 6, 126, 129	25:2	92 n. 3, 99
19:24	92	25:2–7	60 n. 19
19:25	91, 92	25:6	21 n. 20, 44 n. 3
19:26	91	25:8	60 n. 17
19:26–32	91	25:8–17	49
19:30	91	25:13	72
19:31	91	25:23	44 n. 3, 47, 71
19:32	91	25:23–34	49
19:33	44 n. 5, 46 n. 7	25:24	72
19:34	44 n. 5, 91	25:25	72, 99
19:36	91	25:27	72
19:37	91	25:28	72
20	50, 52	25:32	72
20:2	44 n. 4, 44 n. 5, 46 n. 7	25:33	72
20:3	72	25:34	72
20:24–26	33	25:35	44 n. 3, 44 n. 5, 99
21:1–8	62 n. 27	25:39	99
21:14	117 n. 7	25:39–43	44 n. 4
22:1–16	48	25:40	21 n. 20, 44 n. 3
22:10	21 n. 20	25:41	72
22:10–11	46	25:42	47, 59 n. 14
22:12–13	34	25:44–46	43
22:14–16	109 n. 19	25:45	47, 72
22:16	62 n. 27	25:45–46	72 n. 52
22:18	44 n. 4, 44 n. 5	25:46	72
22:27	23 n. 23, 61, 62 n. 26	25:47	44 n. 5, 99
23	24 n. 24	25:47–54	47
23:3	60 n. 15	25:55	47, 59 n. 14
23:4–8	21 n. 19	26	7 n. 20, 9, 10, 80, 97, 98, 99, 101, 102, 103, 104, 104 n. 7, 107, 108, 111, 113, 114, 126, 127, 128
23:9–21	24 n. 24		
23:10	92 n. 3		
23:22	24 n. 24, 44 n. 5	26:3	98
23:27	112	26:3–12	98
23:29	112	26:3–13	102
23:32	112	26:3–46	98
23:33–43	61	26:4	99
23:36	23 n. 23	26:4–8	102
23:39	23 n. 23	26:9	28, 102
23:43	67	26:11–12	102
24	30 n. 8	26:13	98, 107
24:3	30 n. 8	26:14	98, 103, 107
24:8	29, 29 n. 8	26:14–38	102
24:16	44 n. 5	26:14–39	98

INDEX OF PRIMARY SOURCES

26:15	29, 29 n. 7, 38, 39, 99, 103, 123, 124
26:18	98
26:19	108
26:20	99
26:21	98
26:23	98
26:24	99
26:27	98
26:33–39	100 n. 5
26:34	99
26:39	100
26:39–43	100
26:40	98, 100, 108, 111
26:40–41	113
26:40–45	98
26:41	1 n. 4, 8 n. 24, 38, 97, 100, 107, 109, 111, 128
26:41bα	98
26:41bβ	98
26:42	28, 29, 37, 98, 100, 101, 104
26:43	99, 100, 101
26:44	29, 29 n. 7, 99
26:44–45	28, 104
26:45	29, 37, 98
26:46	40 n. 41
28	64

Numbers

1:26–27	84 n. 4
2:3–4	84 n. 4
5:1–4	66
5:5–9	111
5:5–10	109 n. 19
6:6–12	60
6:10	23 n. 23, 64
6:19	66
7:12–17	84 n. 4
7:13	60 n. 18
7:19	60 n. 18
9:1–14	21 n. 19
9:3	72
9:6–13	67
9:6–14	65, 67 n. 40
9:13	47, 66

9:14	44 n. 5, 46 n. 7, 47
15	73 n. 53, 74 n. 56, 75, 103, 109 n. 19, 124
15:2	92 n. 3
15:6	101 n. 5
15:14	44 n. 5, 46 n. 7
15:15	44 n. 5
15:16	44 n. 5
15:22–23	74 n. 55
15:22–29	73 n. 53
15:22–31	73, 109 n. 19
15:24	74 n. 55
15:26	44 n. 5, 46 n. 7
15:27	(74)
15:29	44 n. 5, 46 n. 7
15:30	44 n. 5, 74 n. 55, 74 n. 56, 103
15:30–31	73, 73 n. 53, 74 n. 56
15:31	74 n. 56, 103
18:19	28, 29
19:4	60 n. 15
19:10	44 n. 5, 46 n. 7
19:11	60 n. 15, 64
19:13	72
19:14	60 n. 15
20:1–13	87
20:2–13	84
20:12	87, 88
25	35 n. 27, 84, 88
25:10–13	84
25:11	88
25:12	28, 29
25:12–13	35 n. 27
27:1–11	49
28:2	72
28:11	60 n. 15
28:16–25	21 n. 19
28:19	60 n. 15
28:29	60 n. 15
29:2	60 n. 15
29:4	60 n. 15
29:7	60 n. 15
29:10	60 n. 15
29:12	60 n. 16
29:12–38	61
29:17	60 n. 16

30	48, 49	28–30	98 n. 2
30:4–17	34	29:3	39 n. 39
30:10	49	29:27	39 n. 39
31:19	64	30:2–3	113
33:5–6	67 n. 41	30:6	1 n. 4, 2 n. 5, 97, 105 n. 9, 113, 127
35:15	44 n. 5		
36	71	30:11	74
36:1–12	49	30:19	31
		34:6	39 n. 39

Deuteronomy

2:22	39 n. 39	Joshua	
2:30	39 n. 39	1:8	101 n. 5
3:14	39 n. 39	3–5	68
4–6	31	5	69, 75, 125
4:20	39 n. 39	5:1–2	55 n. 5
4:38	39 n. 39	5:2–9	1 n. 4, 68, 127
5:24	31 n. 16	5:10–12	21 n. 19
6:24	39 n. 39	24	31
7:6	31	24:16–18	28
8:18	39 n. 39	24:21	28
9:3	105, 106	24:21–24	31 n. 16
10:8	39 n. 39		
10:15	39 n. 39	Judges	
10:16	1 n. 4, 97, 105 n. 9, 127	1:3	127 n. 1
11:1	40 n. 41	3:30	105
11:4	39 n. 39	4:23	106 n. 13
12–26	98 n. 2	8:28	105 n. 12
13:2	101 n. 5	11:33	105 n. 12
14	7	14:3	1 n. 4
14:2	31	15:18	1 n. 4, 127 n. 1
15	57, 59	17:6	39
15:12–18	56	18:1	39
15:16–17	58	18:20	88 n. 13
16	95	19:1	39
16:1–8	21 n. 19	19:10	39
16:1–17	67 n. 39	21:25	39
16:4	95		
16:7	66 n. 36	1 Samuel	
20:10–14	43	7:13	105 n. 12
23:16–17	57 n. 12	14:6	1 n. 4, 127 n. 1
25:9	58	17:26	1 n. 4, 127 n. 1
26:13	74	17:36	1 n. 4
26:17–18	31	18:3	28 n. 4
26:18	31	23:18	28 n. 4
27	31	31:4	1 n. 4, 127 n. 1

2 Samuel		9:25–26	127
1:20	1 n. 4, 127 n. 1	17:19–27	116
7:8–16	35	29:1	119 n. 11
8:1	105 n. 12	34:8–21	27
20:20	30 n. 14		
		Ezekiel	
1 Kings		3:15	119 n. 10
1:8	84 n. 4	5:11	66 n. 35
2:10	72	6:9	18 n. 14
3:6	110	8:1	119 n. 11
21:29	106, 107	9:4	56
		14:1	119 n. 11
2 Kings		14:5	18 n. 14
21:27–29	112	14:7	18 n. 14
22:19	106 n. 14, 107	16:59	74
22:21–23	70	17:18–19	74
23	31	20	116
23:1–27	130	20:1	119 n. 11
23:3	28, 31 n. 16	20:3	119 n. 11
23:21–23	21 n. 19, 68 n. 42	20:43	18 n. 14
		28:10	1 n. 4
Isaiah		31:18	1 n. 4
6	83 n. 2	32:19–31	1 n. 4
6:5	83 n. 2	36:22–31	113
24:5	117 n. 6	36:31	18 n. 14
25:5	106 n. 13	43:18–27	62 n. 26
44:5	56	44:7	1 n. 4, 66 n. 35, 118, 127
49:16	56 n. 11	44:9	1 n. 4, 118, 127
51:1–8	116, 116 n. 5	45:21–25	21 n. 19
51:4	117 n. 6		
51:6	117 n. 6	Hosea	
52:1	1 n. 4, 118, 127	2:15	58
56	117 n. 6		
56:2	117 n. 6	Amos	
56:4	117 n. 6	4:6–11	98
56:6	117 n. 6		
58:3	112	Micah	
58:10	112	4:12	110
58:13–14	116		
		Habbakuk	
Jeremiah		2:16	1 n. 4
4:41	n. 4, 2 n. 5, 105 n. 9, 117 n. 6, 127		
		Haggai	
6:10	1 n. 4, 79	1:1	84 n. 4
9:24–25	1 n. 4, 33 n. 23, 118, 118 n. 8	1:12	84 n. 4

Haggai (cont.)		1:6–7	120
1:14	84 n. 4	1:8–16	120
2:2	84 n. 4	2:17	120
		2:36	120
Zechariah		2:47	120
1:3	113	4:31	120
2:14	84 n. 4	6:11	120
9:11	129		
		Ezra	
Malachi		2:1	119
3:7	113	2:21–35	119
		2:59	119 n. 10
Psalms		5:5	119 n. 11
33:11	110	5:9	119 n. 11
35:13	112	6:7	119 n. 11
50:5	30 n. 14, 129	6:8	119 n. 11
51:12	111 n. 23	6:14	119 n. 11
76:6	111 n. 23	6:19–22	21 n. 19, 68 n. 42, 70
81:15	106 n. 13		
89:20–37	35	Nehemiah	
94:15	110 n. 22	7:6	119
97:11	110	7:25–37	119
106:42	106, 111	9:24	106 n. 13
107:12	106, 111	13:15–22	116
119:7	110 n. 22		
132:11–18	35	1 Chronicles	
		1:28–30	33 n. 20
Proverbs		10:4	1 n. 4, 127 n. 1
22:11	111 n. 23	12:6	108
25:12	58	12:7	108
		12:12	108
Job		17:10	106 n. 13
1:1	110	18:1	105 n. 12
10:1	18 n. 14	20:4	105 n. 12
40:12	106	23:15	88 n. 13
42:11	58	23:16	88 n. 13
		26:24	88 n. 13
Ruth			
4:8	58	2 Chronicles	
		7:14	106 n. 15
Lamentations		12:1	107
5:21	113	12:1–12	106 n. 15, 107, 108
		12:5	107
Daniel		13–14	107
1:4	120	13:18	105 n. 12

28:19	108	Targum Neofiti	
29:21	111 n. 23	Gen 17:11	18 n. 14
30	21 n. 19, 70	Exod 6:12, 30	86 n.11
30:1–11	108	Lev 26:41	97
30:1–27	68 n. 42		
30:11	106 n. 15	Targum Pseudo-Jonathan	
32:24–26	108	Gen 17:11	18 n.14
32:26	106 n. 14, 108	Exod 4:24–26	130
33:10–20	108	Exod 12:13	130
33:12	106 n. 14	Lev 19:23	95
33:19	106 n. 14	Lev 26:41	97
33:23	106 n. 14		
34:27	106 n. 14, 112	Targum Prophets	
34:29–33	130	Ezek 16:6	130
35:1–19	21 n. 19, 68 n. 42, 70		
35:13	66 n. 36	Peshitta	
36:11–14	108	Exod 6:12,30	86 n. 11
36:12	106 n. 14		
36:22–23	104		

Versions, Greek

LXX

Gen 17:11	18 n. 14
Lev 19:23	130
Num 15:30–31	73 n. 54
Deut 10:16	79
Deut 30:6	130
Josh 5:4	130
Josh 24:30	55 n. 5
Judg 18:20	88 n. 13
Jer 4:4	130
Hab 2:16	1 n. 4
Esth 5:28	120 n. 13
Esth 8:17	131

Symmachus
Exod 6:12, 30 — 130

Versions, Aramaic

Targum Onqelos
Gen 17:11	18 n. 14
Exod 6:12, 30	86 n. 11
Lev 19:23	95

Ancient Near Eastern Literature

Annals of Sennacherib	45 n. 6
Annals of Tiglath Pileser	45 n. 6
Eshnunna	57 n. 12
Hammurapi	57 n. 12, 94
Lipit Ishar	57 n. 12
Ur Nammu	57 n. 12

Israelite and Jewish Epigraphy

Arad Ostraca	45 n. 5
Cowley	56, 95 n. 12, 112 n. 24

Apocrypha and Pseudepigrapha

2 Baruch
66:5 — 130

Jubilees
1:22–24	129
2:27	71 n. 50
15	130
15:26	71 n. 50
15:34	71 n. 50

Judith		1 Corinthians	
12:1–9	120 n. 13	7:17–20	129
14:10	131		
		Galatians	
1 Maccabees		5:1–15	129
1:13–15	130	6:11–18	129
1:15	128		
1:63	128	Ephesians	
2:46	131	2:11–12	129
Tobit		Phillipians	
1:10–11	120 n. 13	3:2–3	104 n. 7
		3	129

Qumran

		Colossians	
1QpHab 11:8–16	1 n. 4	2:11–12	104 n. 7
Barkhi Nafshi 4Q434 1 I,4	129	2:6–19	129
Dibre Hame'orot 4Q504 4, 11	129		
4Q 458 2 II, 4	130	Barnabas	
		9	129
		9:3–4	129
		10:12	129

Hellenistic Jewish Literature

Josephus, *Jewish Antiquities*		Justin, *Dialogues*	
4.226–227	93 n. 5	16	129
12.241	130	18–19	129
12.278	131	19	129
13.257–58	131	19.92.113	104 n. 7
13.318–19	131	24	129
20.17–96	131	27–29	129
		92	129
		113–114	129

New Testament and Patristics

Classical Literature

Luke			
1:59	129	Celcus, *De Medicina*	131
2:21	129	Horace, *Satirae*	131
		Juvenal, *Satirae*	131
Acts		Martial, *Epigrammaton*	131
15:1–11	129	Petronius, *Satyricon*	131
21:25	129	Strabo, *Geographica*	131
		Suentonius, *Domitianus*	131
Romans		Tacitus, *Historia*	131
2:28–29	104 n. 7		
2:25–5:5	129		

INDEX OF PRIMARY SOURCES

Rabbinic Literature

Mishnah
'Abot 3:11	128, 130
'Arak. 2:2	55 n. 6, 130
'Ed. 5:2	130
Ker. 1:1	74 n. 56
Meg. 2:4	130
Ned. 3:11	27 n. 1, 55 n.6, 131
Neg. 7:5	55 n. 6, 130
'Orlah	95 n. 11
Pesaḥ. 3:7	130
Pesaḥ. 5:3	130
Pesaḥ. 6:2	55 n. 6
Pesaḥ. 8:8	130
Pesaḥ. 9:5	67 n. 37
Šab. 9:3	130
Šab. 18:3–19:6	130
Šab. 19:1–6	55 n. 6
Yebam. 8:1	130
Yoma 8:1	112

Tannaitic Midrash
Mek. Bo' 3	67 n.37
Mek. Bo' 4	67 n.37
Mek. Bo' 11	67 n.37
Mek. Bo' 14	67 n.37
Mek. R. Shimon b. Yoḥai Bo' 12:45	130
Sipre Num. 108	131
'Abot R. Nat A 17	120 n.13

Jerusalem Talmud
Meg. 1:4	39 n. 35
Ned. 3:9	64 n. 30, 129

Babylonian Talmud
Ber. 6a	56 n. 11
Ber. 29a	129
Ker.7a–b	74 n. 56
Ned. 32a	1
'Or.	129
San. 6b	39 n. 35
San. 49b	39 n. 35

Amoraic Midrash
Gen. Rab. 46	130
Exod. Rab. 1:26	83 n. 2
Lev. Rab. 27:1	62 n. 28
Num. Rab. 9	39 n. 35
Cant. Rab. 1	39 n. 35
Ruth Rab. 4	39 n. 35
Lam. Rab. 5:1	113 n. 25
Qoh. Rab. 1	39 n. 35

Medieval Jewish Literature

Abraham Ibn Ezra
Gen 17:11	18
Lev 19:9–10	24 n. 24

Ibn Janah
Lev 26:41	101

Joseph Bechor Shor
	59 n. 14
Lev 19:23–24	79 n. 1

Joseph Kara
Isa 51:4–6	117 n. 6

Maimonides, *Guide* 3:41
	74 n. 56

Rashbam
Lev 19:23–24	79 n. 1

Rashi
Exod 6:12	79
Gen 17:11	18
Lev 26:41	101

Radak (Kimchi)
Isa 51:4, 6	117 n. 6

Nachmanides
Lev 19:9–10	24 n.24
Lev 19:23–24	79 n. 1
Lev 26:41	101

Malbim
	59 n.14

Index of Modern Authors

Ackroyd, P. 116 n. 4
Aharoni, Y. 119 n. 10
Albertz, R. 2 n. 9
Alexander, B. C. 53 n. 1
Alexander, T. 2 n. 5
Althann, R. 2 n. 5
Amit, Y. 6 n. 20
Appiah, K. 8 n. 22
Avi-Yonah, M. 119 n. 10
Baker, D. 15 n. 7
Baltzer, K. 30 n. 9, 34 n. 26
Barr, J. 6 n. 19, 7 n. 21, 30 n. 10, 38 n. 34
Barth, L. 3 n. 12, 131 n. 2
Baumgart, N. 97 n. 1
Bechtel, L. 2 n. 5
Bell, C. 53, 54, 54 n. 2, 54 n. 3
Bernat, D. 64 n. 30, 65 n. 34, 131 n. 2
Bickerman, E. 30 n. 11
Biddick, K. 3 n. 13
Bird, P. 49 n. 12
Bisschops, R. 81 n. 4
Blank, S. 118 n. 8
Blau, J. 2 n. 5
Blenkinsopp, J. 2 n. 9, 83 n. 2, 115
Boling, R. 68
Brettler, M. 2 n. 5, 16 n. 9, 28 n. 5, 81 n. 4, 105 n. 9, 106 n. 13
Bright, J. 34 n. 26
Brueggemann, W. 2 n. 5
Budge, E. 45 n. 6
Carasik, M. 110 n. 21
Carmichael, C. 94 n. 8
Carver, N. 6 n. 19
Childs, B. 83 n. 1
Clements, R. 35 n. 28
Cohen, M. Z. 81 n. 4, 81 n. 5
Cohen, S. J. D. 1 n. 3, 3 n. 12, 26 n. 25, 37 n. 32, 62 n. 28, 63 n. 29, 64 n. 30, 65 n. 34, 69 n. 47, 129, 131 n. 2, 132
Collins, J. 120 n. 15, 131 n. 2
Coppens, J 2 n. 5
Cross, F. M. 30 n. 15, 84, 84 n. 5
Cruse, D. A. 81 n. 5
Crüsemann, F. 6 n. 20
Darby, R. 3 n. 13
Davidson, R. 1 n. 1
Déaut, R. Le 2 n. 5, 97
Dessing, N. 3 n. 13
Di Lella, A. A. 120 n. 15
Douglas, M. 6 n. 19
Dozeman, J. 106 n. 13
Driver, S. R. 58 n. 13, 79, 107 n. 18
Eilberg-Schwartz, H. 2 n. 8, 50, 51, 62 n. 28, 64, 64 n. 30, 93, 95 n. 10
Elliger, K. 91, 97 n. 1
Ephal, I. 119, 119 n. 9, 119 n. 11
Fabry, H.-J. 110 n. 20, 110 n. 21
Fohrer, G. 2 n. 9
Fox, M. 2 n. 5, 3, 5, 36, 37, 51
Fishbane, M. 73 n. 53
Flusser, D. 2 n. 5
Francis, J. 81 n. 4
Freedman, D. N. 28 n. 4
Friedman, R. E. 73 n. 53, 84 n. 5
Gane, R. 5 n. 17, 30 n. 8
Geertz, C. 5 n. 19, 6 n. 19
Geller, S. A. 2 n. 5, 3, 4, 7, 32, 50
Gemser, B. 74 n. 56
Gesenius, W. 18 n. 14

INDEX OF MODERN AUTHORS

Gevirtz, S.   1 n. 2, 2 n. 8, 51
Gilders, W. K.   4 n. 16, 5 n. 17, 6 n. 20, 55 n. 4
Glatt, D. A.   39 n. 37
Glick, L. B.   3 n. 12
Goldingay, J.   103, 104 n. 7
Goody, J.   53 n. 1
Gorman, F.   61 n. 22
Gray, G. B.   73 n. 53
Greenberg, M.   18 n. 14
Greenspahn, F. E.   39 n. 39
Groot, J. de   2 n. 5
Gruber, M.   49 n. 12
Gruenbaum, E.   3 n. 13
Gruenwald, I.   54
Grünwaldt, K.   2 n. 8, 97 n. 1, 115 n. 2
Gunkel, H.   1, 18 n. 14, 31 n. 15, 45
Hall, R. G.   2 n. 6, 79
Hallet, G.   6 n. 19
Haran, M.   28 n. 4, 30 n. 9, 62 n. 25, 67 n. 38
Hartley, J.   79, 91 n. 1, 95 n. 9, 97 n. 1
Hartman, L. F.   120 n. 15
Heger, P.   55 n. 5
Hendel, R.   5 n. 19, 66 n. 36
Hermission, H.   2 n. 8, 104
Hillers, D.   34 n. 26, 37 n. 33
Hoffman, D.   22 n. 22, 63, 63 n. 29, 64, 64 n. 31, 97 n. 1, 101 n. 5
Hoffman, L.   1 n. 3, 3 n. 12, 4 n. 15, 97, 117 n. 7
Holladay, W.   34 n. 23, 118 n. 8
Houtman, C.   2 n. 5
Hurowitz, V.   2 n. 5, 56 n. 9, 87 n. 12
Hurvitz, A.   106 n. 17
Hyatt, J. P.   2 n. 6
Isaac, E.   2 n. 5
Japhet, S.   107 n. 18
Jay, N.   49
Johnson, M.   81, 82
Joosten, J.   29 n. 8
Kalluveettil, P.   30 n. 9, 34 n. 26
Kaminsky, J.   102 n. 6
Kang, S.   106 n. 13
Kaplan, L.   2 n. 5
Kataja, L.   35 n. 29
Keil, Y.   2 n. 7
Kelly, B. E.   107 n. 18
King, L.   45 n. 6
Klawans, J.   6 n. 19
Kline, M.   1 n. 3, 37 n. 33
Klingbeil, G.   5 n. 17, 54, 55
Knohl, I.   3 n. 11, 6 n. 20, 7 n. 20, 28 n. 4, 36 n. 30, 73 n. 53, 91
Kondo, H.   54 n. 2
Korpel, M.   14 n. 5
Kosmala, H.   2 n. 5
Kugler, R.   6 n. 20
Kunin, S.   3 n. 12
Kutsch, E.   28 n. 3, 28 n. 4
Lakoff, G.   81, 82
Lemche, N. P.   2 n. 9
Lesêtre, H.   2 n. 6
Levenson, J.   69 n. 47
Levine, B.   5 n. 19, 6 n. 20, 15 n. 6, 22 n. 22, 44 n. 3, 44 n. 4, 47 n. 8, 62 n. 25, 63, 64, 71, 73 n. 53, 74 n. 56, 79, 79 n. 2, 80, 91 n. 1, 95 n. 10, 97 n. 1, 98, 101 n. 5
Levinson, B. M.   95 n. 8
Levy-Bruhl, L.   6 n. 19
Licht, J.   2 n. 6, 73 n. 53
Lods, A.   2 n. 5
Loewenstamm, S.   30 n. 13
Lohfink, N.   15 n. 8
Long, B.   86 n. 10
Luckenbill, D.   45 n. 6
Magonet, J.   22 n. 22
Marcus, I.   3 n. 12
Mark, E.   3 n. 12
Mayer, G.   2 n. 6, 97
McCarthy, D. J.   34 n. 26
McEvenue, S.   1 n. 2, 14 n. 4, 14 n. 6, 15 n. 6, 15 n. 7, 37 n. 32
Melamed, E.   39 n. 35, 105 n. 9
Mendelsohn, I.   56 n. 9, 58
Mendenhall, G. E.   34 n. 26
Milgrom, J.   3 n. 11, 6 n. 19, 6 n. 20, 22 n. 21, 22 n. 22, 29 n. 7, 30 n. 15, 44 n. 5, 49 n. 12, 60 n. 20, 63 n. 29, 64 n.

Milgrom, J. (cont.)
  31, 65 n. 33, 66, 70 n. 48, 73 n. 53, 74 n. 56, 95 n. 10, 97 n. 1, 109 n. 19, 111
Miller, P.   106 n. 13
Moor, J. de   7 n. 21
Morgenstern, J.   2 n. 5, 2 n. 8, 69 n. 46
Nelson, R.   68
Nicholson, E.   6 n. 20, 28 n. 4, 34 n. 26
Neihoff, M.   131 n. 2
Noth, M.   21, 73 n. 53, 91 n. 1, 95 n. 9, 97 n. 1
Olyan, S.   6 n. 20, 43 n. 1, 45, 46, 71
Paran, M.   14 n. 5
Parker, S.   20 n. 18
Patrick, D.   28 n. 2
Propp, W.   2 n. 5, 2 n. 7, 6 n. 20, 64 n. 30, 65, 65 n. 34, 66 n. 36, 67 n. 37, 69 n. 44, 80 n. 3, 83 n. 1, 84 n. 6, 85 n. 7
Prosic, T.   68 n. 42
Rad, G. von   1, 3, 50, 62 n. 25, 84 n. 3, 116
Ramirez Kidd, J.   44 n. 5
Rendtorff, R.   16 n. 11
Rendtorff, R.   6 n. 20
Richards, I.   81
Ruwe, A.   2 n. 10, 6 n. 20, 13 n. 2
Safrai, S.   2 n. 5
Sarna, N.   1 n. 1, 2 n. 7, 7, 19 n. 16, 28 n. 5, 37 n. 32
Sasson, J.   2 n. 5, 33 n. 23, 50, 69
Schmid, H.   2 n. 5
Schwartz, B.   6 n. 20, 14 n. 4, 19 n. 15, 24 n. 24, 29 n. 7, 30 n. 12, 31 n. 18, 37 n. 32, 38 n. 34, 70, 70 n. 48, 71, 91, 91 n. 1, 92, 92 n. 2, 92 n. 3, 93 n. 5
Shields, M.   2 n. 5
Silverman, E.   3 n. 12
Ska, J.   39 n. 36
Skinner, J.   1, 2 n. 7, 18 n. 14, 37 n. 32
Sklar, J.   38 n. 34
Smith   6 n. 19, 115
Snaith, N. H.   73 n. 53
Soggin, A.   68
Sommer, B.   8 n. 23, 56 n. 11
Sonsino, R.   74 n. 56
Soskice, J.   82, 125
Sperling, S. D.   117 n. 6
Staal, F.   53 n. 1, 54
Stackert, J.   95 n. 8
Steiner, R.   118 n. 8
Sternberg, M.   88
Sun, H.   91 n. 1, 97 n. 1
Talmon, S.   2 n. 5
Tigay, J.   2 n. 5, 85 n. 8
Toeg, A.   73 n. 53, 109 n. 19
Turner, V.   53 n. 1
Van Seters, J.   83 n. 1, 83 n. 2
Vaux, R. de   2 n. 9
Vawter, B.   1 n. 1
Vermes, G.   64 n. 30, 69 n. 45
Viberg, A.   58
Vink, J. G.   6 n. 20
Vriezen, T. C.   2 n. 9
Wagner, S.   105 n. 10
Warning, W.   6 n. 20, 14 n. 4
Warren, A.   81 n. 5
Watson, W.   105 n. 9
Watts, J. W.   4, 4 n. 14, 5, 5 n. 17, 5 n. 18, 28 n. 2
Weber, M.   69
Wegner, J. R.   49 n. 11, 49 n. 12
Weinfeld, M.   16 n. 9, 28 n. 4, 31 n. 17, 35, 116 n. 3, 116 n. 5
Wellek, R.   81 n. 5
Wellhausen, J.   2 n. 9, 84 n. 3, 115 n. 1
Wenham, G.   2 n. 7, 18 n. 14, 24 n. 24, 37 n. 33, 91 n. 1, 97 n. 1
Westermann, C.   2 n. 7, 14 n. 6, 15 n. 6, 15, 16 n. 9, 37 n. 33, 61 n. 24
Wevers, J.   101 n. 5
Whiting, R.   35 n. 29
Williamson, P. R.   14 n. 6, 16 n. 9
Wills, L. M.   120 n. 13
Wittgenstein, L.   6 n. 19
Wold, D. J.   65, 65 n. 33, 70 n. 48, 72, 74 n. 56
Wright, D.   6 n. 20, 53, 53 n. 1, 54 n. 2, 61 n. 21
Wuthnow, R.   54, 54 n. 3
Wyatt, N.   115 n. 2

Wyckoff, C.	20 n. 17
Zadok, R.	119 n. 9, 120
Zakovitch, Y.	60, 92 n. 3, 94 n. 6
Zeusse, E. M.	53 n. 1
Zevit, Z.	5 n. 16

www.ingramcontent.com/pod-product-compliance
Lightning Source LLC
Chambersburg PA
CBHW031314150426
43191CB00005B/228